FREE Study Skills Videos/DVD Offer

Dear Customer,

Thank you for your purchase from Mometrix! We consider it an honor and a privilege that you purchased our product and we want to ensure your satisfaction.

As part of our ongoing effort to meet the needs of test takers, we have developed a set of Study Skills Videos that we would like to give you for FREE. These videos cover our *best practices* for getting ready for your exam, from how to use our study materials to how to best prepare for the day of the test.

All that we ask is that you email us with feedback that would describe your experience so far with our product. Good, bad, or indifferent, we want to know what you think!

To get your FREE Study Skills Videos, you can use the **QR code** below, or send us an **email** at studyvideos@mometrix.com with *FREE VIDEOS* in the subject line and the following information in the body of the email:

- The name of the product you purchased.
- Your product rating on a scale of 1-5, with 5 being the highest rating.
- Your feedback. It can be long, short, or anything in between. We just want to know your impressions and experience so far with our product. (Good feedback might include how our study material met your needs and ways we might be able to make it even better. You could highlight features that you found helpful or features that you think we should add.)

If you have any questions or concerns, please don't hesitate to contact me directly.

Thanks again!

Sincerely,

Jay Willis
Vice President
jay.willis@mometrix.com
1-800-673-8175

RBT

Exam Study Guide 2023 and 2024

3 Full-Length Practice Tests

Secrets Prep Book for the Registered Behavior Technician Certification

[Includes Detailed Answer Explanations]

Written and edited by Matthew Bowling

Printed in the United States of America

This paper meets the requirements of ANSI/NISO Z39.48-1992 (Permanence of Paper).

Mometrix offers volume discount pricing to institutions. For more information or a price quote, please contact our sales department at sales@mometrix.com or 888-248-1219.

Paperback
ISBN 13: 978-1-5167-2376-8
ISBN 10: 1-5167-2376-7

DEAR FUTURE EXAM SUCCESS STORY

First of all, **THANK YOU** for purchasing Mometrix study materials!

Second, congratulations! You are one of the few determined test-takers who are committed to doing whatever it takes to excel on your exam. **You have come to the right place.** We developed these study materials with one goal in mind: to deliver you the information you need in a format that's concise and easy to use.

In addition to optimizing your guide for the content of the test, we've outlined our recommended steps for breaking down the preparation process into small, attainable goals so you can make sure you stay on track.

We've also analyzed the entire test-taking process, identifying the most common pitfalls and showing how you can overcome them and be ready for any curveball the test throws you.

Standardized testing is one of the biggest obstacles on your road to success, which only increases the importance of doing well in the high-pressure, high-stakes environment of test day. Your results on this test could have a significant impact on your future, and this guide provides the information and practical advice to help you achieve your full potential on test day.

Your success is our success

We would love to hear from you! If you would like to share the story of your exam success or if you have any questions or comments in regard to our products, please contact us at **800-673-8175** or **support@mometrix.com**.

Thanks again for your business and we wish you continued success!

Sincerely,
The Mometrix Test Preparation Team

> **Need more help? Check out our flashcards at:**
> **http://mometrixflashcards.com/RBT**

TABLE OF CONTENTS

Introduction

Thank you for purchasing this resource! You have made the choice to prepare yourself for a test that could have a huge impact on your future, and this guide is designed to help you be fully ready for test day. Obviously, it's important to have a solid understanding of the test material, but you also need to be prepared for the unique environment and stressors of the test, so that you can perform to the best of your abilities.

For this purpose, the first section that appears in this guide is the **Secret Keys**. We've devoted countless hours to meticulously researching what works and what doesn't, and we've boiled down our findings to the five most impactful steps you can take to improve your performance on the test. We start at the beginning with study planning and move through the preparation process, all the way to the testing strategies that will help you get the most out of what you know when you're finally sitting in front of the test.

We recommend that you start preparing for your test as far in advance as possible. However, if you've bought this guide as a last-minute study resource and only have a few days before your test, we recommend that you skip over the first two Secret Keys since they address a long-term study plan.

If you struggle with **test anxiety**, we strongly encourage you to check out our recommendations for how you can overcome it. Test anxiety is a formidable foe, but it can be beaten, and we want to make sure you have the tools you need to defeat it.

Secret Key #1 – Plan Big, Study Small

There's a lot riding on your performance. If you want to ace this test, you're going to need to keep your skills sharp and the material fresh in your mind. You need a plan that lets you review everything you need to know while still fitting in your schedule. We'll break this strategy down into three categories.

Information Organization

Start with the information you already have: the official test outline. From this, you can make a complete list of all the concepts you need to cover before the test. Organize these concepts into groups that can be studied together, and create a list of any related vocabulary you need to learn so you can brush up on any difficult terms. You'll want to keep this vocabulary list handy once you actually start studying since you may need to add to it along the way.

Time Management

Once you have your set of study concepts, decide how to spread them out over the time you have left before the test. Break your study plan into small, clear goals so you have a manageable task for each day and know exactly what you're doing. Then just focus on one small step at a time. When you manage your time this way, you don't need to spend hours at a time studying. Studying a small block of content for a short period each day helps you retain information better and avoid stressing over how much you have left to do. You can relax knowing that you have a plan to cover everything in time. In order for this strategy to be effective though, you have to start studying early and stick to your schedule. Avoid the exhaustion and futility that comes from last-minute cramming!

Study Environment

The environment you study in has a big impact on your learning. Studying in a coffee shop, while probably more enjoyable, is not likely to be as fruitful as studying in a quiet room. It's important to keep distractions to a minimum. You're only planning to study for a short block of time, so make the most of it. Don't pause to check your phone or get up to find a snack. It's also important to **avoid multitasking**. Research has consistently shown that multitasking will make your studying dramatically less effective. Your study area should also be comfortable and well-lit so you don't have the distraction of straining your eyes or sitting on an uncomfortable chair.

 The time of day you study is also important. You want to be rested and alert. Don't wait until just before bedtime. Study when you'll be most likely to comprehend and remember. Even better, if you know what time of day your test will be, set that time aside for study. That way your brain will be used to working on that subject at that specific time and you'll have a better chance of recalling information.

Finally, it can be helpful to team up with others who are studying for the same test. Your actual studying should be done in as isolated an environment as possible, but the work of organizing the information and setting up the study plan can be divided up. In between study sessions, you can discuss with your teammates the concepts that you're all studying and quiz each other on the details. Just be sure that your teammates are as serious about the test as you are. If you find that your study time is being replaced with social time, you might need to find a new team.

Secret Key #2 – Make Your Studying Count

You're devoting a lot of time and effort to preparing for this test, so you want to be absolutely certain it will pay off. This means doing more than just reading the content and hoping you can remember it on test day. It's important to make every minute of study count. There are two main areas you can focus on to make your studying count.

Retention

It doesn't matter how much time you study if you can't remember the material. You need to make sure you are retaining the concepts. To check your retention of the information you're learning, try recalling it at later times with minimal prompting. Try carrying around flashcards and glance at one or two from time to time or ask a friend who's also studying for the test to quiz you.

To enhance your retention, look for ways to put the information into practice so that you can apply it rather than simply recalling it. If you're using the information in practical ways, it will be much easier to remember. Similarly, it helps to solidify a concept in your mind if you're not only reading it to yourself but also explaining it to someone else. Ask a friend to let you teach them about a concept you're a little shaky on (or speak aloud to an imaginary audience if necessary). As you try to summarize, define, give examples, and answer your friend's questions, you'll understand the concepts better and they will stay with you longer. Finally, step back for a big picture view and ask yourself how each piece of information fits with the whole subject. When you link the different concepts together and see them working together as a whole, it's easier to remember the individual components.

Finally, practice showing your work on any multi-step problems, even if you're just studying. Writing out each step you take to solve a problem will help solidify the process in your mind, and you'll be more likely to remember it during the test.

Modality

Modality simply refers to the means or method by which you study. Choosing a study modality that fits your own individual learning style is crucial. No two people learn best in exactly the same way, so it's important to know your strengths and use them to your advantage.

For example, if you learn best by visualization, focus on visualizing a concept in your mind and draw an image or a diagram. Try color-coding your notes, illustrating them, or creating symbols that will trigger your mind to recall a learned concept. If you learn best by hearing or discussing information, find a study partner who learns the same way or read aloud to yourself. Think about how to put the information in your own words. Imagine that you are giving a lecture on the topic and record yourself so you can listen to it later.

For any learning style, flashcards can be helpful. Organize the information so you can take advantage of spare moments to review. Underline key words or phrases. Use different colors for different categories. Mnemonic devices (such as creating a short list in which every item starts with the same letter) can also help with retention. Find what works best for you and use it to store the information in your mind most effectively and easily.

3

Secret Key #3 – Practice the Right Way

Your success on test day depends not only on how many hours you put into preparing, but also on whether you prepared the right way. It's good to check along the way to see if your studying is paying off. One of the most effective ways to do this is by taking practice tests to evaluate your progress. Practice tests are useful because they show exactly where you need to improve. Every time you take a practice test, pay special attention to these three groups of questions:

- The questions you got wrong
- The questions you had to guess on, even if you guessed right
- The questions you found difficult or slow to work through

This will show you exactly what your weak areas are, and where you need to devote more study time. Ask yourself why each of these questions gave you trouble. Was it because you didn't understand the material? Was it because you didn't remember the vocabulary? Do you need more repetitions on this type of question to build speed and confidence? Dig into those questions and figure out how you can strengthen your weak areas as you go back to review the material.

 Additionally, many practice tests have a section explaining the answer choices. It can be tempting to read the explanation and think that you now have a good understanding of the concept. However, an explanation likely only covers part of the question's broader context. Even if the explanation makes perfect sense, **go back and investigate** every concept related to the question until you're positive you have a thorough understanding.

As you go along, keep in mind that the practice test is just that: practice. Memorizing these questions and answers will not be very helpful on the actual test because it is unlikely to have any of the same exact questions. If you only know the right answers to the sample questions, you won't be prepared for the real thing. **Study the concepts** until you understand them fully, and then you'll be able to answer any question that shows up on the test.

It's important to wait on the practice tests until you're ready. If you take a test on your first day of study, you may be overwhelmed by the amount of material covered and how much you need to learn. Work up to it gradually.

On test day, you'll need to be prepared for answering questions, managing your time, and using the test-taking strategies you've learned. It's a lot to balance, like a mental marathon that will have a big impact on your future. Like training for a marathon, you'll need to start slowly and work your way up. When test day arrives, you'll be ready.

Start with the strategies you've read in the first two Secret Keys—plan your course and study in the way that works best for you. If you have time, consider using multiple study resources to get different approaches to the same concepts. It can be helpful to see difficult concepts from more than one angle. Then find a good source for practice tests. Many times, the test website will suggest potential study resources or provide sample tests.

Practice Test Strategy

If you're able to find at least three practice tests, we recommend this strategy:

UNTIMED AND OPEN-BOOK PRACTICE

Take the first test with no time constraints and with your notes and study guide handy. Take your time and focus on applying the strategies you've learned.

TIMED AND OPEN-BOOK PRACTICE

Take the second practice test open-book as well, but set a timer and practice pacing yourself to finish in time.

TIMED AND CLOSED-BOOK PRACTICE

Take any other practice tests as if it were test day. Set a timer and put away your study materials. Sit at a table or desk in a quiet room, imagine yourself at the testing center, and answer questions as quickly and accurately as possible.

Keep repeating timed and closed-book tests on a regular basis until you run out of practice tests or it's time for the actual test. Your mind will be ready for the schedule and stress of test day, and you'll be able to focus on recalling the material you've learned.

Secret Key #4 – Pace Yourself

Once you're fully prepared for the material on the test, your biggest challenge on test day will be managing your time. Just knowing that the clock is ticking can make you panic even if you have plenty of time left. Work on pacing yourself so you can build confidence against the time constraints of the exam. Pacing is a difficult skill to master, especially in a high-pressure environment, so **practice is vital**.

Set time expectations for your pace based on how much time is available. For example, if a section has 60 questions and the time limit is 30 minutes, you know you have to average 30 seconds or less per question in order to answer them all. Although 30 seconds is the hard limit, set 25 seconds per question as your goal, so you reserve extra time to spend on harder questions. When you budget extra time for the harder questions, you no longer have any reason to stress when those questions take longer to answer.

Don't let this time expectation distract you from working through the test at a calm, steady pace, but keep it in mind so you don't spend too much time on any one question. Recognize that taking extra time on one question you don't understand may keep you from answering two that you do understand later in the test. If your time limit for a question is up and you're still not sure of the answer, mark it and move on, and come back to it later if the time and the test format allow. If the testing format doesn't allow you to return to earlier questions, just make an educated guess; then put it out of your mind and move on.

On the easier questions, be careful not to rush. It may seem wise to hurry through them so you have more time for the challenging ones, but it's not worth missing one if you know the concept and just didn't take the time to read the question fully. Work efficiently but make sure you understand the question and have looked at all of the answer choices, since more than one may seem right at first.

Even if you're paying attention to the time, you may find yourself a little behind at some point. You should speed up to get back on track, but do so wisely. Don't panic; just take a few seconds less on each question until you're caught up. Don't guess without thinking, but do look through the answer choices and eliminate any you know are wrong. If you can get down to two choices, it is often worthwhile to guess from those. Once you've chosen an answer, move on and don't dwell on any that you skipped or had to hurry through. If a question was taking too long, chances are it was one of the harder ones, so you weren't as likely to get it right anyway.

On the other hand, if you find yourself getting ahead of schedule, it may be beneficial to slow down a little. The more quickly you work, the more likely you are to make a careless mistake that will affect your score. You've budgeted time for each question, so don't be afraid to spend that time. Practice an efficient but careful pace to get the most out of the time you have.

Secret Key #5 – Have a Plan for Guessing

When you're taking the test, you may find yourself stuck on a question. Some of the answer choices seem better than others, but you don't see the one answer choice that is obviously correct. What do you do?

The scenario described above is very common, yet most test takers have not effectively prepared for it. Developing and practicing a plan for guessing may be one of the single most effective uses of your time as you get ready for the exam.

In developing your plan for guessing, there are three questions to address:

- When should you start the guessing process?
- How should you narrow down the choices?
- Which answer should you choose?

When to Start the Guessing Process

Unless your plan for guessing is to select C every time (which, despite its merits, is not what we recommend), you need to leave yourself enough time to apply your answer elimination strategies. Since you have a limited amount of time for each question, that means that if you're going to give yourself the best shot at guessing correctly, you have to decide quickly whether or not you will guess.

Of course, the best-case scenario is that you don't have to guess at all, so first, see if you can answer the question based on your knowledge of the subject and basic reasoning skills. Focus on the key words in the question and try to jog your memory of related topics. Give yourself a chance to bring the knowledge to mind, but once you realize that you don't have (or you can't access) the knowledge you need to answer the question, it's time to start the guessing process.

It's almost always better to start the guessing process too early than too late. It only takes a few seconds to remember something and answer the question from knowledge. Carefully eliminating wrong answer choices takes longer. Plus, going through the process of eliminating answer choices can actually help jog your memory.

Summary: Start the guessing process as soon as you decide that you can't answer the question based on your knowledge.

How to Narrow Down the Choices

The next chapter in this book (**Test-Taking Strategies**) includes a wide range of strategies for how to approach questions and how to look for answer choices to eliminate. You will definitely want to read those carefully, practice them, and figure out which ones work best for you. Here though, we're going to address a mindset rather than a particular strategy.

Your odds of guessing an answer correctly depend on how many options you are choosing from.

Number of options left	5	4	3	2	1
Odds of guessing correctly	20%	25%	33%	50%	100%

You can see from this chart just how valuable it is to be able to eliminate incorrect answers and make an educated guess, but there are two things that many test takers do that cause them to miss out on the benefits of guessing:

- Accidentally eliminating the correct answer
- Selecting an answer based on an impression

We'll look at the first one here, and the second one in the next section.

To avoid accidentally eliminating the correct answer, we recommend a thought exercise called **the $5 challenge**. In this challenge, you only eliminate an answer choice from contention if you are willing to bet $5 on it being wrong. Why $5? Five dollars is a small but not insignificant amount of money. It's an amount you could afford to lose but wouldn't want to throw away. And while losing

$5 once might not hurt too much, doing it twenty times will set you back $100. In the same way, each small decision you make—eliminating a choice here, guessing on a question there—won't by itself impact your score very much, but when you put them all together, they can make a big difference. By holding each answer choice elimination decision to a higher standard, you can reduce the risk of accidentally eliminating the correct answer.

The $5 challenge can also be applied in a positive sense: If you are willing to bet $5 that an answer choice *is* correct, go ahead and mark it as correct.

Summary: Only eliminate an answer choice if you are willing to bet $5 that it is wrong.

Which Answer to Choose

You're taking the test. You've run into a hard question and decided you'll have to guess. You've eliminated all the answer choices you're willing to bet $5 on. Now you have to pick an answer. Why do we even need to talk about this? Why can't you just pick whichever one you feel like when the time comes?

The answer to these questions is that if you don't come into the test with a plan, you'll rely on your impression to select an answer choice, and if you do that, you risk falling into a trap. The test writers know that everyone who takes their test will be guessing on some of the questions, so they intentionally write wrong answer choices to seem plausible. You still have to pick an answer though, and if the wrong answer choices are designed to look right, how can you ever be sure that you're not falling for their trap? The best solution we've found to this dilemma is to take the decision out of your hands entirely. Here is the process we recommend:

Once you've eliminated any choices that you are confident (willing to bet $5) are wrong, select the first remaining choice as your answer.

Whether you choose to select the first remaining choice, the second, or the last, the important thing is that you use some preselected standard. Using this approach guarantees that you will not be enticed into selecting an answer choice that looks right, because you are not basing your decision on how the answer choices look.

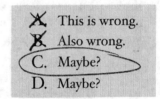

This is not meant to make you question your knowledge. Instead, it is to help you recognize the difference between your knowledge and your impressions. There's a huge difference between thinking an answer is right because of what you know, and thinking an answer is right because it looks or sounds like it should be right.

Summary: To ensure that your selection is appropriately random, make a predetermined selection from among all answer choices you have not eliminated.

Test-Taking Strategies

This section contains a list of test-taking strategies that you may find helpful as you work through the test. By taking what you know and applying logical thought, you can maximize your chances of answering any question correctly!

It is very important to realize that every question is different and every person is different: no single strategy will work on every question, and no single strategy will work for every person. That's why we've included all of them here, so you can try them out and determine which ones work best for different types of questions and which ones work best for you.

Question Strategies

⊘ READ CAREFULLY

Read the question and the answer choices carefully. Don't miss the question because you misread the terms. You have plenty of time to read each question thoroughly and make sure you understand what is being asked. Yet a happy medium must be attained, so don't waste too much time. You must read carefully and efficiently.

⊘ CONTEXTUAL CLUES

Look for contextual clues. If the question includes a word you are not familiar with, look at the immediate context for some indication of what the word might mean. Contextual clues can often give you all the information you need to decipher the meaning of an unfamiliar word. Even if you can't determine the meaning, you may be able to narrow down the possibilities enough to make a solid guess at the answer to the question.

⊘ PREFIXES

If you're having trouble with a word in the question or answer choices, try dissecting it. Take advantage of every clue that the word might include. Prefixes can be a huge help. Usually, they allow you to determine a basic meaning. *Pre-* means before, *post-* means after, *pro-* is positive, *de-* is negative. From prefixes, you can get an idea of the general meaning of the word and try to put it into context.

⊘ HEDGE WORDS

Watch out for critical hedge words, such as *likely, may, can, sometimes, often, almost, mostly, usually, generally, rarely,* and *sometimes.* Question writers insert these hedge phrases to cover every possibility. Often an answer choice will be wrong simply because it leaves no room for exception. Be on guard for answer choices that have definitive words such as *exactly* and *always.*

⊘ SWITCHBACK WORDS

Stay alert for *switchbacks.* These are the words and phrases frequently used to alert you to shifts in thought. The most common switchback words are *but, although,* and *however.* Others include *nevertheless, on the other hand, even though, while, in spite of, despite,* and *regardless of.* Switchback words are important to catch because they can change the direction of the question or an answer choice.

⊘ Face Value

When in doubt, use common sense. Accept the situation in the problem at face value. Don't read too much into it. These problems will not require you to make wild assumptions. If you have to go beyond creativity and warp time or space in order to have an answer choice fit the question, then you should move on and consider the other answer choices. These are normal problems rooted in reality. The applicable relationship or explanation may not be readily apparent, but it is there for you to figure out. Use your common sense to interpret anything that isn't clear.

Answer Choice Strategies

⊘ Answer Selection

The most thorough way to pick an answer choice is to identify and eliminate wrong answers until only one is left, then confirm it is the correct answer. Sometimes an answer choice may immediately seem right, but be careful. The test writers will usually put more than one reasonable answer choice on each question, so take a second to read all of them and make sure that the other choices are not equally obvious. As long as you have time left, it is better to read every answer choice than to pick the first one that looks right without checking the others.

⊘ Answer Choice Families

An answer choice family consists of two (in rare cases, three) answer choices that are very similar in construction and cannot all be true at the same time. If you see two answer choices that are direct opposites or parallels, one of them is usually the correct answer. For instance, if one answer choice says that quantity x increases and another either says that quantity x decreases (opposite) or says that quantity y increases (parallel), then those answer choices would fall into the same family. An answer choice that doesn't match the construction of the answer choice family is more likely to be incorrect. Most questions will not have answer choice families, but when they do appear, you should be prepared to recognize them.

⊘ Eliminate Answers

Eliminate answer choices as soon as you realize they are wrong, but make sure you consider all possibilities. If you are eliminating answer choices and realize that the last one you are left with is also wrong, don't panic. Start over and consider each choice again. There may be something you missed the first time that you will realize on the second pass.

⊘ Avoid Fact Traps

Don't be distracted by an answer choice that is factually true but doesn't answer the question. You are looking for the choice that answers the question. Stay focused on what the question is asking for so you don't accidentally pick an answer that is true but incorrect. Always go back to the question and make sure the answer choice you've selected actually answers the question and is not merely a true statement.

⊘ Extreme Statements

In general, you should avoid answers that put forth extreme actions as standard practice or proclaim controversial ideas as established fact. An answer choice that states the "process should be used in certain situations, if…" is much more likely to be correct than one that states the "process should be discontinued completely." The first is a calm rational statement and doesn't even make a definitive, uncompromising stance, using a hedge word *if* to provide wiggle room, whereas the second choice is far more extreme.

⏱ BENCHMARK

As you read through the answer choices and you come across one that seems to answer the question well, mentally select that answer choice. This is not your final answer, but it's the one that will help you evaluate the other answer choices. The one that you selected is your benchmark or standard for judging each of the other answer choices. Every other answer choice must be compared to your benchmark. That choice is correct until proven otherwise by another answer choice beating it. If you find a better answer, then that one becomes your new benchmark. Once you've decided that no other choice answers the question as well as your benchmark, you have your final answer.

⏱ PREDICT THE ANSWER

Before you even start looking at the answer choices, it is often best to try to predict the answer. When you come up with the answer on your own, it is easier to avoid distractions and traps because you will know exactly what to look for. The right answer choice is unlikely to be word-for-word what you came up with, but it should be a close match. Even if you are confident that you have the right answer, you should still take the time to read each option before moving on.

General Strategies

⏱ TOUGH QUESTIONS

If you are stumped on a problem or it appears too hard or too difficult, don't waste time. Move on! Remember though, if you can quickly check for obviously incorrect answer choices, your chances of guessing correctly are greatly improved. Before you completely give up, at least try to knock out a couple of possible answers. Eliminate what you can and then guess at the remaining answer choices before moving on.

⏱ CHECK YOUR WORK

Since you will probably not know every term listed and the answer to every question, it is important that you get credit for the ones that you do know. Don't miss any questions through careless mistakes. If at all possible, try to take a second to look back over your answer selection and make sure you've selected the correct answer choice and haven't made a costly careless mistake (such as marking an answer choice that you didn't mean to mark). This quick double check should more than pay for itself in caught mistakes for the time it costs.

⏱ PACE YOURSELF

It's easy to be overwhelmed when you're looking at a page full of questions; your mind is confused and full of random thoughts, and the clock is ticking down faster than you would like. Calm down and maintain the pace that you have set for yourself. Especially as you get down to the last few minutes of the test, don't let the small numbers on the clock make you panic. As long as you are on track by monitoring your pace, you are guaranteed to have time for each question.

⏱ DON'T RUSH

It is very easy to make errors when you are in a hurry. Maintaining a fast pace in answering questions is pointless if it makes you miss questions that you would have gotten right otherwise. Test writers like to include distracting information and wrong answers that seem right. Taking a little extra time to avoid careless mistakes can make all the difference in your test score. Find a pace that allows you to be confident in the answers that you select.

⊘ KEEP MOVING

Panicking will not help you pass the test, so do your best to stay calm and keep moving. Taking deep breaths and going through the answer elimination steps you practiced can help to break through a stress barrier and keep your pace.

Final Notes

The combination of a solid foundation of content knowledge and the confidence that comes from practicing your plan for applying that knowledge is the key to maximizing your performance on test day. As your foundation of content knowledge is built up and strengthened, you'll find that the strategies included in this chapter become more and more effective in helping you quickly sift through the distractions and traps of the test to isolate the correct answer.

Now that you're preparing to move forward into the test content chapters of this book, be sure to keep your goal in mind. As you read, think about how you will be able to apply this information on the test. If you've already seen sample questions for the test and you have an idea of the question format and style, try to come up with questions of your own that you can answer based on what you're reading. This will give you valuable practice applying your knowledge in the same ways you can expect to on test day.

Good luck and good studying!

Measurement

Data Collection

PREPARING FOR DATA COLLECTION

Steps in **preparing for data** collection include:

- Receiving directions regarding data collection from a supervisor.
- Discussing the purposes and goals of the data collection.
- Reviewing guidelines regarding data collection protocols and responsibilities.
- Understanding exactly what is required of the data collection, including the type of data collection, the frequency, and the duration as well as the specific beginning and ending times
- Discussing the degree to which clients are aware of data collection.
- Reviewing any ethical issues with the supervisor, including the need for informed consent.
- Preparing all materials needed for data collection, such as electronic monitoring equipment, a stopwatch, or documents.
- Clarifying any information or procedures that are not clear.
- Reviewing time issues to ensure that data collection does not interfere with other client services.

REACTIVITY

Reactivity occurs when clients alter their behavior after becoming aware that they are being observed or recorded as part of an assessment. When reactivity, a common phenomenon, occurs, this can interfere with accurate data collection. The registered behavioral technician (RBT) should be aware of reactivity and take steps to minimize its effects in the following ways:

- Record observations as unobtrusively as possible.
- Increase the frequency or duration of observations so that the client becomes desensitized to them. For example, if recording data with a video camera, the RBT might take video recordings each day for 4 days as part of the daily routine and then only record the data from the 5th day.
- Make observations at a different time if reactivity is evident.
- Consider using a small or hidden camera.
- Use a different form of data collection.

In some cases, reactivity can be used to improve behavior. For example, self-monitoring in which the client records the data often results in improved behavior simply because of the client's having to record his or her behavior.

Continuous Measurement Procedures

OVERVIEW

In **continuous measurement procedures**, the RBT observes the client during specific periods of time and records all instances of the behavior being studied. Although continuous measurement procedures can provide the most information, they can be time-consuming and expensive. Continuous measurement may focus on frequency, duration, latency, and/or intensity. Continuous measurement may involve recording instances not only from direct observation but also from observing video or audio recordings. Many decisions must be made regarding continuous measurement including the following:

- Are the observations natural or contrived (i.e., with interventions)?
- What setting is to be used: natural (e.g., home, school) or clinical?
- Should assessment be unobtrusive (i.e., the client is unaware) or obtrusive (i.e., the client is aware)?
- Should electronic monitoring, direct observation, or some combination of the two be used?
- What should the observation time period be?
- What is the frequency of observation needed to obtain accurate data?
- Should the duration of the behavior be recorded?
- Is the latency (i.e., time delay) between a cue (i.e., stimulus) and the behavior (i.e., response) important to record?
- Is the intensity of the behavior important to record?

FREQUENCY

Frequency measurement is the tallying of the number of times that a particular type of behavior occurs in an observation period. Frequency measurement is used when the number of occurrences is the most important factor. However, to gain reliable data, the observation periods should be of the same duration because, for example, it is difficult to compare the results of an observation period of 5 minutes with one of 20 minutes. In some cases, such as when the behavior depends on a specific stimulus (e.g., instruction, sounds, intervention), in addition to simply tallying the results, the results are often reported as a percentage, so if a client made eye contact three times out of 10 prompts, it is reported as 30%. Frequency is sometimes reported as a rate, which is the frequency divided by the duration of the observation. So, if there were four instances in 60 minutes, it is recorded as 4:60 or 1:15. Frequency measurement is best used when the behavior is discrete and of a similar duration, so it may be used to tally hitting, biting, throwing things, or carrying out specific tasks.

DURATION

Duration measurement is the time that a particular behavior lasts. Duration measurement is used when the duration is the most important aspect, such as when measuring a client's progress in engaging in specific behaviors, such as the length of time that a client can remain seated in a chair. The *onset* is the time when the behavior begins, and the *offset* is the time it ends. Duration measurement is best suited for behaviors that the client carries out for various lengths of time, such as exercising, rather than short-duration behavior, such as hitting. Duration measurement may also be used to measure behavioral states, such as agitation or withdrawal. A stopwatch is often used for duration measurement. In some cases, video monitoring is used during the observation period and then the videotape is reviewed and the frequency and onset and offset of the behavior being studied are recorded. Duration may be reported as a percentage of the observation time (the duration of the behavior divided by the duration of the observation period).

Measurement

LATENCY

Latency measurement is the time between a cue (i.e., a stimulus) and the target behavior (i.e., the response). For example, if an RBT asks a client to open a book, the time before the client carries out the task is the latency period. Latency measurement may be used when the goal is to shorten the latency period, such as when trying to get a child to put away toys more quickly after a request. Latency measurement may also be used when trying to lengthen the latency period, such as when trying to extend the time before a client engages in aggressive behavior during periods of interaction with others. Latency measurement is always used for specific relationships: stimulus and response. Latency measurement involves continuous measurement and is often used when assessing the need for intervention or when determining the effectiveness of interventions used to modify behavior.

INTENSITY

Intensity measurement is the strength, force, or magnitude of a response rather than a dimension of time. Because of this, intensity is used less frequently than other measures and may be more difficult to measure and may require the use of monitoring devices (such as a decibel meter) or a point system that categorizes variations in behavior, such as may occur during a tantrum. Each point on a rating scale must be clearly defined so that different observers will score the intensity in the same way. Intensity measurement may be used, for example, to measure such things as the volume of a client's voice or the intensity of a tantrum. The point system may be used as part of interventions as well as for monitoring. For example, a client may earn points toward a reward when he or she decreases the intensity of the response.

DISCRETE CATEGORIZATION

Discrete categorization is similar to frequency and duration measurements because it involves continuous measurement and beginning (i.e., onset) and ending (i.e., offset) times. However, whereas other continuous measurements focus on one behavior or response, discrete categorization focuses on a series of behaviors leading to one goal or outcome, such as the ability of a client to complete a task or carry out activities. For example, when teaching a client to dress, the first step may be to gather clothing, and many steps may follow before the client is actually clothed. For that reason, a checklist is often used for assessment and it becomes a tool that guides intervention. The client is assessed according to how many items are achieved from the checklist. Discrete categorization is flexible and may involve apparently unrelated behaviors that are necessary to achieve the goal.

Discontinuous Measurement Procedures

PARTIAL INTERVAL

Discontinuous measurement occurs during only part of a day or session in scheduled intervals. For example, scheduled intervals for observations may vary, such as 30 seconds every hour or 15 seconds every 10 minutes, depending on the target behavior. Because the data reflect only part of the time, they are less reliable than continuous data. With **partial interval** measurement, the frequency of the behavior during the interval is recorded, but the purpose is only to determine if the behavior is present or not during the interval, not to record the total number of behaviors. For example, observing eye contact during five 60-second intervals yields this result:

- First interval: Zero instances of eye contact.
- Second interval: One instance of eye contact.
- Third interval: Two instances of eye contact.
- Fourth interval: Three instances of eye contact.
- Fifth interval: Zero instances of eye contact.

When recording the partial interval results, the number of intervals during which eye contact is made is counted (not the total behaviors), so the client's response rate is three out of five (3/5), or 60%.

WHOLE INTERVAL

Whole interval measurement is a form of discontinuous measurement in that the measurement occurs during scheduled intervals of observation, not the entire day or session. With partial interval measurement, any behavior observed for any part of the interval is counted as a response; however, for whole interval measurement, the behavior must occur throughout the entire interval to be counted as a response. For example, observing attention to task for five 20-second intervals yields this result:

- First interval: 15 seconds on task.
- Second interval: 12 seconds on task.
- Third interval: 20 seconds on task.
- Fourth interval: 9 seconds on task.
- Fifth interval: 13 seconds on task.

When recording the whole interval results, only one response, or 20%, is recorded for the intervals because during the other four intervals the client did not stay on task during the entire interval. Whole interval measurement may thus result in underestimation of behaviors because the client did in fact stay on task for a significant portion of each interval.

MOMENTARY TIME SAMPLING

Momentary time sampling is a form of discontinuous measurement because it measures only whether a behavior is present or absent at scheduled points in time. Momentary time sampling is best suited for behaviors that are of long duration. For example, if a client engages in stimming (i.e., repetitive noises or body movement, such as waving the hands or rocking), a timer may be set for every 15 seconds for six intervals; when the timer goes off, the RBT notes only if the behavior is present or absent—for example:

- First interval: Present.
- Second interval: Present.

- Third interval: Present.
- Fourth interval: Present.
- Fifth interval: Absent.
- Sixth interval: Absent.

When recording the momentary sampling results, four responses are recorded. Momentary time sampling can provide information about the duration of the behavior. In this case, the behavior stopped after the fourth interval, or 60 seconds. For whole time sampling, intervals of 10–60 seconds tend to provide more accurate results than longer intervals.

Measurement

19

Permanent-Product Recording Procedures

Permanent product recording procedures are indirect methods for assessing behavior that produce an outcome or a tangible product, such as assembled devices, completed worksheets, or toys left on the floor. Permanent product recording differs from other measures because it does not require direct or real-time observation, so the RBT does not need to be present to observe the behavior, only to count and record the results (or products) of the behavior after the fact. One disadvantage is that, because the behavior is not observed, it is not always clear who is producing the permanent product. For example, sometimes clients may receive assistance from caregivers who want the client to appear to do well. Additionally, permanent product recording provides no information about what may be influencing a client's outcome or production.

Data and Graphs

LINE GRAPHS

Line graphs are often used to plot progress over time and are the most common graphs used by RBTs. Line graphs have an *x* and a *y* axis, with the *y* axis, vertical, typically used to indicate behavior, and the *x* axis, horizontal, used to indicate time. In this graph, the *x* axis represents the workweek, Monday through Friday, and the *y* axis represents the frequency of a desired positive behavior, with a low incidence of 3 at baseline. The first data point entered is usually the baseline data that are taken before any intervention takes place. A data point (count) is entered for each day, and the lines are connected between the data points. In this graph, the client has showed a slow and irregular improvement in behavior from baseline.

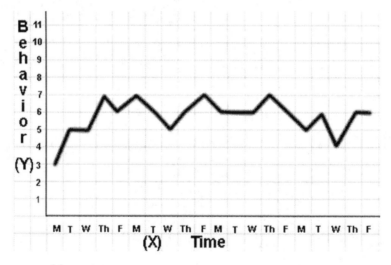

LINE GRAPH LEVELS AND VARIABILITY

Data exhibited in a line graph may show high variability (having a significant difference between the high and low data points) or low variability (having little difference between the high and low data points). High-level data points are near the top of the *y* axis, middle-level data points are near the middle of the *y* axis, and low-level data points are near the bottom of the *y* axis. Interpreting the graph involves visual analysis. The data are reviewed to determine if they are increasing, decreasing, or if no trend is obvious (i.e., the data are stable).

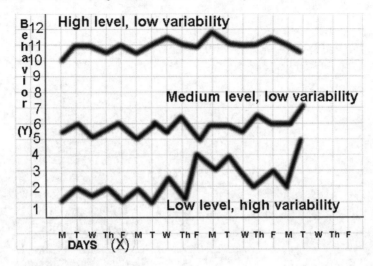

BAR GRAPHS

A **bar graph** is a simple visual method of displaying data. The bar graph may be arranged horizontally or vertically. The bar graph is commonly used to demonstrate performance under different conditions or times or comparisons among different individuals or events. For example, this graph shows the number of responses (such as complying with requests) that a client makes during weekly visits. The first bar represents the baseline data before the intervention, and the subsequent bars show the number of appropriate responses given each week. The bar graph is an easy method of quickly displaying data to others.

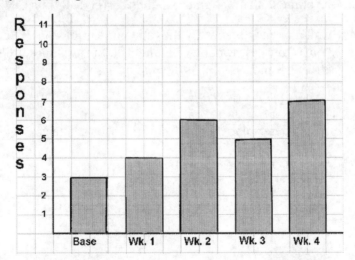

CUMULATIVE GRAPHS

A **cumulative graph** is used to display totals rather than incremental data. This type of graph is useful when graphing something when the goal is to increase a total, such as when a client is to read independently each day. In this case, the client read two pages on the first day and three pages on the second day, so the graph shows five pages for day 2 (not three pages). On day 3, the client again read three pages, so the total is eight pages (five plus three). When a plateau occurs, such as the one between days 6 and 7 and the one between days 8 and 9, this indicates that the client read no pages on those days. If daily performance is more important than total performance, then a line graph provides information that can be more quickly accessed.

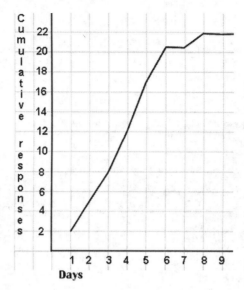

CALCULATING PERCENTAGES AND AVERAGES

A **percentage** is often used to document or describe how frequently or for what time duration of a session a client carries out a behavior. The formula for calculating percentages is as follows:

- Correct responses are divided by the total number of opportunities.
- Thus, if a client is prompted 20 times and responds correctly 8 times, 8/20 = 0.4 = 40%.

The **average** is the sum of all numbers divided by the total number of values. For example, if a client scores 6, 8, 5, and 3 on a daily assessment, the sum of all the numbers is 6 + 8 + 5 + 3 = 22. There are 4 total numbers (6, 8, 5, and 3), so 22 is divided by 4:

- 22/4 = 5.5 is the average score.

Calculating an average can help determine if there is low, high, or stable variability.

Behavior and Environment

DESCRIPTIONS OF BEHAVIOR AND ENVIRONMENT

Descriptions of behavior and environment must be in observable and measurable terms. That is, do not make descriptions of behavior in terms of thoughts, emotions, or feelings (i.e., subjective) but rather in terms of what can be observed and heard (i.e., objective). For example, if a client appears angry, the description should avoid the word "angry" because this implies a feeling, but it should include the observable behavior that suggests that the client is angry: "Client ignored directions, threw papers on the floor, and screamed that she hated school." Descriptions of events should also be measurable. Instead of saying "The client completed most tasks successfully," the description should be, "The client correctly identified primary colors 8 times out of 10." Descriptions of the environment can include anything that can be perceived through one of the senses: hearing, seeing, feeling, smelling, and tasting. Again, the descriptions should be objective and measurable. Instead of "The client's desk was cluttered," the description should be "The client's desk contained three books, a stack of worksheets, four small toys, and a box of crayons."

BARRIERS TO ACCURATE MEASUREMENT/DATA COLLECTION

Measurements should be accurate, reliable, and valid. Potential **barriers to accurate measurement/data collection** include the following:

- Expectations: If the observer focuses too much on expected outcomes and behavior goals, the observer may inadvertently overlook behavior that does not meet those expected outcomes and overvalue behavior that does, resulting in data that are unreliable and inaccurate.
- Observer influences: Different observers come with preconceived ideas and biases that may interfere with accurate measurement. The number of observers can also affect measurement. If one observer has been monitoring responses and a second observer comes to participate, this can affect reliability and accuracy, which may be better or worse.
- Observer drift: Prolonged measurement may result in boredom or fatigue, which can affect the results, so long periods of measurement should be avoided.
- Client reaction: In some cases, if clients are aware that they are being observed/measured in some way, this may alter their responses; therefore, unobtrusive measurement methods should be used whenever possible.

Assessment

Preference Assessments

OVERVIEW

Preference assessments are carried out to help determine what will motivate a client to carry out an appropriate response. A reinforcer is provided following an appropriate response to increase the chance that the same response will occur in a similar circumstance. Preference assessments help to identify those reinforcers that will be the most valuable in different situations. Reinforcers are those things—toys, foods, items, videos, TV viewing, video games, praise—that increase a target behavior. However, reinforcers may change depending on the situation and the client's frame of mind, so what may work as a reinforcer one day may not work the next. Reinforcers are often used when helping the client attain new skills or to reduce unwanted behaviors. To be effective, the reinforcer must only be provided when the client performs the desired response. Many different preference assessment methods can be used to determine the most effective reinforcers, including asking the client, indirect assessment, free operant assessment, and trial-based assessments.

IDENTIFYING REINFORCERS

INDIRECT ASSESSMENT AND FREE OPERANT

Preference assessment methods include the following:

- **Ask the client:** When appropriate, ask the client directly what he or she likes to do in his or her free time (e.g., "What is your favorite toy to play with?") or provide choices of two rewards (e.g., "Would you like a new hair tie or a chocolate?") Some clients may be able to rank order a list of items.
- **Indirect assessment:** Ask a parent/caregiver what the client likes or prefers (e.g., "What seems to keep the child's attention?" or "What is the child's favorite toy?").
- **Free operant** (i.e., the longer the duration with an item, the greater the preference):
  - Contrived: Place a number of items, such as toys, on the floor, and observe the client interacting with the items, noting which items the client chooses, the order of choice, and the duration of interaction with the items.
  - Naturalistic: Observe the client in the natural environment, such as in his or her home, and note the client's behavior and interactions with items as well as the duration of time spent with each item.

SINGLE STIMULUS AND PAIRED STIMULI

Preference assessments include trial-based methods. Note: It is important to allow the client time to interact/play with the chosen items after they are selected rather than rushing to the next trial. Trial-based methods:

- **Single stimulus:** Present the client with one item at a time, and note the type of interaction that occurs. Does the client approach the item? Ignore the item? Push it away? Consume it (if it is food)? Record the duration of engagement with the item. With repeated trials, record the number of times that the client interacts with the item out of the total trials: "Picked up the toy three out of five times." This approach is useful for clients who have difficulty making choices.

24

- **Paired stimuli (Forced choice):** Present the client with a choice of two items of similar size (such as two toys). Note the response (as above) and the item selected. With repeated trials, alter the side that an item is placed on and note whether the client tends to always select the item on one side. If this occurs, then paired stimuli is not an effective assessment for this client.

MULTIPLE STIMULI

Preference assessment includes trial-based methods, such as **multiple stimuli.** With multiple stimuli, the client is presented with three to eight items and is asked to choose one. The choice is noted as well as the type of interaction with the item and its duration. The client is given time to interact with the chosen item, and then the items are removed. Repeat multiple stimuli trials (usually approximately three to five total) are carried out in the following ways:

- **Multiple stimulus without replacement:** Remove the item that was selected first, present the remaining items in a different arrangement, and continue removing the chosen items one at a time until through with all of the items. Note the order of preference as the client chooses items.
- **Multiple stimulus with replacement:** Keep the chosen item in the array, but replace the other items. Each item should be included in the array at least two times in order to establish an order of preference. Note that if a client has a strong preference for one item, the client may choose that item repeatedly. In that case, that item may be omitted from repeat trials.

Assessment

25

Individualized Assessment Procedures

OVERVIEW

Although **individualized assessments** are implemented by the board certified behavior analyst (BCBA), the RBT should have an understanding of the assessment process and be prepared to assist with assessments. The purpose of the assessment is to gather information about a client and determine the client's skill level, needs, and barriers. The assessment is used to develop and update goals, so performing a baseline assessment is essential at the beginning of services so that progress toward goals can be measured. Informal assessments are carried out at each session, and the RBT communicates these assessments through objective documentation and verbal reports during supervisory visits. Formal assessments, typically using an assessment tool, are carried out at regular intervals, such as monthly, quarterly, and annually. Insurance companies may require periodic assessments. Assessment should also always be carried out at the end of service to demonstrate progress. Skills and behaviors are likely to vary over time, and current treatment may become inadequate if the client is not frequently assessed. Assessment should always be selected based on the client's individualized needs and age.

NORM-REFERENCED AND CRITERION-REFERENCED

Individualized assessment procedures may include formal assessments such as the following:

- **Norm-referenced:** This assessment uses standardized tests to determine how the client's performance ranks in relation to peers taking the test. Norm-referenced tests include the SAT and ACT. If, for example, a client scores 25% on a norm-referenced test, this means that 75% of the test takers scored higher and 24% scored lower. These scores do not, however, provide information about the specific skill deficits that the client might have.
- **Criterion-referenced:** This assessment does not compare clients with peers but rather with a predetermined criteria or skill level. Criterion-based tests include the Verbal Behavior Milestones Assessment and Placement Program and the Assessment of Basic Language and Learning Skills, Revised. For the results to be valid, the skill level being tested should be appropriate for the client because setting it too low or too high can result in scores that do not accurately reflect the client's skills.

CURRICULUM-BASED, DEVELOPMENTAL, AND SOCIAL SKILLS

Individualized assessment procedures include the following:

- **Curriculum-based:** Criterion-referenced assessment is based on the curriculum that a client has been taught, so the assessment is individualized for the client (or a group of clients who have received the same instructions). The results can provide information about the success of the instructions or the need to use a different approach with one or more clients. Many different tools are used for curriculum-based assessments.
- **Developmental:** Focuses on milestones of development corresponding to the client's age. For example, developmental assessment of a child includes physical (grasping, rolling over, crawling, walking), intellectual (comprehension, communication), emotional (response, eye contact), and social (interaction, parallel play).
- **Social skills**: Focuses on the client's ability to interact with others, perceptions of social interactions, and coping with social situations.

NORMAL GROWTH AND DEVELOPMENT DURING CHILDHOOD

AGES 2–3

The **2–3-year-old** makes significant changes over the course of a year, including the following:

- **Growth**: Gains 3–5 lb of body weight and 3.5–5.0 in of height.
- **Mobility**: Can run steadily, jump on two feet, and climb. Scribbling becomes more intentional and can draw simple shapes. Makes an effort to color in the lines. Able to undress at age 2 and dress at age 3. Can throw a ball overhand. Plays side by side, and begins to interact with others.
- **Diet**: Can switch to low-fat milk, two to three cups daily along with a regular well-balanced meal of meat, fruits, vegetables, and grains. Should limit fruit juice to 2–4 oz/day because of the high sugar content. Should not be receiving bottle feedings.
- **Toileting**: Most children become potty trained at some time during this year.
- **Communication/cognition:** Begins to talk in short three-word sentences and to understand rules. Begins to use pronouns (e.g., I, me, you) and can talk about feelings. Usually knows the names of at least five body parts and five colors and can categorize objects by size (big or little).

AGES 3–6

Between ages **3 and 6**, the child moves from being a toddler to a child as noted by the following developments:

- **Growth**: Gains 3–5 lb of body weight per year and 1.5–2.5 in of height per year. Most growth occurs in the long bones as the child increases in stature and the head size decreases proportionately.
- **Mobility**: Becomes increasingly adept, drawing various shapes, coloring in the lines, using scissors to cut along lines on paper. Can brush teeth. Can tie shoes by age 6. Able to climb, run, jump, balance, and ride a tricycle or bicycle with training wheels. Interacts with others.
- **Diet**: Eats three meals a day with snacks and can manage a spoon, fork, and knife independently by age 6.
- **Communication/Cognition:** Becomes increasingly verbal and social and commands a large complex vocabulary by age 6. Understands concepts of right and wrong and good and bad and can lie. Learns letters and numbers and by age 6 is beginning to read. May focus on one thing to the exclusion of others.

INDICATIONS OF DEVELOPMENTAL DELAYS

AGES 6–12

During the years of **6–12,** routine health assessments should be done at ages 6, 8, 10, 11, and 12 to determine if there are developmental delays or problems, which may include the following:

- **6 years**: Peer problems, depression, cruelty to animals, poor academic progress, speech problems, lack of fine motor skills, and inability to catch a ball or state age.
- **8 years:** No close friends; depression; cruelty to animals; interest in fires; very poor academic progress with inability to do math, read, or write adequately; and poor coordination.

27

- **10 years:** No team sports and poor choices in peers (gangs); failure to follow rules; cruelty to animals; interest in fires; depression; failure to understand causal relationships; poor academic progress in reading, writing, math, and penmanship; and problems throwing or catching.
- **12 years:** Continuation of problems at 10 years with increasing risk-taking behaviors (e.g., drinking, drugs, sex) and continued poor academic progress in reading, following directions, doing homework, and organization.

AGES 11–14

Early adolescence, ages **11–14,** is a transitional time for children as their hormones and their bodies go through changes. Children mature at varying rates, so there are wide differences. Emotions may be labile, and the child may feel isolated and confused at times, trying to find an identity. Peers gain influence, and the child may challenge the values of the family. Children may have great anxiety about their bodies and sexuality as their secondary sexual characteristics develop. Developmental concerns include the following:

- Delayed maturation.
- Short stature (in females).
- Spinal curvature (in females)
- Poor dental status (e.g., caries, malocclusion)
- Chronic illnesses, such as diabetes.
- Lack of adequate physical activity.
- Poor nutrition, anorexia.
- Concerns about sexual identity.
- Negative self-image.
- Depression.
- Lack of close friends, fighting or violent episodes.
- Poor academic progress with truancy and failure to complete assignments.
- Lack of impulse control.
- Obesity.

AGES 15–17

In middle adolescence, ages **15–17,** most body changes have occurred, and there is less concern about this but more concern about the image teens are projecting to others. Girls may worry about weight and boys about muscle development. Teenagers are interested in sexuality and many begin sexual experimentation. There is strong identification with peer groups, including codes of dress and behavior, often putting teens at odds with their families. Developmental concerns include the following:

- Spinal curvature (in females) and short stature (in males).
- Lack of testicular maturation/Persistent gynecomastia.
- Acne.
- Anorexia, obesity.
- Sexual experimentation, multiple sex partners, and unprotected sex.
- Sexual identification concerns.
- Depression, poor self-image.
- Lack of adequate exercise, poor nutrition, and poor dental health.
- Chronic diseases.
- Experimentation with drugs and alcohol and problems with authority figures.

- Lack of peer group identification, gang associations.
- Poor academic progress, failing classes, truancy, attention deficits and disruptive class behaviors, and poor judgment and impulse control.

AGES 18–21

Late adolescence, ages **18–21,** is the time when adolescents begin to take on more adult roles and responsibilities, entering the world of work or going to college. Most have come to terms with their sexuality and have a more mature understanding of people's motivations. Some young people will continue to engage in high-risk behaviors. Many of the problems associated with middle adolescence may continue if unresolved, interfering with the transition to adulthood. Developmental concerns include the following:

- Failure to take on adult roles, no life goals or future plans.
- Low self-esteem.
- Lack of intimate relationships, sexual identification concerns.
- Gang association.
- Continued identification with peer group or dependence on parents.
- High-risk sexual behaviors, multiple sex partners, and unprotected sex.
- Poor academic progress or ability.
- Psychosomatic complaints and depression.
- Lack of impulse control.
- Poor nutrition, obesity, and anorexia.
- Poor dental health.
- Chronic disease.
- Lack of exercise.

THE VERBAL BEHAVIOR MILESTONES ASSESSMENT AND PLACEMENT PROGRAM

The **Verbal Behavior Milestones Assessment and Placement Program** is a criterion-referenced curriculum guide/skills assessment tool intended for clients ages 2–6 years who have autism or other types of language delay. Skills testing is conducted every 6 months and covers the assessment of expected milestones at different ages to determine if the client has a particular skill. Skills that are tested include mand (i.e., making a request or an indication to get something), tact (i.e., naming an item), echoic (i.e., verbally repeating words/phrases/sounds), intraverbal (i.e., making an appropriate response in response to a vocal prompt), independent play (i.e., the ability to play alone), and social/social play (i.e., the ability to interact with others with eye contact, parallel play, etc.). More complex skills are assessed with older children, including imitation, following directions, reading, writing, and math. This tool also assesses 24 barriers to learning (such as behavioral problems) and transition assessment, which helps to determine if the client is ready to transition to a less restrictive environment (such as to a regular class instead of to a special education class).

THE ASSESSMENT OF BASIC LANGUAGE AND LEARNING SKILLS, REVISED AND THE PROMOTING THE EMERGENCE OF ADVANCED KNOWLEDGE SYSTEM

Common **assessment tools** include the following:

- **Assessment of Basic Language and Learning Skills, Revised:** A criterion-referenced assessment intended for clients ages 0–12 years. This tool assesses 25 skill areas, including language, self-help, academic, motor skills, and social skills. This tool assesses the skills that most children need to begin kindergarten and to communicate and learn. This tool is similar to the Verbal Behavior Milestones Assessment and Placement Program, but it assesses a greater number of skills.

- The **Promoting the Emergence of Advanced Knowledge system:** This assessment tool is intended for children of ages 18 months through adolescence with autism to test language and other skills such as problem solving and application of knowledge they have learned. A client's skills are assessed, and then a curriculum is put in place based on the client's needs and goals in language and communication, social skills, and behavior. The tool contains four modules that focus on target skills: direct training (on foundational skills), generalization (i.e., the ability to use skills in different ways), equivalence (i.e., the use of all senses), and transformation (i.e., problem solving, reasoning).

Functional Assessment Procedures

FUNCTIONAL BEHAVIORAL ASSESSMENTS

Functional behavioral assessments are carried out to determine the reason why a behavior is repeatedly occurring or what function the behavior serves for the client. In order to fully understand a behavior, it is important to know the circumstances associated with the behavior, or the ABCs:

- **Antecedent**: What happens before the behavior occurs.
- **Behavior**: The target response.
- **Consequence**: What follows the behavior.

Once the ABCs are determined, this information can be used to design interventions to decrease the problem behavior. Assessments can be carried out in different manners: direct/descriptive (i.e., observing the behavior in the natural environment without intervening), functional analysis (i.e., contriving interventions and situations to try to trigger the behavior), and indirect (i.e., interviewing, using questionnaires or surveys). Probing, that is, asking the client to carry out a skill and then observing to see if the client is able to do so, is often used. The RBT may assist with assessment under the guidance of the BCBA.

MAKING ANTECEDENT, BEHAVIOR, CONSEQUENCE (ABC) OBSERVATIONS

The RBT may be asked to assist with determining a client's **ABCs** through observation as follows:

- **Antecedent:** Observe for possible triggers for behavior, which may include sensory stimulation (e.g., noise, lights, smells), confusion (e.g., inadequate prompt or explanation), biological distress (e.g., headache, hunger, fatigue, pain), shame/embarrassment (loss of game, bullying, criticism), lack of attention, and delayed gratification.
- **Behavior:** Explain behavior in objective detail.
- **Consequences:** Observe how others respond to the client's behavior and what the client appears to gain or lose: Avoidance of an unpleasant/unwanted situation, attention getting, obtaining a tangible item (e.g., a toy, food), self-soothing, or relief of frustration and anxiety.

Date/Time	A	B	C
3/28 1:10 PM	Class bell rings.	Ignores bell and throws books.	Placed in time-out.

THE ASSESSMENT OF FUNCTIONAL LIVING SKILLS AND ESSENTIAL FOR LIVING

Individualized **functional assessment** tools include:

- **Assessment of Functional Living Skills:** This is a criterion-referenced assessment intended for school-aged children to adults. The tool contains six different assessment protocols, so the person assessing can choose which protocols are most appropriate for the client. The protocols include (1) basic living skills (e.g., bathing, dressing), (2) home skills (e.g., laundry, meal preparation), (3) community participation (e.g., handling money, social awareness, shopping), (4) school skills (e.g., social skills, ability to use technology), (5) independent living skills (e.g., self-care, cleaning, traveling), and (6) vocational skills (i.e., the ability to engage in employment).

- **Essential for Living:** Assesses functional living skills that everyone is expected to have. This tool is appropriate for those ages 2 years and older. This tool contains a protocol to assess skills as well as teaching guidelines if a client lacks a skill. Skills assessed include communication, daily living, vocational, academic, language, and social.

KEYSTONE BEHAVIORS

Keystone behaviors are those that, when changed, also affect other behaviors. For example, if a client is frustrated with a task, the client may also be angry because he or she cannot achieve the task and sad because of feeling like a failure, resulting in the client lashing out or withdrawing. If the source of the frustration is identified and altered to reduce frustration, the client is likely to no longer feel angry and sad, and the associated behavior (e.g., lashing out or withdrawing) will change without further intervention. Keystone behavior assessment differs from functional assessment in that functional assessment looks primarily at the stimulus-response relationship whereas keystone behavior assessment focuses more on the response-response relationship. Keystone behaviors may be positively or negatively correlated with other behaviors, so keystone behaviors are considered pivotal in changing behavior. Thus, when looking at a series of associated behaviors, it is important to assess which change in behavior would be most beneficial in changing multiple behaviors: That is the keystone behavior.

CRITICAL THINKING SKILLS

The main purposes of **critical thinking** are to think and question about a goal or solution and then to exercise good judgment based on evidence rather than on subjective opinion. Critical thinking includes the ability to think logically and to apply reason. Steps to critical thinking include the following:

- Ask a question.
- Gather evidence, such as observations or data and advice of others.
- Review evidence and determine strengths and weaknesses, trends.
- Identify any assumptions or biases.
- Make a decision based on the evidence.

Critical thinking means that one should recognize and avoid logical fallacies and other common errors in reasoning such as the following:

- **Hasty generalization**: Assuming that one example applies to a whole group. For example, if a young client dislikes the sound of bells, assuming that all children of that age dislike the sound of bells.
- **Overgeneralization**: Extending conclusions beyond what is reasonable. For example, if one client is resistive to a training technique, assuming that there is something wrong with the technique.
- **Post hoc fallacy**: Making the assumption that if one thing occurs before another, the first thing causes the second without evidence to support that assumption. For example, if a phone rings and a client throws a toy immediately afterward, it is a post hoc fallacy to assume that the phone ringing is the cause. (In reality, there could be many different reasons for the client to throw a toy.)

GROUPS

Working with clients in a **group** is a good way to assess an individual client's interactions with others and to work on the client's group skills, such as turn-taking, sharing, and communicating. In the case of young clients, such as a group of children on the autism spectrum, typically each client has a dedicated RBT to provide individualized attention and reinforcement as the clients interact and to assess their progress. However, in some cases, one RBT may work with two or more individuals in a group, and this can present challenges in making observations and collecting data, either electronically or manually. The larger the group, the more difficult the data collection because of the potential for some group participants to become aggressive or resistive and the general chaos that can occur with a larger group with different sets of behavior. Small group instruction is practical and may be time-saving and helps promote maintenance and generalization of skills.

Assessment

33

Skill Acquisition

BEHAVIORAL CHARACTERISTICS

ASSOCIATED WITH AUTISM SPECTRUM DISORDERS

People with **autism spectrum disorders** present with a wide range of symptoms. These individuals, usually exhibiting symptoms within the first 2 years of life, are often isolated with an inability to socialize. Approximately 25% suffer seizure disorders. Some degree of mental impairment is present in up to 75%, but there is a wide range—from nonverbal and completely dependent to highly functioning (formerly Asperger's). Early diagnosis helps maximize a child's potential and may allow the child to live independently as an adult. Common characteristics include the following:

- Impairment of social interactions (in at least two areas): Inability to use/understand nonverbal communication, inability to establish peer relationships, lack of socialization skills, and inability to express emotions. Because they lack social skills, children are often isolated and bullied.
- Impairment of communication (in at least one area): Delay or lack of spoken language without attempt to compensate, such as through gestures, inability to carry out a conversation with others, repetitive use of language (i.e., echolalia), and inability to carry out make-believe play or imitation appropriate to developmental level.
- Restrictive repetitive or stereotyped behavior (in at least one area): Preoccupation with some behavior patterns (e.g., head banging, rituals, stimming), inflexibility, and/or preoccupation with objects.

ASSOCIATED WITH ATTENTION-DEFICIT HYPERACTIVITY/DISORDER

Attention-deficit hyperactivity/disorder affects 2–3% of children and often lasts into adulthood. This disorder usually has the following three characteristics:

- **Inattention**: Daydreaming, mind wandering.
- **Impulsivity**: Making careless mistakes, gets along poorly with others, has trouble taking turns, loses things, forgets things (such as handing in assignments).
- **Hyperactivity**: Talking too much, squirming, fidgeting.

These behaviors make it difficult for the client to pay attention in school and keep track of assignments and often result in behavioral and social problems. Additionally, Attention-deficit hyperactivity/disorder may be accompanied by learning disabilities, such as dyslexia, as well as depression or other mood disorders. Diagnosis often includes observation and surveys of family and teachers to determine patterns of behavior. Intervention includes medications and coping and organizing skills. Studies of different treatments indicate that a combined approach with medications and behavioral therapy is more effective than either medication alone or behavioral therapy alone. The combined approach may allow lower medication dosages.

FRAGILE X SYNDROME

Fragile X syndrome, a genetic X-linked disorder, is the most commonly inherited form of mental impairment and autism. The disorder primarily affects males, but some female carriers may exhibit mild symptoms. One of the genes that should repeat (i.e., copy) 6–50 times overexpands (i.e., makes too many copies), inhibiting production of the fragile X mental retardation protein, which is necessary for development of the brain and other organs. Risks associated with fragile X syndrome correlate with the number of repeats. Most children with fragile X live a normal life span without serious medical problems related to fragile X.

Fragile X syndrome: Indications		
Mental	**Physical**	**Behavioral**
• Cognitive impairment (a low IQ) • Learning disabilities • Slow/delayed speech	• Facial abnormalities: A large, long head and ears with prominent forehead and a square jaw • Lax joints • Flat feet • Abnormally large testicles (in males) • Seizure disorders • Visual disturbances • Heart valve abnormalities (mitral valve prolapse)	• Autistic-like behavior • Hyperactivity and short attention span • Shyness • Difficulty/inability to make eye contact • Difficulty adjusting to changes

CLASSIFICATIONS BY IQ

Intellectual disability (ID) is usually diagnosed before age 18. Individuals may have difficulty adapting to changing environments, need guidance in decision making, and have self-care or communication deficits. Behaviors range from shy and passive to hyperactive or aggressive. Those with associated physical characteristics (e.g., Down syndrome) or problems are often diagnosed early. ID may be inherited (e.g., in Tay-Sachs disease), toxin-related (e.g., in maternal alcohol consumption), perinatal (e.g., with a lack of oxygen), environmental (e.g., due to a lack of stimulation/neglect), or acquired (e.g., in encephalitis, brain injury). Diagnosis involves performance results from standardized tests along with behavior analysis. ID classifications are based on IQ:

Classifications (IQ)	Description
55–69: mild (85%)	Educable to approximately the 6th-grade level. May not be diagnosed until adolescence. Usually able to learn skills and be self-supporting but may need assistance and supervision.
40–54: moderate (10%)	Trainable and may be able to work and live in sheltered environments or with supervision.
25–39: severe (3–4%)	Language is usually delayed. Can learn only basic academic skills and perform only simple tasks.
≤25: profound (1–2%)	Usually associated with a neurological disorder with sensorimotor dysfunction. Require constant care and supervision.

Skill Acquisition

FETAL ALCOHOL SYNDROME

Fetal alcohol syndrome is a syndrome of birth defects including brain damage and physical abnormalities (e.g., facial abnormalities, neurological impairments, slow growth) and develops as the result of maternal ingestion of alcohol. Despite campaigns to inform the public, women continue to drink during pregnancy, but no safe amount of alcohol ingestion has been determined. fetal alcohol syndrome includes the following:

- **Neurological deficits:** May include microcephaly (i.e., small head), intellectual disability, motor delay, hearing deficits. Learning disorders may include problems with visual-spatial (i.e., the ability to tell where things are in space) and verbal learning, attention disorders, and delayed reaction. Clients often have poor memory and difficulty with problem solving and understanding the consequences of their actions.
- **Behavioral problems:** Clients may exhibit irritability and hyperactivity as well as poor judgment in behavior and lack of impulse control. They may have difficulty getting along with others because of poor social skills. In school, they may have difficulty staying on task and paying attention and changing from one task to a different one. Their concept of time may be poor.

TRISOMY 21

Trisomy 21 (i.e., **Down syndrome**) is the most common chromosomal disorder in humans and is one of the leading causes of intellectual disability (which is usually mild to moderate). Common physical characteristics include a short, broad head; short stature; and epicanthic skin folds in the upper eyelids. Orthopedic problems, dental abnormalities, and conductive hearing loss are common, and 40–50% have congenital heart defects. Behavioral characteristics include the following:

- Those with a mild intellectual disability can usually learn to read and take care of activities of daily living and may be able to hold a job as an adult. Some can live independently or with some assistance. Those with a moderate to more severe intellectual disability may need support for most activities.
- Having a short attention span is common, and many have difficulty with memory of spoken words (such as directions) but are good visual learners, so using pictures and diagrams is more effective than giving verbal directions or explanations. Some clients talk out loud to themselves to help them understand information.
- Clients with Down syndrome often have good social skills and are friendly, loving, and trusting with others
- Some clients may exhibit stubbornness and throw temper tantrums when frustrated.

OPPOSITIONAL DEFIANT DISORDER (ODD)

Having **oppositional defiant disorder** (ODD) means that the client has an abnormally intense disregard for authority figures, primarily parents or guardians or people that the client knows well. This behavior usually starts before age 8 up to age 12. Behavior with ODD usually does not involve aggressive behavior or violence toward people, property, or animals. The ODD client challenges authority figures because of learned behaviors, such as negative reinforcement. A pattern of mutual negative reinforcement occurs between the client and authority figures in such a manner that the client confronts all requests with extreme defiance. Typical patterns of behavior may consist of having frequent losses of temper, arguing with authority figures, showing defiance, blaming others, and annoying others. The behavior is so problematic as to cause problems at work, school, or play. The client with ODD exhibits social and academic impairments that are not the result of a psychotic or mood disorder.

CONDUCT DISORDER

Conduct disorder is characterized by a blatant disregard for other people's feelings and property, societal norms, and etiquette. Its onset may be during childhood or adolescence. Conduct disorder likely develops when an individual has a genetic predisposition or weakness and experiences childhood stresses such as abuse, neglect, harsh parenting, or poverty. Individuals who are predisposed to conduct disorder often develop psychosis, depression, violent mood swings, and irritability. Conduct disorder is more prevalent in males than females. The diagnostic criteria for conduct disorder require a relentless pattern of behavior that shows a lack of respect for the rights of others as well as social norms. Indications include aggression to people or animals (e.g., bullying, abuse), destruction of property (e.g., fire-setting, destruction), deceitfulness or theft (including criminal acts), and serious violations of rules (e.g., defiance before age 13, spitefulness, truancy, running away, blaming others).

OBSESSIVE-COMPULSIVE DISORDER

Obsessive-compulsive disorder is a disorder in which individuals are plagued by obsessions and/or compulsions that interfere with employment (as adults) and social, interpersonal, and other daily activities and last more than 1 hour daily. Its onset is most often between ages 10 and 12 or during late adolescence and early adulthood. Characteristics include the following:

- Obsessions are unwanted, repeated, and uncontrollable ideas, images, or urges that come to mind involuntarily despite attempts to ignore or suppress them.
- Compulsions are repeated, unwanted pattern(s) of behavior (impulses) to perform apparently irrational or useless acts that are often responses to obsessions and are done to reduce stress (e.g., cleaning and washing repeatedly, repeated checking or counting, and arranging and rearranging items).

A sense of dread may develop if the compulsion is resisted, and some try to ignore or suppress these thoughts/behaviors. Behavioral interventions include the following:

- Combined exposure with training to delay obsessive responses. Best used in conjunction with pharmacotherapy (i.e., medications).
- Steady decrease of rituals by exposure to anxiety-producing situations until the client has learned to control the related obsessive compulsion.
- Reducing obsessive thoughts by the use of reminders or noxious stimuli to stop chain-of-thought patterns, such as snapping a rubber band on the wrist when obsessive thoughts occur.
- Helping family to avoiding triggering obsessive-compulsive disorder responses and reinforcing the behavior.

CEREBRAL PALSY

Cerebral palsy requires a multidisciplinary approach to treatment, depending upon the type and extent of impairment. This neurological disorder may not be detected until 4–6 months or more after birth when developmental delays or spastic movements become apparent. Some children will

Skill Acquisition

remain dependent on others and require lifetime assistance with activities of daily living, but others will be able to function independently. Management issues include the following:

Issue	Interventions
Visual defects	Glasses, eye exercises, and/or surgical repair.
Hearing loss	Hearing aids and/or speech therapy.
Limited mobility	Physical and occupational therapy to help maximize physical potential. Muscles and joints are often stiff and contracted. Client may have rigidity, tremors, and twisting with impaired voluntary control of muscles.
Bowel and bladder incontinence	Persistent efforts at training, but may not be complete until 3–10 years of age.
Cognitive impairment and emotional issues	Special education, tutoring, learning accommodations, and behavior modification. Clients may have difficulty controlling emotions and may be resistive to personal hygiene and activities.

REACTIVE ATTACHMENT DISORDER

Reactive attachment disorder is common in children who have been abused or neglected during their first 2 or 3 years and fail to establish emotional bonds with caregivers. It can also result from prolonged separation from caregivers, such as with hospitalization or death of a caregiver. This disorder is often observed in clients who are in foster care. Behavioral and emotional problems often persist despite a change in environment and interfere with clients' ability to establish emotional bonds and manage emotions and behavior. Behavioral characteristics may vary and may include the following:

- Violent, aggressive behavior, irritability.
- Withdrawn, refusal to smile or engage.
- Sad and depressed, listless appearance.
- Failure to seek or accept comfort.
- Watching but not interacting.
- Inability to trust.

The first step in behavioral modification is to identify the undesirable behaviors and identify what situations or events trigger the behaviors. It is especially important to provide emotional support when introducing reinforcement to modify the behavior.

TOURETTE'S SYNDROME

Tourette's syndrome is a chronic tic disorder (persisting for more than 1 year) characterized by vocal and motor tics that occur multiple times a day or intermittently. Although Tourette's syndrome has a genetic component, the exact cause has not been identified. The average age of onset is between 6 and 7 with motor tics occurring first. Typical signs and symptoms include tics, obsessive compulsive disorder, Attention-deficit hyperactivity/disorder, and behavioral problems. Mood disorders, migraines, sleep disorders, and learning disabilities are also common. Approximately 10% of patients exhibit coprolalia, with onset during adolescence, and >50% engage in self-injurious behavior. Symptoms subside at approximately age 18 in many patients, although they persist indefinitely in some patients. Many patients do not require medications, but low-dose neuroleptics are the most commonly prescribed. Behavioral therapy, such as habit reversal therapy, may help patients manage symptoms.

TIC DISORDERS

Tic disorders may vary and may result from medical conditions (such as head injury) or drug use. Provisional tic disorder occurs during early childhood in up to approximately 25% of children at some point but usually does not persist for more than 1 year. Persistent tics are most often associated with Tourette's syndrome. Different types of tics include the following:

- Simple motor tics: Brief movements, eye blinking, head jerking, grimacing, shrugging shoulders, pursing lips.
- Complex motor tics: Abrupt movements usually involving a series of movements such as touching oneself, hitting, flapping arms, sniffing, making obscene gestures, jumping.
- Simple vocal tics: Various sounds such as clucking, sniffing, clearing throat, grunting, hissing.
  - Complex vocal tics that may be single or repeated.
  - Various syllables.
  - Phrases ("Get out!).
  - Echolalia: Repeating what another person has said.
  - Palilalia: Repeating one's own words.
  - Coprolalia: Using obscene words or inappropriate and/or derogatory remarks.

SUBSTANCE ABUSE

Many clients with substance abuse (of alcohol or drugs) are reluctant to disclose this information, but there are many indicators that suggest **substance abuse:**

Physical signs	Other signs
• Needle tracks on the arms or legs. • Burns on the fingers or lips. • Pupils are abnormally dilated or constricted; eyes are watery. • Slurring of speech, slow speech. • Lack of coordination, instability of gait. • Tremors. • Sniffing repeatedly, nasal irritation. • Persistent cough. • Weight loss. • Heart rate abnormalities. • Pallor, puffiness in face.	• Odor of alcohol/marijuana on clothing or breath. • Labile (i.e., changeable) emotions, including mood swings, agitation, and anger. • Inappropriate, impulsive, and/or risky behavior. • Lying. • Missing appointments. • Difficulty concentrating/short-term memory loss, disoriented/confused. • Blackouts. • Insomnia or excessive sleeping. • Lack of personal hygiene.

ENCOPRESIS

Encopresis is the voluntary or involuntary passage of stool (feces) in places or manners that are inappropriate for a child, 80% of whom are male, 4 years or older. There are two types of encopresis:

- **Retentive**: Accounts for approximately 80% of those affected and is characterized by a history of long-term painful constipation and the development of overflow diarrhea. The chronic constipation causes distension of the rectum and stretching of the internal and external anal sphincters; as a result, the child may no longer feel the urge to defecate, so stool eventually leaks from the rectum, causing chronic fecal incontinence.

Skill Acquisition

- **Nonretentive**: Accounts for the other 20% of those affected. Nonretentive encopresis, usually involving passage of normally formed stools on a daily basis, does not involve constipation or bowel abnormalities, except in a small subset that may have irritable bowel syndrome, but is generally a behavioral/psychological problem. When encopresis is deliberate, the child may have conduct disorder or oppositional defiant disorder (ODD).

SEPARATION ANXIETY DISORDER

Separation anxiety disorder is more severe than normal separation and stranger anxiety, which start around the age of 7 months and persist until approximately age 2. Separation anxiety disorder is excessive concern regarding separation from the principal caregiver and lasts longer, with the following components:

- Safety concerns and excessive worry about being lost
- Sleep disturbances, such as nightmares centered around the theme of separation and refusal to go to sleep
- School refusal and reluctance to play with friends
- Clinginess to family members
- Psychosomatic complaints (e.g., headache, stomachache)
- Temper tantrums
- Panic attacks

These symptoms must last >4 weeks and must cause functional impairment to be diagnosed as separation anxiety disorder. The exact cause of separation anxiety disorder is unknown. Environment, genotype (i.e., the genetic makeup of the individual), and family history all influence the development of separation anxiety disorder.

Skill Acquisition Plan

COMPONENTS OF A WRITTEN SKILL ACQUISITION PLAN

A **skill acquisition plan** contains a detailed description of the patient's learning goals and how to teach the client as well as program guides. The plan, developed by the BCBA, should include the following steps:

- Determine a skill deficit and a goal to attend to that deficit.
- Outline prompting and reinforcement strategies and consequences.
- Determine appropriate measures to assess progress.
- Collect baseline data to guide intervention.
- Select interventions used to teach skills.
- Gather the necessary supplies and materials.
- Implement the interventions.
- Measure progress/Collect data to assess the effectiveness of interventions performed.
- Carry out the necessary modifications.
- Develop a plan for maintenance.

As part of the development and implementation, the registered behavioral technician (RBT) helps collect baseline and ongoing data, implements the plan, and provides feedback to the board certified behavior analyst (BCBA)/board certified assistant behavior analyst (BCaBA) regarding progress and the need for modification. However, the RBT does not implement modifications independently.

PREPARATION FOR THE SESSION

All **preparation for the session** as required by the skill acquisition plan should be completed before arriving to serve the client so that the RBT is prepared and confident and the plan is correctly implemented. Steps to preparing for the session include the following:

- Carefully read through the plan making sure to understand any program that is to be run with the client.
- Practice interventions as necessary, especially if they are new interventions that the RBT is inexperienced with using.
- Review the program to determine if it contains elements that the RBT has questions about, and clarify them with the supervisor.
- Ask the supervisor for guidance and modeling if necessary.
- Gather the supplies and materials needed for the session.
- Write out a brief personal performance plan or checklist to ensure that no necessary elements of the plan are overlooked during the session.
- Prepare the materials needed for documentation.

Contingencies of Reinforcement

OVERVIEW

Reinforcement is when a behavior takes place and is immediately followed by a consequence that strengthens the behavior so that the behavior is more likely to occur again. Thus, reinforcement requires the following components:

- A behavior or response must have a consequence.
- The behavior or response is more likely to occur with the consequence than without.
- An increase in a behavior or response is directly related to the consequence.

One important factor to remember is that reinforcement may apply to not only the behavior that occurred directly before the reinforcement but also to behaviors that occurred immediately before that. For example, if a child throws food off a tray four times in a row and then receives a reinforcer when taking a bite of the food, the reinforcer can encourage not only eating the food but also throwing it. Thus, it is better to wait and reinforce a series of correct responses rather than to reinforce a single correct response that follows a series of incorrect responses. Additionally, reinforcement may be reversible. That is, if a child is allowed to watch TV only after eating all of the food on her plate, then she may associate watching TV with eating.

ESTABLISHING A CONTINGENCY

Reinforcement is based on **establishing a contingency**, which is an "If...then" statement (e.g., "If you complete your worksheets, then you can play with your toys"). Thus, contingencies are response-consequence relationships. If the response (i.e., an appropriate behavior) results in the consequence (i.e., the reinforcing reward), then a contingent relationship is present between the response and the consequence. The reinforcement, which may be unconditioned or conditioned, must always follow the target behavior in order to be motivating. If, for example, the child is given a toy and then told that in order to keep the toy, the child must complete the worksheets, then the toy is no longer a reinforcer but is essentially a bribe. Contingency contracts may be developed with a client so the client has some input. These contracts generally include a description of behaviors, reinforcers, sanctions for failure to meet the terms of the contract, and any bonuses for consistent compliance.

CONDITIONED VERSUS UNCONDITIONED REINFORCEMENT

Unconditioned reinforcement is also sometimes referred to as primary reinforcement because the reinforcers are necessary for basic survival. Natural positive reinforcers include food, shelter, security, oxygen, water, and sex. Natural negative reinforcers include escaping hunger, thirst, fear, pain, cold, or heat. Access to positive unconditioned reinforcers or avoidance of negative unconditioned reinforcers is highly motivating for individuals.

Conditioned reinforcement, also referred to as secondary reinforcement, involves a reinforcer that is initially neutral (i.e., it has no effect) but becomes a reinforcer when paired with an unconditioned or other conditioned reinforcer. For example, money is a common conditioned reinforcer for adults because it can buy such things as food and shelter. For children, attention is a common conditioned reinforcer because it provides a sense of security and love. Conditioned reinforcers may be edible (e.g., candy), sensory (e.g., music), an activity (e.g., watching TV), tangible (e.g., a toy), or social (e.g., an interaction with a friend). If, for example, a child has a favorite toy (i.e., an established conditioned reinforcer), a new conditioned reinforcer may be stickers that the child can earn and then can exchange for a toy.

CONTINUOUS VERSUS INTERMITTENT SCHEDULES

Reinforcement is based on a **schedule of reinforcement**, that is, a plan for how many responses or which responses will be reinforced. Reinforcement may be on a continuous schedule, in which the reinforcement is provided with each appropriate response during a session, or on an intermittent schedule, in which the reinforcement is provided on some predetermined schedule, such as every 5 or 10 minutes or at every fourth occurrence.

During the initial treatment period, continuous reinforcement tends to result in faster acquisition of the target behavior; therefore, it is a good beginning strategy. However, during the extinction phase (i.e., when all reinforcement stops), the behavior tends to diminish more quickly if it resulted from continuous rather than intermittent reinforcement. For that reason, early continuous reinforcement is usually changed to intermittent once a high rate of appropriate behavior is achieved. The schedule of reinforcement may be set up as a fixed ratio (i.e., a constant number of responses), fixed interval (i.e., of a constant duration), variable ratio (i.e., a changing number of responses), or variable interval (i.e., of a changing duration).

FIXED AND VARIABLE RATIO SCHEDULES

Different schedules of reinforcement that may be used include:

- **Fixed ratio (FR):** Reinforcers are delivered only after a specified number of responses, such as every fifth response—designated as FR:5. (Note that continuous reinforcement is designated as FR:1 because reinforcement is given after every response.) The interresponse time (the duration required for the client to carry out a task) is typically short and uniform. This schedule may result in performance that is inconsistent, and there is often a pause after reinforcement—the greater the ratio (i.e., the frequency of reinforcement), the longer the pause. If the ratio of responses and reinforcement is too high, the client may also begin to pause before responding prior to the reinforcement—an example of ratio strain.
- **Variable ratio (VR):** Similar to FR except that the ratio changes unpredictably from one occasion to another. The average number of responses required before reinforcement is indicated by a number, for example, VR:4. This means that an *average* of four responses is required (2, 4, 3, 6, 5 responses). The response rate is typically high, and the interresponse time is short and uniform. There is a short pause or no pause after reinforcement unless a very high average ratio is used. Performance tends to be more consistent with VR than with FR, and behavior extinguishes more slowly with VR than with FR.

FIXED INTERVAL AND VARIABLE INTERVAL SCHEDULES

Different schedules of reinforcement include the following:

- **Fixed interval (FI):** Reinforcement is delivered after the first response after a specified period of time has elapsed. The time interval remains consistent. For example, for an interval schedule of FI:2, the client has an opportunity to respond every 2 minutes and the first response after the 2-minute period is reinforced. Responses before 2 minutes are not reinforced. This schedule tends to result in inconsistent performance and a long pause after the reinforcement.
- **Variable interval (VI):** Similar to FI in that a reinforcement is delivered after the first response following a specific period of time has elapsed, but these time periods vary from one occasion to the next. VI:4, for example, indicates that an *average* of 4 minutes must elapse before a response can be reinforced (2, 4, 3, 6, 5 minutes). VI tends to result in performance that is more consistent than that of FI with little or no pause after reinforcement; however, interresponse times tend to be longer than with ratio schedules.

Skill Acquisition

NONCONTINGENT REINFORCEMENT

Noncontingent reinforcement is independent of responses and is delivered noncontingently, meaning that it requires no preceding behavior/response. Noncontingent reinforcement may be delivered on a fixed (e.g., every 5 minutes) or variable (i.e., random) schedule. Although contingent reinforcement is usually more effective for modifying behavior, noncontingent reinforcement may be used in some cases, such as to decrease the incidence of an unwanted behavior. For example, if a client throws a tantrum as a means to get attention (i.e., reinforcement), providing reinforcement on a time basis may decrease the client's need to throw a tantrum. Noncontingent reinforcement tries to change the relationship between the behavior (the tantrum) and the reinforcer (the attention). If combined with extinction exercises, the behavior response rate (the unwanted behavior) drops sharply. Noncontingent reinforcement has been used to effectively control such behaviors as aggression, tantrums, inappropriate talk, and refusing to eat. Noncontingent reinforcement may also be used to enrich an environment or to motivate clients.

POSITIVE REINFORCEMENT/PUNISHMENT VS. NEGATIVE REINFORCEMENT/PUNISHMENT

With positive reinforcement or punishment, something is added, whereas with negative reinforcement or punishment, something is removed.

- **Positive reinforcement** involves providing reinforcement to encourage a behavior. For example, if a client makes eye contact when communicating (a desired behavior), he may receive a reinforcer (i.e., a reward), such as a cookie. This differs from positive punishment, which adds something to discourage a behavior. For example, if a client becomes disruptive, he may receive a verbal reprimand. The reprimand is added with the intention of decreasing the disruptive behavior.
- **Negative reinforcement** involves taking away something unpleasant in order to increase the probability that a behavior will continue or reoccur. For example, if a client has shown that she is responsible enough to handle mature content on the internet, then parental controls may be removed. **Negative punishment,** on the other hand, involves taking away something pleasant until a behavior changes in order to discourage the unwanted behavior. For example, if a client refuses to cooperate with a training session, she may lose TV privileges until she begins to cooperate.

FACTORS INFLUENCING THE EFFECTIVENESS OF REINFORCERS

There are many factors that influence the effectiveness of reinforcers, such as the following:

- **Establishing operations and abolishing operations**: Deprivation increases the value of reinforcers, whereas satiation decreases the value of reinforcers.
- **Immediacy**: Reinforcers are more effective when they are delivered immediately after a behavior. If the reinforcer is delayed, the client may not realize that the behavior and the reinforcer are connected. Additionally, a delay may mean that an intervening behavior may have occurred, and the reinforcer may become associated with the intervening behavior.
- **Contingency**: The reinforcer is stronger if its delivery is contingent on a specific behavior.
- **Size/Magnitude**: The larger or more intense the reinforcer is, the stronger it is.
- **Individual differences/perceptions**: Individuals may widely vary in their responses to reinforcers.

USING AVERSIVE STIMULI

The use of **aversive stimuli** (i.e., **punishment**) is usually avoided because the results tend to be temporary; and, in some cases, the aversive stimuli act as reinforcement for the unwanted behaviors that they are intended to control. Aversive stimuli that have been used include such

44

things as squirting lemon juice into a client's mouth, spraying water in a client's face, and physically blocking or preventing a client from carrying out a behavior, usually when the behavior is dangerous to the client or others. There is controversy regarding the use of some forms of aversive stimuli, such as the use of electric shock to treat clients who engage in self-harming. The US Food and Drug Administration banned the use of this treatment, but the ban was overturned by a federal appellate court decision in 2021—although very few treatment centers support the use of electric shock therapy. However, in the natural environment, aversive stimuli are common—for example, a child puts a finger in an electrical socket and gets a shock or a child runs into the street and a parent yells "NO!" and grabs the child. These examples of aversive stimuli serve an immediate purpose, that is, protecting the child from harm. Many, however, serve only to punish, such as when a parent spanks a child for misbehaving.

USING AVERSIVE STATEMENTS

Aversive statements include not only the word "no," but also reprimands (e.g., "You are not supposed to run in the room") and warnings (e.g., "If you don't quiet down, you will lose internet privileges"). The primary problems with aversive statements are that they may not work, may work only temporarily, or may serve as reinforcements for the behavior that they are intended to control. Aversive statements tend to be more effective when accompanied by eye contact and/or touch, and the tone of voice may also affect how the message is received. Additionally, unless tied to a consequence, aversive statements tend to lose their effectiveness over time. For example, if a caregiver frequently shouts at or threatens a client with some type of punishment but does not follow through, the client often begins to disregard the caregiver's threats. Although aversive statements are generally avoided in therapy because they are so often ineffective, they are frequently used in the child's natural environment and may be a factor in undesirable behavior or conflicts between a client and a parent, teacher, or caregiver.

USING PHYSICAL RESTRAINT

Physical restraint should be used only in emergency situations and for the shortest time necessary because it is a form of punishment, and a description of the type of restraint and the reason must be documented. Different types of physical restraint include the following:

- **Personal restraint**: Holding a body part to prevent a behavior, such as holding a client's arm for a minute to prevent the client from hitting someone. This is usually done as a consequence after the behavior has already started, but it may also be done as an antecedent if, for example, a certain situation often triggers the client to hit others.
- **Protective equipment**: This type of restraint typically allows the client to move freely but prevents injury from behavior, such as wearing a helmet to protect the client's head if a client engages in headbanging.
- **Response blocking**: This involves preventing an unwanted behavior from occurring, such as by using some type of barrier. For example, if a client tries to eat crayons, a blocking response would be to place a hand in front of the client's mouth.

USING TIME-OUTS

Time-outs are a form of negative reinforcement or punishment because something is taken away. For a time-out, the client is removed from a situation and placed in a different place for a specified period of time during which the client should receive no reinforcement, negative or positive. Time-outs may be exclusionary (e.g., the client is removed from the room to an area with no reinforcement) or nonexclusionary (e.g., the client remains in the same room but has access to no positive reinforcement). If time-outs are used, the time should be appropriate for the age and developmental level of the client. A 5-minute time out, for example, may be too long for a 3-year-old and too short for a 13-year-old, although extended time-outs tend to be no more effective than shorter time-outs. Time-outs are frequently used in the home environment and in schools to deal with unwanted behavior. In some cases, time-outs are nonproductive. For example, parents frequently send children to their rooms, but if the rooms contain cell phones, TVs, toys, or other desirable items, these may serve as reinforcers for the behavior rather than deterrents.

POSITIVE REINFORCERS

Many different things may serve as **positive reinforcers.** Using the same reinforcer every time may result in reinforcer satiation (when too much of the same thing leads to a loss of effectiveness); therefore, sometimes giving a client a choice of reinforcers may provide some variation and decrease the risk of reinforcer satiation. Some typical reinforcers include the following:

- **Consumables**: These include food items such as cookies, candies, or a favorite food such as crackers, grapes, or cereal. For example, if a client is reluctant to eat anything other than a favorite food, he or she may be rewarded with the favorite food whenever taking a bite of a different food.
- **Social reinforcers**: These vary widely and include attention, indications of approval, touch, praise, and positive facial expressions (e.g., smiling).
- **Tangible items**: These are usually small items such as toys or coins.
- **Activity privileges**: These may include such things as playtime, TV viewing, tablet use, going to the movies, fishing, playing ball, and jumping on a trampoline.
- **Sensory reinforcers**: These include anything that involves the senses, such as listening to music, smelling a desirable fragrance, and looking at pictures.

AUTOMATIC POSITIVE REINFORCEMENT VS. AUTOMATIC NEGATIVE REINFORCEMENT

Automatic positive reinforcement is a response that occurs as a result of a behavior, such as a feeling of sensory stimulation from spinning objects or self-soothing from stimming. The reward that the client gets from carrying out the behavior reinforces that behavior so that it is more likely to recur. **Automatic negative reinforcement** occurs when a behavior reduces or stops an aversive stimulus. For example, if a client feels anxiety and hair pulling relieves this anxiety, the client is more likely to engage in hair pulling when feeling anxious. Both forms of automatic reinforcement can be difficult to manage. One method of modifying behavior includes providing a substitute that provides similar stimulation or relief. For example, if a client engages in continual stimming, some type of manipulative, such as a toy that the client can push back and forth, may serve as an alternative reinforcement.

SELF-MONITORING AND SELF-REINFORCEMENT

Self-monitoring is a method that encourages clients to observe their own behavior on several different occasions over a period of time. For example, if a client has difficulty remembering to carry out a series of tasks, the client and an RBT may develop a checklist for the client to review and determine what tasks need to be accomplished and then check them off as they are completed. In some cases, the use of a timer may be appropriate, such as if a client needs to remember to take medications at a certain time.

Self-reinforcement involves the client administering his or her own consequences for behavior rather than an outside agent, such as the RBT. For example, a client may give him- or herself a sticker each time a homework assignment is completed. This may be done as part of a token economy so that a specified number of stickers results in a bigger and more desirable backup reinforcer.

Discrete Trial Training (DTT) Procedures

ELEMENTS

Discrete trial training (DTT) is a highly structured teaching strategy based on antecedent, behavior, and consequence (ABC) contingencies and is used for behavioral modification and education; it is commonly used with clients on the autism spectrum. Discrete means that it has a specific beginning and end. Skills are broken down into components with each component taught until the client masters it before moving to another component. For example, DTT may be used to teach a client the names of colors or to ask for something (e.g., "May I please have a crayon?"). Typically, DTT is carried out with the RBT sitting at a table across from the client. Elements of DTT include the following:

- **Discriminative stimulus (S^D):** This an event that indicates that a behavior will be reinforced, so an event that occurs before a response (a behavior) and reinforcement is a discriminative stimulus for reinforcement.
- **Prompt**: "Which one of the cards is yellow?"
- **Response**: The client's response or answer to the prompt (e.g., he or she points to the blue card).
- **Consequence**: This will either be a reinforcer (such as a candy or the RBT saying, e.g., "That's right!") if the response is correct or feedback if the response is incorrect (e.g., the RBT saying "This is a yellow card"). The RBT may also guide the client's hand to touch the correct card.
- **Intertrial interval**: There is a brief pause before the next S^D: "Which one of the cards is purple?"

TYPES

Discrete trial training (DTT) procedures may vary in the following ways:

Massed trial: A client is asked the same question or repeatedly given the same prompt for a predetermined number of times (5–10). This is often used in the beginning of training with a client when repetition helps the client learn, especially if the client is struggling with learning. However, clients can get bored with too much massed practice.

Random rotation trial: The client is given multiple different targets, such as pictures of different items to identify. If the client answers correctly, then the RBT moves on to the next target. To master a skill, the client has to be able to identify the item in random rotation.

Block trial: An already mastered stimulus (such as the name of a toy) is presented for a specified duration or number of responses in a block of time, and then a new stimulus is presented in a separate trial for a block of time.

MANDING TRIALS

Manding trials involve teaching a client to ask for something (or point or otherwise indicate a desire, especially if nonverbal) rather than alternative methods of grabbing or crying. The client should be observed to determine if an item is desired. For example, if a client cries out and grabs toward a toy (a type of mand), this indicates desire. The behavior is first modeled so the client knows what is expected (e.g., by saying "This is a toy" several times while giving the client the toy). The number of times and the duration will vary depending on the client. The next step is to show the client the desired item. If the client exhibits interest, the toy is withheld, and the RBT waits a few seconds to determine if the client will ask for it independently. If the client does not, then the

Skill Acquisition

RBT prompts by saying "toy" and waits for the client to respond. The toy is withheld until the client gives the correct mand. This process is repeated many times during each session until the client is able to mand consistently.

TYPES OF VERBAL OPERANTS

Verbal operants (described by BF Skinner) are advanced components of language, and the RBT may work with all of these. Verbal operants include the following:

Copying a text	Able to see and copy a written word: Sees the word "car" and writes "car."
Echoic	Able to repeat words that are heard: Hears the word "cookie" and says "cookie."
Intraverbal	Able to think about something and respond appropriately: "What do you want?" The client says "I want a cookie."
Mand	Able to ask for something: The client wants a cookie and says "cookie."
Tact	Able to label things appropriately: The client sees a picture of a dog and says "dog."
Textual	Able to see a written word and say it (read): Sees the word "orange" and says "orange."
Transcriptive	Able to hear a word and write it (spell): Hears the word "apple" and writes "apple."

80/20 RULE

Motivation is an important aspect of learning. If a client feels frustrated and overwhelmed at the beginning of a task, then he or she is more likely to become resistive. According to the **80/20 rule,** the first 80% of the tasks should be achievable and then the latter 20% can be more challenging. Although the RBT cannot always follow this rule, in general, it is best to allow the client some successes before potential failures. Frustration is a normal part of learning, but it interferes with the learning process, so every effort should be made to avoid the client becoming frustrated and engaging in a power struggle with the RBT. Additionally, if a client is presented with challenging tasks for an extended period of time without success, this can increase his or her frustration and anger so that he or she is no longer able to learn and may become more resistive in the following sessions.

Naturalistic Teaching Procedures

INCIDENTAL TEACHING

Incidental teaching is a form of naturalistic teaching that is carried out in the natural environment rather than in contrived conditions, such as a treatment center or classroom. Natural environments may include the home, school, park, or a store. With incidental teaching, the teaching opportunities often cannot be identified in advance, so the contingency planning is not as clear as it is with discrete trial training (DTT). The RBT spends time with the client in the natural environment and makes direct observations and uses these observations as opportunities for teaching. For example, if a client is in the home, the RBT may observe the client getting ready for the day. When the client needs to get dressed, the RBT might say "What do you need to do first to get dressed?" This type of teaching encourages communication and helps the client to learn skills that are useful in everyday life. The RBT can help the client recognize that skills learned in contrived conditions can apply to everyday life.

Task Analyzed Chaining Procedures

OVERVIEW

Most behavior comprises a series or **chain** of steps rather than a single step. For example, putting on a pair of pants requires many steps: opening a drawer, taking out a pair of pants, unfolding the pants, and so on. Each step becomes a stimulus (or a discriminative stimulus [S^D]) for a response, which is reinforced.

- S^D 1—The pants are in the drawer. Response 1—opens drawer. ("Great job!")
- S^D 2—The drawer is open. Response 2—takes out a pair of pants. ("That's right!)
- S^D 3—The client is holding the pants: Response 3—unfolds pants. ("Good!")

Therefore, a behavior chain is a series of discriminative stimuli and responses. Before developing a behavior chain, a task analysis must be carried out to determine each step in the chain and the correct sequence. A task analysis may be carried out by direct observation of someone doing the task, by asking an expert to outline the steps, or by personally carrying out the task. A task analysis data sheet that lists each S^D and the appropriate response (i.e., action) is developed:

	S^D	Response	Trials
1	The pants are in the drawer.	Open the drawer.	1 1 1 1 1 1 1 1 1 1 1 1 1 1 1
2	The drawer is open.	Take out the pants.	2 2 2 2 2 2 2 2 2 2 2 2 2 2 2

STRATEGIES FOR CHAINING PROCEDURES

FORWARD CHAINING

Forward chaining is a method of teaching a client how to carry out the steps of a behavior chain in order, beginning with the first step and moving on through the steps one by one. Each step is repeated until it is mastered and then the next step is added, so when step two is added, the client will carry out step one and two each time and so on until the behavior chain is completed. Both prompting and fading are used during chaining. Prompting may consist of telling the client what to do (e.g., "Open the drawer"), or it may be actually guiding the client's hand and helping him or her to open the drawer. As the client begins to master the steps, the RBT begins to fade the prompts;

that is, the RBT lessens the frequency of the prompts or no longer gives the prompts when they are no longer needed because the goal is for the client to carry out all of the steps without prompting.

BACKWARD CHAINING

Backward chaining, in which the last step in a behavior chain is taught first, is sometimes used for clients whose abilities are limited. Backward chaining produces natural reinforcement through the completion of each step. Prompting and fading are used to teach the steps. For example, if the client is learning to put on a pair of pants, then the RBT would assist the client in putting on the pants until both feet are in the pants legs and the client is ready for the last step—pulling up the pants. At this point, the RBT would prompt the client with words (e.g., by saying "Pull up your pants") or the RBT would use action (e.g., by guiding the client's hands down to grasp the pants and pull them up). This step is repeated and the prompting is faded until the client is able to master the step and carry it out without prompting. Then, the next-to-last step is added and the client carries out these two steps each time, and so on, until all of the steps are mastered.

BACKWARD CHAINING WITH A LEAP AHEAD

Backward chaining with a leap ahead is a variation in which the RBT carries out an ongoing assessment and allows the client to perform some steps without training if he or she is able to do so rather than taking the time to train each step. This procedure is a modification of backward chaining in order to save time, although the client must complete each step properly to receive reinforcement.

REVERSE CHAINING

Reverse chaining is another modification in which the RBT guides the hands of the client physically through all but the last step (beginning with step one) in a behavior chain and then prompts the client to perform the last step independently. Once the client has mastered the last step, the RBT follows the same procedure but prompts the client to complete the last two steps independently, and so on, until all of the tasks are completed independently from beginning to end.

TOTAL TASK PRESENTATION

Total task presentation is one method of teaching a behavior chain when there is a small number of steps or when the chain is not complex and the client has the ability to carry out the steps. With total task presentation, all of the steps are carried out each time with the RBT providing whatever type of prompting is necessary to guide the client through the steps. Graduated guidance, or hand-over-hand physical prompting in which the RBT guides the client's hands, is often used initially with total task presentation. As the client begins to master the steps, shadowing (i.e., holding the hands over the client's hands so that they are in place to provide guidance when necessary) is then used. The shadowing is faded until the client is able to carry out all of the steps independently.

Discrimination Training

Discrimination means that the client responds differently to different stimuli. For example, a young client may exhibit one type of behavior when a parent is present but another type of behavior when only the RBT is present. The stimulus (i.e., the parent or the RBT) that evokes the specific response is the stimulus control for that event. Stimulus controls may be many different things: individuals, smells, items, places, colors, animals, shapes. **Discrimination training** focuses on reinforcement of the appropriate response (i.e., the differential reinforcement) to one stimulus control and not another. When teaching a client to discriminate among items, the client needs to already be familiar with them. For example, if asking the client to discriminate among colors, the client should be familiar with colors. If the RBT shows different colored cards, including a yellow card (i.e., the discriminative stimulus [S^D]) and asks (i.e., prompts) the client to identify the yellow card and the client responds appropriately, reinforcement is given (by saying, e.g., "That's right!"); but, if the client responds inappropriately and picks the blue card (i.e., the stimulus delta), no reinforcement is given (by saying, e.g., "Wrong"). When the client has achieved mastery of the item 80–90% of the time, then another item is taught.

Stimulus Control Transfer Procedures

OVERVIEW

Stimulus control refers to behavior that results from the presence or absence of a stimulus. That stimulus exerts "stimulus control" over the behavior. This occurs because the behavior has only been reinforced when the stimulus was present or absent. Typically, this reinforcing of behavior must occur many times before stimulus control develops. For example, if a client's father always rewards the child with attention if she stops throwing toys but the child's mother does not, the father becomes the stimulus that exerts stimulus control over the behavior (i.e., stopping throwing toys). In some cases, clients limit the response to a narrow stimulus control, such as only modifying behavior when the father is present; that is, the client may exhibit the desired behavior only when the father is the stimulus control and she may have difficulty transferring stimulus control to other people or situations. In this case, stimulus control transfer strategies are indicated.

STIMULUS CONTROL TRANSFER STRATEGIES

Stimulus control transfer occurs when the client's response to one discriminative stimulus switches to another discriminative stimulus. Essentially, the client responds to a different stimulus with the same action. Stimulus control transfer may be used to switch from the RBT giving prompts to a parent giving them, from verbal commands to hand signals, from behavior learned in a session to other social situations. Stimulus control transfer involves prompt fading and prompt delay and changing the stimulus that brings about a response. If, for example, a client has been appropriately responding to a verbal prompt (e.g., "Say mama") and the prompts have faded, then the client may be asked to respond to a picture of the mother (e.g., by asking "Who is this?"), so the discriminative stimulus switches from the verbal prompt to the visual prompt. In this case, both discriminative stimuli should evoke the correct response—"mama." It is important that the client have mastery of the first discriminative stimulus before attempting stimulus control transfer.

Prompts and Prompt Fading Procedures

STIMULUS PROMPTS

A **stimulus prompt** is a temporary antecedent discriminative stimulus (S^D), something that evokes a response; that is, the prompt (e.g., the RBT saying "Pick up the cup") controls the response initially, but the prompt should fade so that the client is responding to the actual discriminative stimulus (i.e., the cup itself) and not the prompt. There are stimulus prompts and response prompts. With stimulus prompts, some characteristic of the stimulus is altered in order to make the correct response more likely. For example, if asking the client to identify an object in a picture, the picture of the target object may be larger than the other pictures. Types of **stimulus prompts** include the following:

Within-stimulus prompts involve a change in some characteristic of the stimulus: size, color, shape, dimensions, placement, or sound.

Extrastimulus prompts involve adding another prompt to an existing prompt. For example, when teaching a client to discriminate between the right and left hands, one prompt may be saying "Show me your left hand," and a second prompt may be an X written on the top of the client's left hand.

RESPONSE PROMPTS

Both stimulus prompts and response prompts are used in behavior modification. **Response prompts** include (from strongest to weakest in the prompt hierarchy) the following:

- **Physical**: Full physical prompts involve the RBT physically guiding the client, such as by holding and moving the client's hands. This is the most intrusive prompt. Partial physical prompts involve providing physical prompting only as necessary and may include shadowing.
- **Modeling**: The RBT demonstrates the correct behavior so the client can then imitate the behavior. This is best used with instructions and time for the client to practice with role-playing.
- **Gestural**: The RBT uses some type of gesture—nodding the head, pointing, looking at something, or imitating a behavior (e.g., miming picking up a cup)—as a prompt.
- **Verbal**: The RBT provides a verbal cue, such as saying "Show me the dog."
- **Visual**: The RBT uses visual media—such as pictures, videos, posters—as prompts. This is, for most clients, the weakest type of prompt.

PROMPT FADING

Clients can become dependent on prompts to guide them through a behavior or behavior chain, so it is important to fade prompts by decreasing and eventually eliminating the prompts. Different methods of **prompt fading** include:

- **Least to most:** The RBT allows the client to respond independently without prompts unless prompts are needed and then begins with a small prompt, adding more intrusive prompts if needed.
- **Most to least:** The RBT begins by providing prompts and decreases or increases them as necessary.
- **Time-delay fading:** This is a modification of most-to-least fading in which there is an increasing time delay between the stimulus and the prompt. With constant time delay, a fixed delayed time is used, but with progressive time delay, the delay time is slowly increased with each prompt.

- **Simultaneous prompting:** In this case, the RBT gives the prompt immediately after describing the task, so there is no delay.
- **Graduated guidance:** The RBT gradually only uses prompts as needed and gradually stops using the prompts.

SIMULTANEOUS PROMPTING

Simultaneous prompting is an error-free form of prompting used during instructional trials (i.e., teaching) in which a prompt is given immediately after the directions for a task that the RBT knows the client can successfully carry out every time. For example, if the RBT has been teaching the client to clap his hands:

- Directions: "I want you to clap your hands."
- Prompt: Mimics hand clapping.
- Response: The client claps his hands.
- Reinforcement: Praise and/or other reinforcement

This type of prompting is carried out with prompting only during instructional trials when teaching is occurring, but during assessment trials (i.e., testing), the directions are given without the prompt to determine if the client can follow the directions without further prompting:

- Directions: "I want you to clap your hands."
- Response:
  - o The client claps his hands: Provide praise/reinforcement.
  - o Does not clap his hands: End the trial with no consequences or reinforcement.

NO-NO PROMPTING

No-no prompting involves giving directions without a further prompt up to three times, giving the client repeated tries to respond appropriately. The RBT provides reinforcement for correct responses and feedback for incorrect responses:

Trial 1 with a correct response:

- Directions: "I want you to clap your hands."
- Response: The client claps her hands—Give praise/reinforcement and stop the trial.

Trial 1 with an incorrect response:

- Directions: "I want you to clap your hands."
- Response: The client does not clap her hands.

Trial 2 without further directions:

- Feedback: "No, try again."
- Response: The client does not clap her hands.

Trial 3:

- Feedback: "No, try again."
- Correct response:
  - o The client claps her hands: Give praise/reinforcement and stop the trial.
- Incorrect response (the procedure is the same as simultaneous prompting):

Skill Acquisition

- Directions: "I want you to clap your hands."
  - o Prompt: Mimic hand clapping or provide some prompt that usually causes the client to carry out the desired behavior.
  - o Response:
    - ❖ The client claps her hands: Give praise/reinforcement and stop the trial.
    - ❖ The client does not clap her hands: End the trial with no consequences or reinforcement.

ERROR CORRECTION PROCEDURES AND TRANSFER TRIALS

Error correction is used when a client makes a mistake of some type, such as an error of identification or of action or when the client engages in scrolling, trying many different responses one after another (e.g., "cat, dog, horse, cow") trying to give the correct response. For example, the client's task is to correctly identify the picture of a dog.

Trial 1:

- Direction (S^D): "Touch the picture of the dog."
- Response: The client touches the picture of the cat.

Transfer trial (up to three times): Remove the cards, and then replace them.

- Direction (S^D): "Touch the picture of the dog."
- Prompt: Point toward the picture of the dog.
- Response: The client touches the picture of the cat.

Prompts should be more directive at first and then fade. For example, the RBT may touch the correct card the first time and then point at it the second time and just hold a finger up but not near the card on the last try. Each time the client responds correctly, the RBT provides some differential reinforcement. Prompted correct responses should receive mild reinforcement (e.g., by saying "That's right; that's the dog"), but a response without the prompt should receive a greater reinforcement (e.g., by saying "Yes, that's great. You pointed at the dog!") Once the transfer trials are completed, repeat trial 1 and collect data, providing reinforcement if the client's response is correct or repeating transfer trials if it is incorrect.

GUIDED COMPLIANCE

Guided compliance is a form of positive punishment (i.e., something is added to prevent an undesirable behavior) for noncompliance that involves providing prompts so that the client must engage in the desirable behavior and he or she cannot practice behavioral escape or avoidance. Typically, the prompts become more intrusive if the client fails to comply. For example, if the client is in class and needs to sit in a chair but persists in standing, the first prompt may be to remind the client verbally. If the client continues to stand, the next prompt may involve gesturing or modeling sitting in a chair. The most intrusive prompting, physically guiding the client to the chair, is usually the last type of prompting used. It is critically important that the prompting does not result in coercion or physically forcing the client to carry out the desired behavior.

Stimulus Generalization and Response Maintenance Procedures

STIMULUS GENERALIZATION

The stimulus that typically comes before the response and the reinforcer is the control stimulus. **Stimulus generalization** (multiple stimuli), which is the opposite of discrimination, occurs when a response (the behavior) occurs in the presence of other control stimuli, usually stimuli that are similar; that is, a response learned in training transfers to other situations or settings that are untrained. For example, an RBT has been teaching a client to sit on request. The RBT asks the client to sit down (the discriminative stimulus), the client complies (the response), and the RBT praises the client (the reinforcement). Then, the client goes to school and the teacher asks the client to sit down, and the client again complies. This represents stimulus generalization because the client is able to respond the same way to similar commands from the RBT and from the teacher. Additionally, if a control stimulus is usually accompanied by other stimuli (such as background noise or lighting), the client may respond to these other stimuli in the same way as to the control stimulus. It is important to plan for generalization as part of training rather than simply training and hoping.

RESPONSE GENERALIZATION

Response generalization (multiple responses) occurs when a client alters additional behaviors or responses to those that were trained or developed in response to one stimulus, but the behaviors are similar to the target behavior. For example, if a client is trained to reduce headbanging in response to stressful situations, the client may also reduce hand-flapping and finger-licking as well. That is, the intervention (the training) generalizes from altering one response (the headbanging) to encompass altering similar responses (e.g., hand flapping, finger licking) that are untrained. The term used to describe a tendency toward behaviors changing together is *response covariation*. For example, studies have shown that there is a correlation between hair pulling and thumb sucking, so treating one behavior may result in a change in the other one as well, representing indirect training. Response generalization is common. For example, if a young client learns to fasten the hook-and-loop (Velcro) fasteners on his shirt and is then able to fasten the Velcro fasteners on his shoes, that is response generalization.

REINFORCEMENT OF GENERALIZATION

To **reinforce generalization**, it is important that the generalized behavior be reinforced as often as possible. This means that although training for generalization often begins in a training situation, such as a treatment center rather than the natural environment, it should be reinforced often in all environments. If possible, some training should take place in different environments. Parents, caregivers, and teachers should receive training in what behaviors to look for and methods of reinforcement. Clients may also be trained to carry out self-recruitment of reinforcement because the more reinforcement, the more likely the client is to maintain generalization. If a client is learning to put items away after use, for example, the client might be taught to say "I put away my toys" because this usually brings a response such as "That's good." A token economy system may also be used to as a reinforcement every time a client exhibits generalization.

Skill Acquisition

Shaping Procedures

Shaping involves the differential reinforcement (i.e., reinforcing the target behavior and extinction for other behavior) of successive approximations of a target behavior until the target behavior is gradually achieved. Shaping begins by identifying a starting behavior, which is then reinforced until the behavior occurs more frequently. Once this occurs, reinforcement is withdrawn, and a novel (i.e., new) response that more closely approximates the target behavior is reinforced as part of gradually shaping the starting behavior into the desired behavior. For example, if training a client to say "mama," the starting behavior might be the client verbalizing, "mm." This is reinforced until the client reliably says "mm" when asked to say "mama." At this point, "mm" is no longer reinforced but a new sound that is closer to the target, such as babbling "mumumumu" is reinforced. The number of approximations may vary, but the target behavior is always the goal. Each approximation replaces the one that came before. Care should be taken to avoid overreinforcing the approximations. Two types of shaping are described below:

- Across response topography (i.e., how the behavior appears): Changing the appearance of the behavior.
- Within response topography: Changing some other characteristic of the behavior, such as its duration, intensity, or rate.

Token Economy Procedures

Token economy procedures use conditioned reinforcers, such as check marks, stickers, or poker chips, to provide reinforcement for target behavior. The tokens have no real value but serve as temporary reinforcers, which can be exchanged for a backup reinforcer, such as a privilege, a cookie, or a piece of candy. When using tokens, it is important to (1) specify the target behavior (while avoiding ambiguous targets such as "improved behavior"), (2) identify a reinforcement schedule, (3) identify the tokens and the number of tokens needed for the exchange, and (4) identify the backup reinforcers. The type of tokens will vary according to the target behavior. For example, if the target behavior is for a client to focus on quiet reading, interrupting this by handing the client a poker chip may interfere. A better choice may be a check mark on a behavior card. Too long a delay between receiving tokens and exchanging them for the backup reinforcer decreases the effectiveness of the token system. The number of tokens required for exchange is typically low initially to motivate the client and increases gradually. With the response cost, which represents a negative punishment, a token is removed with unwanted responses.

Behavior Reduction

BEHAVIORAL MODIFICATION

OVERVIEW

Behavioral modification is a psychotherapeutic intervention that is used to modify or eliminate undesired behaviors and/or to teach new or desired behaviors for children and adults. Whereas cognitive behavioral therapy focuses on altering how an individual thinks about events and thus altering his or her behavior, and psychoanalysis focuses on the underlying causes of behavior, behavioral modification focuses primarily on the behavior itself. Therefore, some clients may receive more than one type of therapy. Behavioral modification is based on the work of BF Skinner and involves positive and negative reinforcement. Behavioral modification begins with a functional assessment of the target behavior (i.e., the behavior to be changed) and a description of its antecedents, behavior (the response), and consequences (ABCs) so that an individualized plan can be developed.

PARENT-CHILD INTERACTION THERAPY

Parent-child interaction therapy is designed for preschool children with conduct disorder, oppositional defiant disorder (ODD), and autism. This therapy style may be used with other behavioral reduction techniques. Sessions are usually 1 hour per week for 10–16 weeks. The therapist observes the parent-child interaction from outside the room (usually with a two-way mirror) and provides feedback. Parent-child interaction therapy has two phases:

- **Child-directed interaction:** Parents learn specific skills to use when engaging children in free play, including reflecting the child's statements and describing and praising (i.e., positive reinforcement) appropriate behavior while ignoring undesirable behavior. The goal is to strengthen the parent-child bond and eliminate undesirable behaviors.
- **Parent-directed interaction:** During this phase, positive behaviors are increased and undesirable behaviors are decreased. Parents learn to give clear commands, provide consistent positive reinforcement, and use time-outs (i.e., negative reinforcement) for noncompliance.

EARLY AND INTENSIVE BEHAVIORAL INTERVENTIONS

Early and intensive behavioral interventions are available free of charge in every state and US territory for autism and other developmental delays and disabilities. These services are best begun before the child is 4 years old and typically continue for 2–3 years. The child can be assessed and provided interventions as needed, such as speech therapy, hearing impairment services, occupational therapy, family training, and behavioral modification (applied behavior analysis) therapy. Treatment is usually carried out for 30–40 hours per week with one-on-one assistance. These programs help the child develop basic skills that most children acquire in their first 2 years. Enrollment:

- Children younger than 3 years of age: Contact the local early intervention program. Each state runs its own program; for example, California's program is called Early Start and Idaho's program is the Infant Toddler Program.
- Children 3 years and older: Contact a local public elementary school and ask to speak to the district's special education director about preschool special education services.

SELF-INJURIOUS BEHAVIOR

Self-injurious behavior is fairly common in clients with autism (up to 15%) and other intellectual disabilities, such as fragile X syndrome. Self-injurious behaviors may include headbanging, hand-/wrist-biting, head hitting, scratching, hair pulling, and repeatedly rubbing the skin. Observations are typically carried out to try to identify not only triggers for the behavior (e.g., anxiety, boredom, anger) but also reinforcers (e.g., attention, self-stimulation, pleasure) and the frequency, duration, and intensity of the behavior. During observations, it is important to take note of the environment, including lighting and sounds. Some clients may engage in more than one type of self-injurious behavior. In that case, the triggers and reinforcers should be identified for each type because they may be quite different. For example, a client may engage in hair pulling (the behavior/response) when environmental noise increases (the antecedent/trigger), resulting in relief of anxiety (the reinforcer), but the client may also engage in repeatedly rubbing the skin (the response/behavior) when bored (the antecedent/trigger) resulting in self-stimulation (the reinforcer).

Written Behavior Reduction Plan

IDENTIFYING ESSENTIAL COMPONENTS

WRITTEN BEHAVIOR REDUCTION PLAN

A written **behavior reduction plan** outlines how to prevent unwanted behavior and how to handle it when it occurs. Behavior reduction plans are required for students whose behavior interferes with their own or others' learning. Behavior reduction plans are also used for any clients whose unwanted behaviors need to decrease. Components of a written behavior reduction plan typically include the following:

- An operational definition of the target (i.e., unwanted) behavior that needs to decrease: This section needs to be written objectively, and the behavior should be clearly described.
- The function that the target behavior serves: Attention, tangible items, avoidance, and sensory stimulation are examples.
- Antecedent modifications: Preventive strategies are listed.
- Replacement behaviors: Skill acquisition plans are made.
- Consequence modifications: Strategies are identified for responding to the target behavior.
- List of persons responsible: The point person is clearly identified.
- Emergency responses: A crisis intervention plan is formed to deal with dangerous behavior(s).

BEHAVIOR CONTRACT

A **behavior contract** is similar to a behavior reduction plan except the client often has a more active role in development of the plan and the plan may depend on some degree of self-management. A behavior contract should be individualized and is usually developed when initial interventions have been unsuccessful in changing behavior. Components of the behavior contract include the following:

- Identify the target (i.e., undesired) behaviors that need to be changed, usually limited to one or two per behavior contract.
- Outline who will be in charge of enforcing the contract, such as parents, teachers, caregivers, or the client (if self-managing).
- Identify desirable behaviors and reinforcers (by type, quantity, and frequency).
- Identify consequences for undesired behaviors that continue.
- Establish expectations, including limits.
- Determine how progress will be assessed and measured.

The focus of a behavior contract should be to make the client more accountable for his or her own behavior, but it should focus on positive behaviors and rewards rather than on punishments in order to motivate the client.

Behavior Reduction

Common Functions of Behavior

The most common **functions of behavior** include the following:

- **Attention getting:** This may include a child who cries to get attention of the parent and a student who goofs off in class to make others laugh. Common attention-getting behaviors include tantrums. Clients will often respond to positive (i.e., praise) and negative (i.e., scolding, punishing) attention.
- **Access to tangible items**: Clients engage in behaviors in order to gain access to a desirable item, such as a toy or a cookie. Behaviors may include crying, grabbing, begging, hitting, or biting in order to gain the desired item.
- **Avoidance or escape:** The client may want to avoid a session and may try to hide, run away, or refuse to cooperate.
- **Sensory stimulation:** This is a form of automatic reinforcement, such as when a client rocks back and forth, flaps hands, or picks at a scab.

ESCAPE BEHAVIOR VS. AVOIDANCE BEHAVIOR

Escape behavior and **avoidance behavior** may be used as responses to aversive (i.e., unpleasant or negative) stimuli:

- **Escape behavior:** A behavior is strengthened if it results in escape from an aversive event and ends the event. For example, if a client is distressed by loud noise and puts on noise-cancelling headphones, this is a form of negative reinforcement (because the noise is removed) that increases the likelihood that the client will use the headphones in the future to escape excess noise.
- **Avoidance behavior:** This behavior prevents exposure to an aversive stimulus that the client can predict. This type of behavior may develop following escape behavior. For example, if the client who is distressed by noise refuses to go to a noisy classroom and thus avoids any exposure to the noise, this reinforces the avoidance behavior. Another example of avoidance behavior is when a client dislikes skin-to-skin contact with others and wears long-sleeved shirts and pants to prevent inadvertent touching.

COVERT BEHAVIOR VS. OVERT BEHAVIOR

Covert behavior is behavior that occurs but cannot be observed because it involves the thought processes of the mind, such as thinking, daydreaming, dreaming, remembering, calculating, and processing information, rather than physical actions. Covert behaviors can occur while the individual is inactive or active. This covert behavior is what triggers overt behavior. First, an action is conceived in the mind (either consciously or unconsciously) and then it is carried out as an overt behavior. Covert behaviors cannot be assessed or measured. **Overt behaviors**, on the other hand, are those behaviors that are observable, typically through physical actions, gestures, facial expressions, or spoken words. When making client observations, it is these overt behaviors that are assessed and measured because they can be readily seen or heard. Although they are triggered by covert behaviors, overt behaviors in turn trigger covert behaviors. That is, an overt behavior is carried out, and then the mind processes the action and the consequences.

BEHAVIORAL CUSPS

Behavioral cusps are behaviors or changes in behavior that lead to important new behaviors. Behavioral cusps are therefore considered gateway behaviors, and one behavioral cusp tends to lead to another one. For example, if a client learns the alphabet, she then begins to connect sounds to the letters, begins to identify objects, and eventually begins to read—another behavioral cusp

that brings about many new behaviors. Some of these behaviors may be predictable, but others may not. When teaching new skills or behaviors to clients, each new skill or behavior should be viewed as a potential behavioral cusp that will lead to the client gaining more new skills and behaviors. A typical behavioral cusp for adolescents is learning to drive, which opens up a world of possibilities—getting a job, dating, engaging in risk-taking behavior, and becoming more independent.

Interventions Based on Modification of Antecedents

OVERVIEW

An antecedent is an observable stimulus that occurs before a behavior (the response).
Modification of antecedents (i.e., changing something in the environment) is done to prevent a behavior from occurring, so this occurs before the discriminative stimulus. For example, if a client throws a tantrum when music is playing in a room, an antecedent modification might include turning the music off before the client enters the room. Implementing the modification of antecedents involves the following components:

- Observing the client carefully to identify undesirable behavior (B), such as throwing items, hiding, or spitting.
- Carefully make note of antecedents (A), that is, triggering events that occur immediately before the behavior. These may include an environmental trigger (e.g., noise, lighting, setting) or the actions of another person (e.g., bullying, touching, speaking, standing too close).
- Note the consequences that result from the behavior (e.g., time-outs, attention, comforting, reprimands).
- Make repeated observations to determine if there is a consistent pattern to the behavior.
- Outline the desired behavior.
- Determine what possible changes to the antecedent may alter the behavior.
- Implement the modification of antecedents, and monitor the results.

MOTIVATING OPERATIONS AND DISCRIMINATIVE STIMULI

Motivating operations (i.e., the motivations behind behaviors) refer to the desires or feelings of the client that affect the value of a stimulus. Motivating operations can be classified as abolishing operations if they lower the value of a reinforcer or as establishing operations if they increase its value, thus affecting behavior. A **discriminative stimulus** is the stimulus (or signal) that controls a behavior because the behavior was previously reinforced when the stimulus was present. Motivating operations include the following:

- Abolishing operations are changes that decrease the likelihood that a discriminative stimulus will cause a behavior to occur. For example, if a client has just eaten a large lunch, this decreases the chance that food can be used to reinforce a desired behavior.
- Establishing operations are changes that increase the likelihood that a discriminative stimulus will cause a behavior to occur. For example, if a client is thirsty, this increases the likelihood that a glass of water will reinforce a desired behavior.

Motivating operations may be difficult to determine for some clients. For example, clients with autism may appear to lack motivation or may exhibit motivation that is atypical.

TYPES OF ANTECEDENT INTERVENTIONS

Antecedent interventions, those that occur before a behavior, may include the following:

- **Offer a choice**: Do you want to color or play with a toy?
- **Prompt (P)**: This follows motivating operations (MO) and discriminative stimulus (S^D) and precedes the behavior (the response [R]) and consequence (C) ($MO > S^D > P > R > C$). Prompting is frequently used to evoke a behavior.
- **Prime**: Providing information on what to expect: "We will finish this session in 5 minutes."

62

- **High-probability sequence**: Beginning with easy instructions and leading to more difficult instructions.
- **Noncontingent reinforcement**: Reinforcing before behavior occurs in order to change the connection between a behavior and reinforcement. For example, if a child gets parental attention each time she cries, the child begins to cry to get attention; therefore, to modify this behavior, the parent provides the child with attention on a regular schedule (e.g., every 5 or 10 minutes) regardless of her behavior, so the child loses the association between crying and attention.
- **Time delay**: Varying the times for reinforcement.

COMPETING RESPONSE TRAINING

Competing response training is teaching a client to substitute a different behavior for the target behavior (a type of habit reversal training). Competing response training may be used for such things as nail biting, hair pulling, repeatedly touching the face, or sticking out the tongue. The steps to competing response training include the following:

- The first step is identifying the target behavior and helping the client to describe the behavior in detail, including antecedent movements, to increase awareness. For example, if a client repeatedly licks his lips and has developed red irritated skin about his lips, the client should be aware of first opening his mouth and then sticks out his tongue.
- The next step is for the client to acknowledge each time the urge or behavior occurs: "I feel like licking my lips." The client should receive positive reinforcement if this is acknowledged or a reminder if the behavior occurs without acknowledgement.
- The last step is to use competing behaviors that prevent the target behavior. The competing behavior should not be intrusive or noticeable. For example, when the client feels the urge to lick his lips, he may be taught to purse his lips or tighten them until the urge passes.

VISUALIZATION AND RELAXATION

Visualization (i.e., therapeutic imagery) is used primarily for relaxation and reduction of stress as well as performance improvement. Visualization may be used in conjunction with other types of therapy, such as exposure therapy or behavior modification to help a client relax. Visualization is creating a visual image in the mind of a desired outcome and imagining or "feeling" oneself in that place or situation. All of the senses may be used to imagine the feeling of being in a place and feeling very relaxed—what it looks, smells, feels, and sounds like. Basic techniques include the following:

- Sit or lie comfortably in a quiet place away from distractions.
- Concentrate on breathing while taking long, slow breaths.
- Close the eyes to shut out distractions, and create an image in the mind of the desired place or situation.
- Concentrate on that image, engaging as many senses as possible, and imagining details.
- If the mind wanders, breathe deeply and bring the consciousness back to the imagery or concentrate on breathing for a few moments and then return to the imagery.
- End with positive imagery.

Sometimes, clients are resistive at first or have a hard time maintaining focus, so guiding them through visualization for the first few times can be helpful.

Behavior Reduction

PROGRESSIVE MUSCLE RELAXATION

Progressive muscle relaxation is a technique that is used to reduce stress, anxiety, or fear, which often causes muscles to become tense (tight). This technique involves purposely tensing one muscle group at a time and then relaxing it. During progressive muscle relaxation, the client should be in a quiet environment free from distractions and should sit or lie comfortably while wearing comfortable clothes and removing his or her shoes. The cycle of tensing and relaxing is approximately 5 seconds of tensing followed by 10 seconds of relaxing. The sequence is typically done as follows:

- Right hand/forearm followed by the right upper arm.
- Left hand/forearm followed by the left upper arm.
- Forehead, followed by the eyes (squeeze them tight and then open) and cheeks.
- Mouth/jaw followed by the neck.
- Shoulders.
- Shoulder blades and back.
- Chest and abdomen.
- Hips and buttocks.
- Right upper leg followed by the right lower leg and then the right foot.
- Left upper leg followed by the left lower leg and then the left foot.

Differential Reinforcement Procedures

ALTERNATIVE/INCOMPATIBLE BEHAVIOR

Differential reinforcement of alternative behavior is used to increase desirable behavior and decrease undesirable behavior. With this technique, the undesirable behavior as well as one or more alternative behaviors are identified. Alternative behaviors are typically the opposite of the undesired behavior. If a young client persists in chewing on crayons, but, instead of chewing the crayon, the client simply twirls the crayon, this alternative behavior would be reinforced. In some cases, multiple alternative behaviors (both already identified and nonidentified) are reinforced. **Differential reinforcement of incompatible behavior** is a variation that involves an incompatible behavior that makes the undesired behavior difficult or impossible to carry out. For example, for the crayon-chewing client, an incompatible behavior would be chewing gum, which would make chewing crayons difficult and would thus be reinforced. Steps to using differential reinforcement of alternative/incompatible behavior include identifying the desirable and undesirable behaviors and identifying the reinforcers for both types of behavior. Desirable behaviors should be reinforced immediately, and no reinforcement is given for undesirable behaviors. During the initial training, continuous reinforcement is used, but as the client shows progress, intermittent reinforcement should be used because this helps maintain the desired behavior and promotes generalization.

OTHER BEHAVIOR AND DIFFERENTIAL REINFORCEMENT OF LOW RATES

Differential reinforcement of other behavior is used to decrease undesirable behavior. With this technique, an undesirable behavior is identified and then any other (hopefully one that is more desirable) behavior is reinforced, basically teaching the client what behavior to avoid. For example, if a client persistently yells out during class time (an undesirable behavior), any other behavior (e.g., staring at the ceiling, twirling a pencil, grunting) is reinforced. Reinforcement may be provided whenever another behavior is observed (a momentary reinforcement), but it is commonly done on an interval schedule, such as every 2 minutes. With interval reinforcement, when the 2-minute timer sounds, reinforcement is provided if the undesired behavior is absent and another behavior is present at that moment. Interval reinforcement does not account for undesirable behavior that occurs before the timer goes off during the 2-minute interval and also does not provide training in desirable behaviors. With **differential reinforcement of low rates**, the goal is to decrease but not eliminate a behavior, which is potentially positive. For example, if a client repeatedly raises his/her hand in class 12 times every 15 minutes to answer or ask questions, reinforcement may be given each time the number decreases over the course of a 15-minute period, such as being reduced to 8 times every 15 minutes.

OVERCORRECTION

Overcorrection involves applying a penalty for an undesirable behavior either by performing restitution, through positive practice, or a combination:

- **Restitution:** Correcting the effects of the undesirable behavior. If, for example, a client took another client's lunch and ate part of it, a *simple correction* would be to return the remaining food. *Overcorrection* would require not only that the client return the unneatened food but also provide additional food to compensate for what the client already ate.
- **Positive practice:** Repeatedly practicing the desired behavior. If, for example, a client dislikes putting books away and throws many books out of a bookshelf, and the client replaces the books (i.e., restitution) but also is required to straighten all of the bookshelves and return all books used in the room to the proper bookshelves, this represents positive practice.

Restitution and positive practice are often used together. Overcorrection differs from aversive stimulus (such as a reprimand) or response cost in that the client must make an effort to correct the behavior.

BEHAVIORAL DEFICITS AND BEHAVIORAL EXCESSES

A **behavioral deficit** is a desirable behavior that the client needs to increase in frequency, intensity, or duration. That is, behavioral deficits are behaviors that do not occur often enough. For example, if a client is learning to turn in classwork but only does so half of the time, the client has a deficit in this behavior. A behavioral deficit can also refer to mental or physical functioning that is less than expected for the client's age. For example, a 10-year-old child may be unable to read.

A **behavioral excess** is an undesirable behavior that the client needs to decrease in frequency, intensity, or duration. That is, behavioral excesses are behaviors that occur too often. For example, if a client consistently overeats and hoards food, this is a behavioral excess that may be targeted for intervention. Other types of common behavioral excesses include throwing tantrums and telling lies. Clients with Attention-deficit hyperactivity/disorder frequently exhibit behavioral excesses.

IMPLICATIONS OF SHORT-CIRCUITING THE CONTINGENCY

In behavior reduction, reinforcement is normally contingent on an appropriate response (the behavior). **Short-circuiting the contingency** means that reinforcement is provided or taken (with self-management) without first carrying out the response. In this case, the reinforcement can actually reinforce NOT carrying out the appropriate behavior. Short-circuiting the contingency also occurs when, for example, a parent tells a client to do homework or lose TV time and then allows TV time even though the client has not done the homework. This is a fairly common situation in the home environment or when reinforcement is applied inconsistently with different people and in different environments, and it can lead to persistent undesirable behavior. It is important that all of those involved in delivering reinforcement (e.g., the RBT, teachers, caregivers, and parents) understand the purpose and importance of consistency in reinforcement.

BEHAVIOR TRAP

A **behavior trap** occurs when unwanted behavior is accidentally reinforced and then becomes habitual. Behavior traps are very common in the natural environment (e.g., home, school) and often result from some type of punishment. For example, if a parent asks a child to put away toys and the child refuses and throws a tantrum, the parent responds by placing the child in a time-out. Because the child did not want to put away the toys, being put in time-out solves the child's problem and reinforces the child's behavior. If this same pattern repeats many times, the unwanted behavior becomes habitual so that whenever the child does not want to cooperate, the child throws a tantrum and sits in time-out, successfully avoiding the tasks. The only way out of the behavior trap is through extinction—that is, to stop providing the reinforcement. In this case, the parent needs to continue to insist that the child cooperate and stop giving the time-outs that are reinforcing the behavior.

Extinction Procedures

Extinction refers to removing a reinforcer after each episode of problem behavior in order to decrease the problem behavior. For this method to be effective, the reinforcer must be clearly identified. For example, a child often refuses to do chores, so the child is rewarded upon completion of chores with a piece of candy as the reinforcer. It is easy to assume that the candy is the reinforcer. However, the child frequently complains of a stomachache when beginning the chores, so the parent often completes the chores for the child. In this case, the reinforcer that needs to be removed may be the parent completing the child's chores. Not all reinforcers are contrived or conditioned (such as the piece of candy). In many cases, reinforcers may be increased attention, escape from activities/chores, or something else that can be difficult to identify without careful observation. Extinction is different from punishment, and it typically takes longer to reduce a response (the problem behavior) with extinction; therefore, if the problem behavior puts the client at risk (such as for self-injurious behavior), then extinction may not be the most appropriate approach. Extinction also refers to the phase of behavioral modification during which reinforcement is no longer provided.

FACTORS INFLUENCING EXTINCTION

The primary purpose of **extinction** is to stop an undesirable behavior. Extinction, removing a reinforcer of a behavior, is different from ignoring a behavior. For example, if a client repeatedly throws food on the floor and is reprimanded by a parent or caregiver, the reprimand may serve as a reinforcer because the client gains attention. In this case, removing the reprimand may aid extinction. However, if the parent or caregiver simply ignores the behavior, the behavior may be more likely to continue. Factors that influence extinction include the intervention schedule. Continuous intervention achieves more rapid extinction than intermittent intervention. Additionally, if reinforcement occurs after extinction begins, this may increase the time needed for extinction. For example, if a client has been undergoing extinction to eliminate tantrums by the parent standing by and not intervening in any way but the grandmother visits and soothes the client during a tantrum, this reinforces tantrum throwing and will set back extinction. Extinction is usually more effective if it is combined with reinforcement of desired behaviors. That is, reinforcement is withheld with undesired behavior while desired behavior is reinforced.

RESPONSE PATTERNS ASSOCIATED WITH EXTINCTION
EXTINCTION BURST AND RESPONSE VARIATION

Clients may respond in different ways to extinction, especially if they have become in some way dependent on the reinforcer:

- **Extinction burst:** After reinforcement is stopped, some clients will experience an increase in the frequency, intensity, and duration of the target (i.e., the unwanted) behavior. This increase is usually temporary, but it can put the client or others at danger if the target behavior is aggression or self-injury; if the RBT does not recognize this worsening of behavior as temporary, reinforcers may be reintroduced, interfering with extinction.
- **Response variation:** During extinction, some clients may begin to respond in different manners. For example, if a client does not receive the expected reinforcement (the attention) for failing to put her toys away, she may begin to scatter even more toys around the room. On the other hand, in some cases the response may be an improvement, such as if the client begins to put items away in an attempt to obtain reinforcement. This improved behavior can then be built on with shaping.

Behavior Reduction

67

AGGRESSION, EMOTIONAL RESPONSE, AND SPONTANEOUS RECOVERY

Clients may respond in different ways to **extinction**, especially if they have become in some way dependent on the reinforcer:

Aggression: Some clients may respond to extinction with anger and aggression, so the RBT should always be alert to prevent injury of the RBT or self-injury of the clients.

Emotional response: Crying, arguing, and begging are common responses to extinction and indicate that the client is emotionally upset at the loss of reinforcement.

Spontaneous recovery: Following extinction, it is common for clients to undergo periods of spontaneous recovery of previously extinguished behaviors even after an extended period of time. In this case, extinguishing is reintroduced. Generally, the behavior in these periods of spontaneous recovery is shorter in duration and less intense than the original behavior. If extinction is still in place (i.e., no reinforcement is provided for the unwanted behavior), then the recovery period is usually short.

FLOODING AND SYSTEMATIC DESENSITIZATION

Flooding, a form of exposure therapy, is a technique used in behavioral therapy in which the client is exposed directly (in real life) or through imagery (via pictures, virtual reality) to things or situations that cause anxiety in order to lessen the anxiety response. With flooding, no attempt is made to lessen the anxiety or the associated fear during the exposure. This differs from **systematic desensitization**, which is carried out in small, progressive steps. The flooding technique is used primarily for clients with phobias, but it may also be used with post-traumatic stress disorder and panic disorder. For example, if a client is afraid of cats, with flooding, the client may go to an animal shelter and enter a room full of cats and kittens in real life, in virtual reality, or by watching cat videos or looking at cat pictures. Not all clients are willing to participate in flooding because of their fears. Systematic desensitization would more likely begin with exposure to a picture of a cat and then, perhaps, a video before progressing to exposure to one real-life cat—first at a distance and then closer. Although flooding shows short-term effectiveness, the results are more short lived than when the exposure is spaced.

SETTING EVENTS THAT AFFECT BEHAVIOR

Setting events are internal or external factors or conditions that affect behavior or "set the stage" for unwanted behavior and do not necessarily occur at the same time as the behavior. Setting events may be conditions within the client, such as hunger, thirst, pain, poor sleep, illness, medications, and allergies. If, for example, a client has an earache, the client may exhibit unwanted behavior because of the discomfort. Setting events may also be associated with the situation or environment itself, such as who is giving prompts, what activities are going on, the behavior of others, environmental temperature, location, or exposure to arguments. Whereas trigger events usually occur immediately before a behavior, setting events may occur hours, days, weeks, or even months before a behavior. Some setting events occur only occasionally (e.g., an accident), whereas others may occur frequently (e.g., domestic violence). Two specific types of setting events include establishing operations and abolishing operations.

ESTABLISHING OPERATIONS AND ABOLISHING OPERATIONS

Establishing operations are motivating or setting events that increase the value or potency of a reinforcer in a particular situation and evoke the behavior that results in that reinforcer. For example, if a client is thirsty, the value of water (the reinforcer) is increased; therefore, this increases the chance that the client will engage in a behavior (such as asking verbally) that results in getting a glass of water. Deprivation is, thus, one type of establishing operation. If a client has gone without a reinforcer, such as food, money, shelter, or water, for an extended period, then these things become stronger reinforcers.

Abolishing operations, another type of setting event, are the opposite in that the events decrease the value or potency of a reinforcer and thus decrease the likelihood of the behavior that results in the reinforcer. Satiation is a type of abolishing operation. If, for example, the client just drank a large soda, the value of another soda or glass of water is reduced, and the client will not be motivated to ask for one.

Crisis/Emergency Procedures

Crisis/emergency procedures are triggered when the client, the RBT, or others are in danger because of a health problem (e.g., seizure, injury, illness), behavioral problem (e.g., violence, aggressive behavior, elopement, hair pulling, hitting, scratching, threatening), or environmental problem (e.g., fire, flood, storm, a lack of heating/air conditioning, a lack of water, a lack of electricity). A written plan should be in place that outlines what to do in case of emergency for all clients; additionally, the RBT, parents, caregivers, and others who interact with clients should all be trained in the crisis/emergency procedures. The written plan should stress the importance of preventive measures for known unwanted behavior, such as wearing hair up or under a cap or hat if a client engages in hair pulling. Note that restraint should only be used as a last resort and only for the shortest duration necessary. RBTs should be aware of the location of fire extinguishers, shelters (in areas where they are needed), and escape routes. In all crisis/emergency procedures, the safety and welfare of the clients should be the primary concern.

PERSONAL PREVENTIVE MEASURES

It is important to use nonprovoking behaviors and to be aware of precursor behaviors and triggers in order to use preventive measures effectively. **Personal preventive measures** include the following:

- Avoid wearing jewelry that might be pulled, grabbed, or used to choke (e.g., earrings, necklaces). Avoid scarves around the neck.
- Avoid wearing clothing that make it difficult to retreat or run, such as tight-fitting clothes, flip flops, and high heels.
- Wear clothing with long sleeves.
- Keep hair up and out of reach (e.g., tied back, in a bun, under a cap).
- Avoid clutter to reduce the chance of tripping and falling.
- Keep objects that could be used as weapons (e.g., hot drinks, sharp objects) out of the environment.
- If precursor (i.e., warning) behavior is present, maintain one to two arms' length of distance from client and avoid any further demands that may trigger more violent behavior.
- Keep hands near the waistline with children and near the chest for older or taller clients.
- Have two staff members present if indicated to ensure safety.
- Call 911 if necessary to prevent injury to the client or others.

USING DISTRACTION IN CRISIS SITUATIONS

Distraction is often used in a crisis to shift a client's attention from something that is causing the client to exhibit undesirable behavior, such as a meltdown or tantrum, to something that engages the client. Young clients may be easier to distract than older ones. For example, a toddler may respond readily to toys or personal attention, such as hugging or holding, whereas a school-age client may be distracted by the introduction of something that the client especially values, such as a particular video game. Distraction should not be depended on repeatedly to modify the same behavior. Rather, the underlying cause for the behavior should be assessed. Additionally, if the same distraction (e.g., a toy) is used repeatedly, it may begin to serve as a reinforcer for the undesirable behavior. If a distraction is used to allow a client to avoid doing a task, this should not occur more than once with that same task.

HABIT BEHAVIORAL PROBLEMS AND HABIT REVERSAL TRAINING

Clients may exhibit various types of **habit** (i.e., **repetitive**) **behavioral problems**:

- **Nervous habits**: Biting nails, scratching, pulling hair, biting fingers, tapping feet, cracking knuckles.
- **Tics (both motor and verbal):** Grimacing, twitching, head jerking, grunting, humming, clearing the throat.
- **Stuttering:** Word repetitions, prolongation of sounds.

When habits are the result of a neurological condition, such as Tourette's syndrome, they may persist even with **habit reversal training**, but the client may be better able to control them. Some habits are primarily behavioral and may be more responsive to treatment. Behavioral interventions include:

- **Awareness training**: Teaching the client to recognize triggers for the habit and to avoid or modify them when possible.
- **Self-monitoring**: Having the client keep a record of habitual behaviors including the time, duration, circumstances.
- **Differential reinforcement** of other behavior and response cost (removing a reinforcer) for habitual behavior.
- **Relaxation training**: Using deep breathing and muscle relaxation to decrease stress.
- **Response prevention**: Applying barriers such as mittens to prevent hair pulling or scratching.
- **Competing/Alternative response**: Substituting another behavior for the habitual behavior to prevent or interfere with the habitual behavior.

POSITIVE STRATEGIES TO PREVENT UNWANTED BEHAVIOR

Using **positive strategies** can help prevent unwanted behavior in the following ways:

- **Establishing a routine:** Some clients, especially those on the autism spectrum, like order and do better when they have a set routine or specific procedures that they can anticipate and follow.
- **Using silent signals to communicate:** These signals should be developed with the client so the client knows what the signal means. For example, if the client finishes early, the RBT may point at a clock and hold up so many fingers to indicate how much time the client has to wait, or the RBT may wave a hand to indicate that a client has responded appropriately.
- **Outlining expectations:** Clients need to know what is expected of them and the end goal, and these goals should be developed with clients when possible so that they have ownership.

Behavior Reduction

71

Documentation and Reporting

COMMON TERMINOLOGY

Common **terminology** includes the following:

- **ABC**: Antecedents, behaviors, and consequences.
- **Acquisition**: Acquiring a new behavior through reinforcement.
- **Antecedent**: A stimulus, setting, or event that precedes a behavior.
- **Aversive stimulus (the punisher)**: An unpleasant stimulus that is presented as a consequence and tends to decrease the likelihood that the behavior will repeat because it evokes avoidance/escape behavior.
- **Backup reinforcer**: A tangible reward that can be purchased with tokens.
- **Backward chaining**: Teaching the last behavior or component of a behavior chain first and then teaching additional behaviors in continued reverse order.
- **Baseline**: Beginning data before any interventions.
- **Behavior chain (aka the stimulus-response chain)**: A sequence of behaviors that make up a complex task, with each behavior having a discriminative stimulus and a response.
- **Cognitive processes**: Events associated with the mind, such as thoughts, beliefs, and expectations.
- **Conditioned reinforcer**: A stimulus that was previously neutral but when paired repeatedly with an existing reinforcer begins to function as the reinforcer.
- **Conditioned stimulus**: A stimulus that was previously neutral but when paired repeatedly with an unconditioned stimulus it begins to function the same as the unconditioned stimulus.
- **Contingency**: The relationship among antecedents, behaviors, and consequences, specifically the relationship between a behavior and its consequence when the consequence occurs only if the behavior occurs, so the consequence is "contingent upon" the behavior.
- **Contrived setting**: A setting that is not part of the client's normal routine, that is, a controlled environment.
- **Covert behavior**: Private or hidden behavior that is not observable by others.
- **Deprivation**: A condition characterized by withdrawal of a reinforcer for a period of time to make the reinforcer more powerful when it is reinstated.
- **Escape behavior**: A behavior that terminates (i.e., ends) an aversive (i.e., unpleasant) event.
- **Extinction**: A previously reinforced behavior is no longer reinforced in order to decrease the behavior.
- **Fading**: Gradual removal of some aspect of contingencies of reinforcement, such as slowly removing prompts or reinforcers in order to maintain behavior.
- **Feedback**: Providing information about performance.
- **Forward chaining**: Teaching the first behavior or component of a behavior chain first and then proceeding in the order in which the behaviors are to be performed.
- **Intensity**: The strength or magnitude of a behavior.
- **Interresponse time**: The average time between responses.
- **Latency**: The time period between a stimulus and the onset of a behavior.
- **Maintenance**: Continuing a behavior for an extended period after the behavior modification program has ended.
- **Mand**: A request (i.e., a demand/command) for something.

- **Negative punishment**: A type of punishment that involves removing a reinforcer after a behavior occurs.
- **Negative reinforcement**: A type of reinforcement in which a behavior is followed by removal or avoidance an aversive (i.e., unpleasant) stimulus.
- **Overcorrection**: A type of punishment in which the client either makes restitutions (i.e., corrects the consequences of the behavior) or carries out positive practice, that is, repeatedly practicing the correct behavior.
- **Rate**: Frequency of a behavior divided by time, typically the number of responses per minute.
- **Reinforcer**: A stimulus, event, or reward that increases the likelihood that a behavior will recur.
- **Response**: Another word used for behavior.
- **Shaping**: Developing a new behavior by reinforcing successive approximations of the target behavior.
- **Stimulus**: An event that can be perceived by the senses and evokes a response.
- **Tact**: Commenting about something perceived by the senses or labeling something in the environment.
- **Target behavior**: The behavior that is to be modified or changed.
- **Time sampling**: Carrying out brief observations at specified times during the day rather than during a long block of time.
- **Token economy**: A form of reinforcement in which tokens are earned for desired behavior; these tokens can then be exchanged for a more desirable backup reinforcer.
- **Unconditioned response**: A reflex response evoked by an unconditioned stimulus.
- **Unconditioned stimulus**: A stimulus that evokes an unconditioned reflex response, such as a loud noise eliciting a startle response.

Documentation and Reporting

Supervisor Communication

Effective communication between an RBT and his or her supervisor is essential to providing optimal client care and improving RBT skills. Communication is important because the supervisor is responsible for client care and is also liable. Communication should focus on the client and the client's needs and progress. The RBT should use professional behavioral terminology and should respond positively to feedback and ask questions to clarify information that is not clear. When communicating, the RBT should be organized, respecting the supervisor's boundaries and time constraints, and should report the client's functional progress by summarizing highlights in measurable terms with regard to progress, setbacks, concerns, and other incidents (e.g., aggressive behavior, caregiver negligence/abuse, unexpected toileting accidents). The RBT should express opinions respectfully and make suggestions based on observations, experience, and client progress while keeping in mind the need to comply with the supervisor's plan of care. The RBT should never communicate confidential information without the permission of the individual involved.

RECEPTIVE AND EXPRESSIVE LANGUAGE SKILLS

Effective communication requires **receptive** and **expressive language skills**, which are often viewed as listening and talking, but these skills are more complex, as detailed below:

- **Receptive**: Active listening is part of receptive language skills, so the RBT should focus on what others are saying, nod, ask clarification questions, and respond appropriately. Receptive skills also include the ability to read, comprehend, understand pictures, signs, symbols, graphs, and objects, understand nonverbal responses and body language, and follow directions. One's receptive vocabulary is often larger than one's expressive vocabulary. Electronic communications cannot transfer a person's real emotion and feelings and can rob the listener of valuable clues about the message sender's tone and intent.
- **Expressive**: The ability to communicate clearly is central to expressive language skills, but this includes not only verbal communication but also command of turn-taking, pausing, body language, eye contact, and other nonverbal communication. Expressive language skills include direct statements and assertions and questions. Much expressive communication is now delivered by email or direct messaging, which can require simplification of the message and can constrain communications.

ACTIVE LISTENING

Active listening requires more than just passively listening to another individual. Active listening includes observing the other individual carefully for nonverbal behaviors, such as posture, eye contact, and facial expression, as well as understanding and reflecting on what the person is saying. The listener should carefully observe for inconsistencies in what the individual is saying or comments that require clarification. Feedback is critical for active listening because it shows the speaker that the listener is paying attention and is showing interest and respect. Feedback may be as simple as nodding the head in agreement, but it should also include asking questions or making comments to show full engagement. Listening with empathy is especially important because it helps build a connection with the speaker. The listener should communicate empathy with words by saying, for example, "You feel (emotion) because (experience)" because the speaker may not be sensitive to what the listener is comprehending.

CLINICAL DIRECTION

When an issue arises regarding **clinical direction**, the RBT should determine whether the issue is urgent and requires immediate or very soon communication with the supervisor or whether communication can wait until the next session with the supervisor. The RBT should use his or her best judgment regarding contacting the supervisor about urgent situations during the visit or immediately after. Urgent situations may include the following:

- The RBT is unsure of how to proceed or does not understand elements of the client's plan of care. The RBT should avoid guessing about intent and should clarify information with the supervisor.
- The client has a sudden, unexpected change—either positive or negative.
- The client has an environmental change (such as a new medication or a different caregiver) that is affecting the client or the plan of care.
- Issues regarding mandatory reporting (e.g., abuse, negligence) are evident.
- Safety issues (e.g., hitting, biting, threatening, alcohol/drug abuse) have arisen.

OTHER VARIABLES THAT MIGHT AFFECT THE CLIENT

Numerous unanticipated **variables** might affect the client and should be reported to the supervisor immediately as appropriate or following a session. Variables may include the following:

- New or a change in a medical condition, such as an infection or new diagnosis.
- New or a change in medications and any adverse effects that have occurred or may occur.
- Change in caregiver (e.g., family, hired caregiver).
- Change in the place of service, such as with a client whose parents are divorced and the client goes from one house to another or with a change of address.
- Change in family dynamics, such as upon the birth of a child or another child leaving for college.
- Environmental changes, such as home remodeling, new furniture, prolonged power outages, that may affect the client.
- Death or illness in the family.
- Change in behavioral symptoms.
- Loss of a pet or acquisition of a new pet.
- Financial instability, such as from a family member's loss of a job or inability to work.
- Change in insurance coverage for treatments that were previously covered.
- Lack of sleep, nightmares, or night terrors.

Documentation and Reporting

Session Notes for Service Verification

ELEMENTS TO INCLUDE IN SESSION DOCUMENTATION

Session documentation should be completed immediately after completion of a session, if possible, or at least within 24 hours because important information may be forgotten or overlooked if the documentation is delayed. Records, which are legal documents, may not be deleted or altered, although errors can be marked with a line through the error that is then initialed and dated. Documentation must be legible, concise, accurate, and honest. Avoid using subjective descriptions, making suggestions for changes, or commenting on behaviors. Necessary elements include the following:

- Patient identification number, name, and birthdate.
- Date of service.
- Beginning and ending times for the session.
- Client diagnosis.
- Session location.
- Description of therapy provided and progress toward goals in objective, measurable terms.
- Information should be objective and behavioral.
- Description of any variables affecting the client or caregivers.
- Description of new observations, such as changes in behavior or condition.
- Legal signature of the RBT.

SUBJECTIVE VS. OBJECTIVE OBSERVATIONS

Subjective observations are based on opinion and are therefore always open to interpretation and are not always reliable because they are not based on fact. Subjective observations may be colored by biases, either for or against someone or something. For example, a parent may say "My child is showing so much improvement in behavior" because the parent wants this to be true and focuses only on a few positive responses rather than including the negative ones. Additionally, subjective observations often tend to be quite general rather than specific: "The client was very excited to try a new game"; however, it is not clear how the client expressed this excitement.

Objective observations, on the other hand, are based on verifiable facts and data. Objective observations should not be affected by biases or preconceived ideas and should be measurable whenever possible. Thus, instead of noting that a child is showing improvement in behavior, objectively state that "the child has had two episodes of tantrums each day for the past 2 days compared to three to five tantrums daily in the preceding week." Instead of noting that the client was excited, an objective observation is that "the client ran to the table and started to open the game independently, shouting, 'Game! Game!'"

Documentation Requirements

HEALTH INSURANCE PORTABILITY AND ACCOUNTABILITY ACT OF 1986 (HIPAA)

The Health Insurance Portability and Accountability Act of 1986 (HIPAA) addresses the rights of the individual related to privacy of health information. Healthcare providers must not release any information or documentation about a client's condition or treatment without consent because the individual has the right to determine who has access to his or her personal information. Personal information about the client is considered protected health information and consists of any identifying or personal information about the patient, such as health history, condition, or treatments in any form, and any documentation, including electronic, verbal, or written. Personal information can be shared with a spouse, legal guardians, custodial parents, those with durable power of attorney for the client, and those involved in the care of the client, such as physicians, without a specific release, but the client should always be consulted if personal information is to be discussed with others who are present or shared with others to ensure that there is no objection. Failure to comply with HIPAA regulations can make a healthcare provider liable for legal action.

- HIPAA **Privacy Rule**: Protected information includes information included in the medical record (either electronic or paper), conversations between the doctor and other healthcare providers, billing information, and any other form of health information.

LEGAL IMPLICATIONS

AMERICANS WITH DISABILITIES ACT (ADA)

The 1992 Americans with Disabilities Act (ADA) is civil rights legislation that provides the disabled, including those with mental impairment, access to employment and to the community. Although employers must make reasonable accommodations for the disabled, the provisions related to the community often apply to all. The ADA covers not only obvious disabilities but also disorders such as arthritis, seizure disorders, and cardiovascular and respiratory disorders. Communities must provide transportation services for the disabled, including accommodations for persons in wheelchairs. Public facilities (e.g., schools, museums, physician offices, post offices, and restaurants) must be accessible with ramps and elevators in place as needed. Telecommunications must also be accessible through devices or accommodations for the deaf and blind. Compliance is not yet complete because older buildings are required to provide access that is possible without "undue hardship," but newer construction of public facilities must meet ADA regulations.

INDIVIDUALS WITH DISABILITIES EDUCATION ACT (IDEA)

The **Individuals with Disabilities Education Act (IDEA)** ensures that children with disabilities receive free and appropriate public education, including early intervention, special education, and related services to include the following:

- Birth through age 2 (Part C), Early intervention services: Family training, occupation therapy, physical therapy, speech therapy, hearing services, nutritional services, social workers, assistive technology and devices, counseling, and home visits.
- Ages 3–21 (or older if the state authorizes) (Part B): Special education and related services, supplementary aids, adaptive equipment, special communication systems, occupational therapy, physical therapy, speech therapy, and development of an individualized education plan (IEP) that focuses on the client's goals.

Children must be placed in the least restrictive environment for educational services. IDEA requires that youth with disabilities also receive plans for transition from high school. Educational services must include academic content as well as self-help and vocational skills. IDEA provides approaches

Documentation and Reporting

77

for conflict resolution to resolve problems between educators and parents/caregivers: IEP review, facilitated IEP meeting, mediation, filing a complaint, and due process.

MANDATORY REPORTING, ALLOWABLE BREACH OF CONFIDENTIALITY

The RBT is included in laws regarding **mandatory reporting** of abuse or neglect. Suspected abuse of any kind (e.g., physical, emotional, financial, sexual) that affects minors or other vulnerable populations, such as older adults and people who are disabled, must be immediately reported to the supervisor and the appropriate authorities—typically child protective services or adult protective services agencies—and must be carefully documented. States vary on the time frame during which abuse must be reported (often up to 48 hours) and how the report is made, so the RBT should learn the state requirements. Abuse should be reported if it is witnessed directly, if the RBT received evidence or information about the abuse, or if the abuse is divulged by a victim. Depending on the severity and the state, the abuse may also need to be reported to the police. Although maintaining confidentiality is essential, in cases of neglect, abuse, and imminent danger to an individual or others, an **allowable breach of confidentiality** may be necessary to ensure safety. This breach should be documented, and the reason should be outlined.

BEHAVIORAL AND PHYSICAL INDICATORS OF ABUSE IN CHILDREN

Children rarely admit to being abused and, in fact, typically deny it and attempt to protect the abusing parent. Therefore, the RBT must often rely on physical and behavioral signs, such as listed below, to determine if there is cause to suspect **abuse**:

- **Behavioral indicators of abuse:** The child may be overly compliant or fearful with obvious changes in demeanor when a particular parent/caregiver is present. Some children act out with aggression toward other children or animals. Children may become depressed or suicidal or may present with sleeping or eating disorders. Behaviors may become increasingly self-destructive as the child ages.
- **Physical indicators of abuse:** The type, location, and extent of injuries can raise suspicion of abuse. Head and facial injuries and bruising are common, as are bite or burn marks. There may be handprint marks or grab marks or unusual bruising such as across the buttocks. Any bruising, swelling, or tearing of the genital area is also cause for concern.

IDENTIFYING AND REPORTING NEGLECT OF BASIC NEEDS

ADOLESCENTS AND ADULTS WITH DISABILITIES

Neglect of basic needs is a common problem of adolescents and adults with disabilities who live alone or with reluctant or incapable caregivers. In some cases, passive neglect may occur because an elderly or impaired person is trying to take care of a client and is unable to provide the care needed; in other cases, active neglect reflects a lack of caring and may border on negligence and abuse. Cases of neglect should be reported to the appropriate governmental agency, such as the local adult or child protective services agency. Indications of neglect may include the following:

- Lack of assistive devices, such as a cane or walker, needed for mobility.
- Misplaced or missing glasses or hearing aids.
- Poor dental hygiene and dental care.
- Client is left unattended for extended periods of time, sometimes confined to a bed or chair.
- Client is left in soiled or urine-/feces-stained clothing.
- Inadequate food/fluid/nutrition, resulting in weight loss.
- Inappropriate and unkempt clothing, such as lack of a sweater or coat during the winter and dirty or torn clothing.
- Dirty, messy environment.

CHILDREN

Although some children may not be physically or sexually abused, they may suffer from profound **neglect or lack of supervision** that places them at risk. Indicators of abuse may include the following:

- Appearing dirty and unkempt, sometimes with infestations of lice, and wearing ill-fitting or torn clothing and shoes.
- Being tired and sleepy during the daytime.
- Having untended medical or dental problems, such as dental caries.
- Missing appointments and not receiving proper immunizations.
- Being underweight for height or stage of development.

Neglect can be difficult to assess, especially if the RBT is serving a homeless or very poor population. Visits by a social worker may be needed to determine if there is adequate food, clothing, and supervision, and this determination may be beyond that of the RBT or BCBA; therefore, suspicions should be reported to the appropriate authorities, such as the local child protective services agency, so that social workers can assess the home environment.

TRANSPORTATION AND STORAGE OF CLIENT DATA

Client data are covered under HIPAA regulations regarding confidentiality and privacy and must be protected. When transporting client data, they should be in a locked container or in the most secure place available. Client data, which may be in written, audio, or video form, should only be transported if given permission to do so by the supervisor. Generally, personal health information is contained in records in the client's residence or place of treatment, but if data must be transported and left in a vehicle, they should be locked in the trunk when not in use. Data left inside a car, even if the car is locked, are more vulnerable to theft. Client data (all forms) must be stored securely for a minimum of 7 years according to the Behavior Analyst Certification Board (BACB), although some state laws may differ.

Documentation and Reporting

Professional Conduct and Scope of Practice

SECTIONS OF THE RBT ETHICS CODE (2.0)

The Behavior Analyst Certification Board (BACB) developed the **RBT Ethics Code (2.0)** to guide RBT practice in all settings and enforces it through the BACB's code-enforcement procedures. The RBT Ethics Code is based on the principles of treating others with compassion, dignity, and respect; behaving with integrity; and being responsible for one's own competence. Ethics standards include the following:

- **Section 1**: General responsibilities: Outlines the need to be truthful and professional, to provide services under supervision, to avoid discrimination and harassment, to be aware of personal biases and challenges, to avoid multiple relationships, and to maintain professional boundaries.
- **Section 2**: Responsibilities in providing behavior technician services: Outlines clinical responsibilities, such as working in the best interest of clients; following directions of supervisors; acting professionally; using restrictive or punishment-based procedures only as part of a treatment plan; and protecting clients' legal rights, confidentiality, and privacy.
- **Section 3**: Responsibilities of the BACB and BACB-required supervisor: Outlines the relationship between the RBT and the supervisor, discusses the importance of honesty, and describes the reasons why self-reporting is indicated.

PROFESSIONAL ISSUES

Professional issues associated with RBT conduct include the following:

- **Employment as an independent contractor:** Although some RBTs in the United States advertise their services as independent contractors, this is a violation of the US Internal Revenue Service definition for employees. An independent contractor must be in control of how duties are performed without the need for supervision, but RBT certification specifically requires that the RBT work under supervision; therefore, in the United States, an RBT should not work as an independent contractor. Additionally, working as an independent contractor violates the RBT Ethics Code. RBTs should be wary of any employer that is hiring RBTs as independent contractors.
- **Certification maintenance:** RBT certification must be renewed annually, and the application must include a renewal competency assessment. Application for renewal of certification should be done 45 days prior to the expiration date, and 2 weeks should be allowed for the application to be processed.

RBT REQUIREMENTS FOR SELF-REPORTING

The RBT is required to report to the BACB professional or personal conduct that may pose a risk to others in any of the RBT's roles. **Self-reporting requirements** include:

- Noncompliance with required supervision.
- Critical events:
  - Violations of ethics standards: Failing to ensure continuity of service, engaging in multiple relationships, inappropriate or inaccurate documentation.
  - Physical and mental health conditions and substance use disorders: Having current or within the previous 3 years a mental health condition or substance use disorder for which the RBT does not have an active plan of care and that may impact the ability to provide services, or within the previous 3 years participated in treatment under direction of a court of law because of criminal charges related to a mental health condition or substance abuse disorder.
- Investigations: All investigations (e.g., ethics, billing, audit, criminal) must be reported.
- Agreements/Actions: Termination, denial of licensure, arbitration agreement, required action (e.g., repayment, education, relinquishment of license/certification), public health safety tickets or fines, criminal/civil suits, expungement of court records, probation, parole, pretrial diversion, current detainment, and felony convictions.

EVENTS THAT DO NOT MEET THE RBT REQUIREMENTS FOR SELF-REPORTING

Although the BACB requires that many different events be self-reported, some events are explicitly omitted. Changes in personal information must be updated in the RBT's BACB account but are not otherwise reported. **Events that do not require self-reporting** include the following:

- A new or existing mental health or substance use disorder that is unlikely to impact the safe delivery of care and for which a care plan is in place.
- Any audit that does not result in the need for corrective actions or penalties.
- Credit/Tax hearings.
- Bankruptcy.
- Fines (e.g., tax, revenue, wage garnishment).
- Parking tickets, tickets from traffic camera violations.
- Traffic tickets of $750 or less.
- Family court proceedings (e.g., divorce, child custody).
- Employer layoffs or actions that do not constitute an ethics violation.

RBT, BCABA, BCBA, AND BCBA-D

Registered behavior technician: The RBT is a paraprofessional who works under the supervision of a BCaBA, BCBA, or BCBA-D. The RBT requires a high school diploma or GED, being at least 18 years of age, and completion of 40 hours of RBT training as well as a competency assessment and passing the RBT certification exam.

Board certified assistant behavioral analyst: The BCaBA requires a bachelor's-level certification. The BCaBA professional may directly supervise RBTs but must work under the supervision of a BCBA or BCBA-D to carry out behavior analysis services.

Board certified behavior analyst: The BCBA requires a master's-level certification. This professional serves in a leadership and supervisory role. The BCBA may work as an independent practitioner.

81

Board certified behavior analyst-doctoral: The BCBA-D requires a doctoral- or postdoctoral-level degree and certification. The BCBA's responsibilities are similar to those of the BCBA. BCBA-Ds are often involved in teaching and/or research and policy setting.

Supervision Requirements and the Role of the RBT

BACB's Supervisory Requirements for the RBT

The RBT must work under qualified **supervision** for a minimum of 5% of the hours (or 20 hours) during which the RBT is providing applied behavioral analysis therapy each calendar month. Additionally, it is the RBT's responsibility to keep track of the dates and hours he or she worked and the dates and hours that were under supervision. The RBT must retain a copy of supervision records for 7 years, ideally by scanning them and saving them in an electronic format. If the BACB requests copies of supervision records during an audit, the RBT has 7 days to produce the records. The RBT is also responsible for requesting supervision when needed to remain compliant with requirements. The supervisor is responsible for the work provided by the RBT. The supervisor must have at least two face-to-face real-time contacts with the RBT each month, and one of these visits must be only with the individual RBT. The second contact may be with a small group (not to exceed 10) of RBTs. The supervisor must observe the RBT providing services at least one time each month (preferably on site but it may be conducted via web camera or video conferencing if necessary).

Responsibilities and Activities of RBT Supervisors

RBT supervisors may be a BCBA, BCaBA, BCBA-D, or noncertified (i.e., an individual licensed in a different behavioral health field and competent in applied behavioral analysis). Responsibilities and activities include the following:

- Explaining the purpose of supervision, teaching, and modeling.
- Describing ineffective supervision, strategies and outcomes, and identifying poor performance and unethical behavior.
- Preparing for the role of supervisor, reviewing time and resources, and verifying certification requirements.
- Developing a plan for training and evaluation, setting performance objectives, and reviewing expectations.
- Establishing positive relationships with supervisees and communicating regularly and effectively.
- Using behavioral skills training, modeling, teaching, providing feedback, and assisting supervisees to reach skill mastery.
- Complying with fieldwork requirements, developing a supervision contract, documenting supervision, measuring, identifying opportunities for training, and providing a variety of different fieldwork opportunities.
- Evaluating the effectiveness of supervision, assessing baseline skills, making observations, and identifying outcomes of ineffective supervision.
- Incorporating ethics, discussion of ethical dilemmas, and professional development into the supervision role.

ROLE OF THE RBT IN THE SERVICE DELIVERY SYSTEM

The **role of the RBT** is to work with clients who need behavioral therapy, such as individuals on the autism spectrum, and they also work with clients with mental health disorders, substance abuse, cognitive impairment, and social disorders. The RBT may work in clients' homes or in clinical settings. The RBT works under the direction and supervision of a BCBA to support and implement a plan of care. Activities may include the following:

- Following protocols for behavior modification.
- Providing direct care in individual and group settings.
- Making observations and documenting client behavior.
- Assisting the supervisor and seeking information as needed.
- Communicating with clients, families, and other professionals.
- Measuring and assessing clients.
- Maintaining professional boundaries.
- Providing input to the supervisor regarding client needs and progress.
- Collaborating in modification of the plan of care as indicated by client needs.
- Assisting clients to develop life skills.
- Training clients for employment.
- Providing guidance to families and caregivers.

Response to Feedback

Feedback is an essential element of supervision and is provided directly (during implementation of treatment) and indirectly (from documentation, graphs, progress toward goals). The purpose of feedback is to help the RBT to do the following:

- Improve performance.
- Develop new skills.
- Help solve problems.

In order to meet these goals, the supervisor must provide feedback and should encourage the RBT to carry out self-assessment. The RBT is responsible for asking questions if the feedback is not clear or if it is unclear what response is indicated. The RBT should make note of any feedback and address it in the provision of care. Additionally, the RBT is also responsible for asking for feedback when the RBT has a question about how to deal with different issues, such as a new client's behavior. If the RBT finds that any feedback or guidance is not effective, the RBT should discuss the problem with the supervisor and seek further feedback.

Stakeholder Communication

COMMUNICATING WITH STAKEHOLDERS

Most RBT **communication** with stakeholders (e.g., families, caregivers, and other professionals) is informal and dealing with issues related to immediate provision of care because more formal communication, such as reports, evaluations, and consultations, is typically carried out by the applied behavioral analyst (ABA). If clients or caregivers have questions about the plan of care, the RBT should generally direct these to the BCBA, who is responsible for making clinical decisions. The RBT should communicate with stakeholders in the manner in which the RBT has been directed by the supervisor. In some cases, the RBT may be included in team meetings and may share observations, ask questions, and respectfully make suggestions, keeping in mind that the ABA makes the decisions. The input of the RBT can be invaluable to the ABA who is planning or modifying the plan of care because the RBT spends more time in the direct care of the client.

ASSERTIVE COMMUNICATION

Assertive communication occurs when individuals express opinions directly and their actions correlate with their words. Assertive communicators are respectful of others and not do not bully but are firm and honest about their opinions. They frequently use "I" statements to make their point: "I would like. . . ." Communication usually includes cooperative statements such as "What do you think?" and distinguishes between fact and opinion. Assertive communicators often engender trust in others because they are consistent, honest, and open in their communications. The assertive communicator feels free to express disagreement and anger but does so in a manner that is nonthreatening and respectful of others' feelings. Assertive communication requires a strong sense of self-worth and the belief that personal opinions have value. Assertive communicators tend to have good listening skills because they value the opinions of others and feel comfortable collaborating.

COMMUNICATION USING VERBAL METHODS

Verbal (i.e., **spoken**) **communication** can vary from very formal (such as a conference presentation) to very informal (such as a chat with a friend), but every aspect of the communication process has meaning—the words, posture, tone of voice, facial expression, silent times, and general appearance. Communication of the same words will be very different if heard over the phone, read in an email, or experienced in a face-to-face conversation. In any professional communication, formal or informal, the RBT should come prepared and have some idea of what to say, although memorizing a speech word for word is not advisable because communication should appear spontaneous even when it is not. The average person speaks approximately 200 words per minute, and each sentence is a new creation; therefore, without planning, the message can easily become muddled. For a formal presentation, brief outline notes may be helpful to stay focused on the topic.

COMMUNICATION USING NONVERBAL METHODS

Nonverbal interpersonal communication can convey as much information as verbal communication, both on the RBT's part and the client's part. Nonverbal communication is used for many purposes, such as expressing feelings and attitudes, and it may be a barrier or a facilitator to understanding. Although there are cultural differences, interpretation of nonverbal communication can help the RBT better understand and promote clear communication as evidenced in the following ways:

- **Eye contact:** Making eye contact provides a connection and shows caring and involvement in the communication. Avoiding eye contact may indicate that someone is not telling the truth or is uncomfortable, fearful, ashamed, or is hiding something—although this depends on the individual's culture. Some ethnic groups and those on the autism spectrum are uncomfortable making eye contact or avoid eye contact as a sign of respect (e.g., Asian Americans, African Americans, Native Americans).
- **Tone:** The manner in which words are spoken (e.g., patiently, cheerfully, somberly) affects the listener; when the message and tone do not match, it can interfere with communication. A high-pitched tone of voice may indicate nervousness or stress.
- **Touch:** Reaching out to touch a client's hand or pat a shoulder during communication may be reassuring, but hugging or excessive touching can make clients feel uncomfortable. Some clients, such as those on the autism spectrum, may dislike physical contact. Clients may touch themselves (e.g., lick the lips, pick at the skin, scratch) if they are anxious.
- **Gestures:** Using the hands to emphasize meaning is common and may be particularly helpful during explanations, but excessive gesturing can be distracting. Some gestures alone convey a message, such as a wave goodbye or pointing. Tapping of the foot, moving the legs, or fidgeting may indicate nervousness. Rubbing the hands together is sometimes used as a self-comforting measure. Some gestures, such as handshakes, are part of social rituals. Mixed messages, such as fidgeting but speaking with a calm voice may indicate uncertainty or anxiety.
- **Posture:** Slumping can indicate a lack of interest or withdrawal. Leaning toward the other person while talking indicates interest and facilitates interaction.

Professional Boundaries

OVERVIEW

Professional boundaries are those behaviors that separate a paraprofessional or professional from a personal relationship in order to provide safe and effective care to a client. Although the relationship with a client may seem similar to a friendship, it is a relationship based on client needs. Practices that violate professional boundaries include the following:

- Having sexual contact with a client.
- Injuring or in some way harming a client.
- Using insulting, degrading, or aggressive behavior or comments.
- Violating a client's privacy unnecessarily, such as by watching a client undress.
- Asking a client for personal information that is not relevant to care.
- Sharing personal information with a client.
- Engaging in inappropriate touching, kissing, hugging, and caressing.
- Doing favors for clients outside of working hours or showing favoritism.
- Failing to report important information about a client to colleagues or supervisors in order to protect the client from consequences.
- Accepting money or other gifts.
- Proselytizing or imposing religious or political beliefs.
- Encouraging dependency on the part of the client.
- Misusing or stealing a client's money or other property.
- Spreading rumors or gossiping about a client.
- Posting information about a client on social media.

COERCION

Issues of professional boundaries include the possibility of **coercion**. The relationship between an RBT and a client represents an imbalance of power, so the use of coercion is abusive. Although some clients are compliant, others may be uncooperative, but both may be easily intimidated. Coercion is sometimes used to control behavior and can include threatening punishments, carrying out punishments, or removing punishments (i.e., negative reinforcement) for compliance. Every effort should be made to avoid any type of coercion or forcing a client to do something the client does not want to do, even though this can be challenging. Additionally, coercion is often counterproductive in that it can produce behaviors that are ultimately more problematic than the initial behavior. For example, a client who is punished or threatened for not trying different foods may begin to eat but then vomit. Using a reward system with positive reinforcement is more effective than using negative reinforcement.

DUAL RELATIONSHIPS

The RBT Ethics Code states that the RBT must avoid **dual (aka multiple) relationships** with clients and supervisors. A dual relationship occurs when there is more than one role or relationship between the RBT and the client or others. For example, if an RBT has a social relationship with the parent of a client, this is a multiple relationship (e.g., RBT and child, RBT and parent), and may affect the type of care the RBT provides the child. If a supervisor begins a romantic relationship with an RBT, this is also a multiple relationship (e.g., supervisor and RBT, romantic partner and RBT). The RBT should not engage in a sexual relationship with a client or supervisor for at least 2 years after the end of the professional relationship. In a small community, avoiding all dual relationships can be difficult, but the RBT should report any dual/multiple relationships to the

87

supervisor, and if the dual/multiple relationship includes the supervisor, then the report should be made to the supervisor's immediate supervisor.

CONFLICTS OF INTEREST

A **conflict of interest** occurs when an RBT can receive personal benefit, such as money or favors, from a professional relationship or when the RBT and another party (such as the client or supervisor) hold incompatible goals. In either case, the conflict of interest may affect workplace actions and decisions. Every organization should have a policy in place that applies to all individuals in the organization for disclosure of conflicts of interest, and this policy often includes the issue of gift giving and receiving. A conflict of interest may occur not only with the RBT but also with family, business partners, or close friends of the RBT. Any existing or potential conflicts of interest should be disclosed immediately to a supervisor and appropriately documented. In some cases, the RBT may be recused (i.e., excused or removed from the situation) because of the conflict or a plan devised to manage the conflict.

SOCIAL MEDIA CONTACTS

The RBT Ethics Code prohibits the sharing of any identifying information about clients (e.g., pictures, videos, written information) on **social media**. Identifying information includes not only the obvious (e.g., name, address) but also any information from which identification can be reasonably determined. Organizations should have clear policies about social media, and some organizations prohibit any discussion about the workplace, including the place of employment or staff members, on social media because of concerns about breach of privacy and security. Thus, the best policy is to share nothing about clients or supervisors, even in general terms. If, for example, an RBT has posted the place of employment on a social media site and then describes, even in general terms, problems the RBT is having with a client or supervisor, someone else associated with that place of employment may be able to figure out to whom the RBT is referring, thereby breaching privacy. The RBT should avoid all contact with clients and their families/caregivers on social media.

INFORMED CONSENT

Clients or parents/guardians must provide **informed consent** for all treatment that the client receives. The BCBA is primarily responsible for ensuring informed consent, but the RBT should be knowledgeable and prepared to answer questions and ensure compliance. Informed consent includes a thorough explanation of all procedures and treatments that are part of the plan of care and any associated benefits or risks. Clients and parents/guardians should be informed of all options and allowed input on the type of interventions when appropriate. Although many clients served by the RBT are children or are unable to give consent directly, their parents or other legal representatives should do so and should be advised to the types of interventions planned and their duration, intensity, and frequency. They should be encouraged to ask questions and made to feel they are an integral part of the process because they are more likely to be supportive when they have had input.

Maintaining Client Dignity

Maintaining **client dignity** includes the following considerations:

- Maintain confidentiality and share information only with the client, supervisor, and caregiver.
- Communicate with respect and at an appropriate level of language, depending on the client's communication skills and age. For example, talk to an adolescent as to other adolescents, not as to a child, regardless of the adolescent's communication skills.
- Avoid talking about the client in front of the client as though the client cannot comprehend, even if the client is mentally challenged.
- Encourage clients to discuss their plans of care.
- Avoid talking down to clients, making fun of them, or belittling them.
- Avoid side conversations with other individuals, such as coworkers, while caring for a client.
- Avoid making judgmental statements about the client, caregiver, or lifestyle choices.
- Practice active listening when the client or caregivers are communicating.
- Engage in friendly communication during care of the client.
- Show empathy and understanding.
- Exercise patience.

Professional Conduct and Scope of Practice

RBT Practice Test #1

Want to take this practice test in an online interactive format?
Check out the bonus page, which includes interactive practice questions and much more: **mometrix.com/bonus948/rbt**

1. What is the RBT's role in the development of a written skill acquisition plan?

   a.   Collect baseline and ongoing data.
   b.   Determine skill deficits.
   c.   Outline goals.
   d.   Assess progress.

2. Which one of the following is a requirement of the Americans with Disabilities Act?

   a.   Early intervention services for children with disabilities.
   b.   Transportation services for those with disabilities.
   c.   Protection of the privacy of personal information.
   d.   Vocational training for those with disabilities.

3. The RBT is using total task presentation to teach a young child a simple behavior chain and is beginning with graduated guidance with hand-over-hand physical prompting to guide the client. What should the RBT do as the client first begins to master some steps?

   a.   Stop all prompting.
   b.   Use only verbal prompts.
   c.   Use shadowing.
   d.   Ask the child "What do you do next?"

4. According to the client's schedule of reinforcement, reinforcement for desired behavior should be given with every third occurrence. What type of reinforcement does this represent?

   a.   Continuous.
   b.   Fixed ratio.
   c.   Variable interval.
   d.   Variable ratio.

5. Which one of the following is an example of a setting event?

   a.   The RBT reinforces a desired behavior.
   b.   The RBT greets the client.
   c.   A client enjoys an activity.
   d.   A client has a headache.

6. The RBT has brought a copy of a client's health and treatment records in the automobile to the assisted living facility where the client resides. What is the least that the RBT should do to ensure the security of the records?

    a. Lock them inside the car.
    b. Place the records so they are not visible through the windows.
    c. Take them inside the assisted living facility.
    d. Lock the records in the trunk.

7. A child becomes upset when trying to do a math problem and begins to cry. In response, the parent comforts the child and offers the child a cookie. If conducting a direct observation, what are the ABCs that the RBT records?

    a. A = crying, B = comfort and cookie, and C = math problem.
    b. A = comfort and cookie, B = math problem, and C = crying.
    c. A = math problem, B = comfort and cookie, and C = crying.
    d. A = math problem, B = crying, and C = comfort and cookie.

8. A young child with autism is very uncooperative during a session when the RBT attempts to train the child to ask for items rather than just grabbing them. Which one of the following is the best description when reporting the behavior?

    a. "Child threw himself on the floor, screaming and kicking for 5 minutes."
    b. "Child aggressive and throwing tantrums."
    c. "Child threw a temper tantrum for 5 minutes."
    d. "Training unsuccessful because of child's negative behavior."

9. An RBT is working with a client who has developed motor tics associated with anxiety to reduce the tics. The client exhibits eight motor tics in one 2-hour session and four motor tics in the second 2-hour session. What type of measurement is used to record this information?

    a. Frequency.
    b. Duration.
    c. Intensity.
    d. Latency.

10. The registered behavior technician (RBT) has been asked by the board-certified behavior analyst (BCBA) to collect client data needed for insurance reimbursement, but the RBT is unsure how to proceed with data collection. What should the RBT do first?

    a. Clarify any procedures that are not clear with the BCBA.
    b. Review guidelines regarding data collection protocols.
    c. Prepare materials for data collection.
    d. Discuss the purpose and goals of the data collection.

11. Which one of the following is an example of an unconditioned reinforcer?

    a. Candy.
    b. Water.
    c. Attention.
    d. Toy.

12. Which one of the following is an important factor to ensure that reinforcers are effective?

    a. Delayed reinforcement.
    b. Random reinforcement.
    c. Satiation.
    d. Immediate reinforcement.

13. Informed consent should include which one of the following?

    a. The names of those working with the client.
    b. An explanation of treatments and procedures.
    c. Costs of treatment.
    d. Outcome goals.

14. What is an essential element of active listening?

    a. Feedback.
    b. Summary.
    c. Questions.
    d. Comprehension.

15. The supervisor provides feedback to the RBT after a direct observation. The supervisor is critical of the methods that the RBT used with the client. What is the best response?

    a. "Could you tell me what I should do to improve?"
    b. "I'm sorry. I'll review the procedure."
    c. "I thought I was doing it right."
    d. "I was nervous because you were watching."

16. A child has learned to ask for a cookie by saying "Cookie please," but now he repeatedly asks for a cookie throughout the day. What type of reinforcement is indicated to decrease this behavior?

    a. Differential reinforcement of alternative behavior.
    b. Differential reinforcement of incompatible behavior.
    c. Differential reinforcement of other behavior.
    d. Differential reinforcement of low rates.

17. The RBT works in a small town and discovers that a client is the child of the RBT's spouse's boss. What is the best course of action?

    a. Ask the spouse about the relationship with the boss.
    b. Say nothing because this is not important.
    c. Ask to be assigned a different client.
    d. Disclose this to the supervisor.

18. What type of relationship is in a contingency?

    a. Consequence-consequence.
    b. Response-response.
    c. Antecedent-response.
    d. Response-consequence.

19. According to the Individuals with Disabilities Education Act (IDEA), what is one of the requirements for educational services for children with disabilities?

    a. Least restrictive environment.
    b. Vocational skills only.
    c. One-on-one instruction.
    d. Shared costs.

20. A client engages in skin scratching when he is anxious, and the scratching calms the client and reduces his anxiety. What type of reinforcement is the client using?

    a. Automatic positive reinforcement.
    b. Automatic negative reinforcement.
    c. Noncontingent reinforcement.
    d. Natural negative unconditioned reinforcement.

21. The RBT is using manding trials to teach a child with autism and limited speech to ask for favorite snacks instead of crying or yelling. Initially, if the child is asking for juice, what is the least the child should say in order to receive reinforcement?

    a. "Juice, please."
    b. "I want juice."
    c. "Juice."
    d. "Juuu."

22. A client is trying to improve her reading skills. If her goal is to read 100 pages a week, what type of graph is best used to demonstrate her progress?

    a. Line graph.
    b. Bar graph.
    c. Cumulative graph.
    d. Pie chart.

23. The supervising BCBA has outlined a plan of behavior modification for a client, but the newly certified RBT is not familiar with one of the interventions. What is the best way to communicate this?

    a. "Could I use a different intervention with the client?"
    b. "I'll have to study that intervention a little more."
    c. "What is the purpose of this intervention?"
    d. "I'm not familiar with this intervention. Could you review it with me?"

24. Which type of individualized assessment compares clients with a predetermined skill level?

    a. Norm referenced.
    b. Social.
    c. Criterion referenced.
    d. Developmental.

25. The RBT is using backward chaining to teach a child to wash her hands and has demonstrated the procedure a number of times; the client can carry out the last step without prompting. When should the RBT provide reinforcement?

    a. After each step.
    b. After steps that require minimal prompting.
    c. Before the step that generally requires no prompting.
    d. After the step done without prompting.

26. The RBT is attracted to the supervising BCBA and believes that the attraction is reciprocated. How long after the professional relationship ends is it appropriate to engage in intimate relations with the supervisor?

    a. 6 months.
    b. 12 months.
    c. 2 years.
    d. 4 years.

27. An RBT is carrying out momentary time sampling during six intervals (one interval every 20 seconds) to determine if the client is shortening the duration of stimming. Which one of the following should the RBT record?

    a. The latency of a behavior during each interval.
    b. The number of behaviors during each interval.
    c. The duration of a behavior during each interval.
    d. The presence or absence of a behavior at the beginning of each interval.

28. Which one of the following is an example of receptive language?

    a. Eye contact.
    b. Turn-taking.
    c. The ability to read.
    d. Body language.

29. An RBT is carrying out partial interval discontinuous measurement of a client who experiences vocal tics. The RBT is making observations during five 60-second intervals with the following results:

- First interval: 0 tics.
- Second interval: 8 tics.
- Third interval: 4 tics.
- Fourth interval: 1 tic.
- Fifth interval: 6 tics.

Which is the correct recording of these results?

    a. 1.
    b. 1/5, or 20%.
    c. 4/5, or 80%.
    d. 19.

30. The RBT accompanies a client with an intellectual disability to the grocery store to help him learn to shop for groceries and finds opportunities for teaching from direct observation of the client in that environment. What type of teaching does this represent?

    a. Discrete trial.
    b. Incidental.
    c. Pivotal response.
    d. Contingent observation.

31. The RBT is using discrete trial training to help a child identify items. The RBT lays out three picture cards at a time and asks the child to identify one item, such as the picture of a cow, each time. When she answers correctly, the RBT provides reinforcement. When the RBT asks her to identify the fox, she points to the picture of a cat. What should the RBT do in response to this incorrect response?

    a. Ignore it and move on to the next trial.
    b. Point and say "This is a fox."
    c. Say "No, try again."
    d. Show the child a picture of a cat and say "This is a cat."

32. A client is learning to work under supervision to wrap and box manufactured items for shipment. Which method of assessment is likely the most effective in determining the client's progress?

    a. Permanent product recording.
    b. Frequency measurement.
    c. Discrete categorization.
    d. Whole interval measurement.

33. The RBT is fading prompts by slowly increasing the time between the stimulus and the prompt. What type of prompt fading is this?

    a. Time delay.
    b. Least to most.
    c. Graduated guidance.
    d. Most to least.

34. When working with a young boy, the RBT notes bruising around his face and legs as well as what appear to be grab marks on his arms, and the child reacts fearfully when the RBT reaches a hand toward him. What is the best response?

    a. Ask the parent/guardian about the marks.
    b. Ask the child what happened.
    c. Report the observations to the local child protective services agency.
    d. Wait and observe the interactions of the parent/guardian and child.

35. A client's parent asks the RBT frequent questions about the client's progress. To which one of the following questions can the RBT appropriately respond with an explanation?

    a. "Can you modify this procedure a little?"
    b. "What is the purpose of fading?"
    c. "When will the behavioral intervention plan be updated?"
    d. "What can we do to speed up my child's learning?"

36. When preparing session notes, which one of the following statements is objective?

    a. "The client was very unhappy and upset during the session."
    b. "Today was nonproductive because the client was uncooperative."
    c. "When prompted to read a word, the child picked up the book and threw it at the RBT."
    d. "The client is not interested in learning to dress herself."

37. The RBT observes that a 5-year-old child who has previously been cooperative when playing with other children begins to grab toys and tries to bite another child. When should the RBT communicate this with the supervisor?

    a. During the session.
    b. At the end of the session.
    c. After a few days of observation.
    d. At the next supervisory visit.

38. Which one of the following measurements is generally most difficult to measure accurately?

    a. Latency.
    b. Frequency.
    c. Duration.
    d. Intensity.

39. Which one of the following is an example of a professional boundary violation?

    a. The RBT pats a client's hand when the client responds appropriately.
    b. The RBT bows her head and stands quietly when a client prays.
    c. The RBT tells another RBT that a client is sexually active.
    d. The RBT tells a parent that the RBT has 3 years of experience.

40. Which one of the following is part of the duties of the RBT?

    a. Modify the intervention plan according to client needs.
    b. Design the intervention plan.
    c. Implement the intervention plan.
    d. Assess client progress.

41. A client has been repeatedly throwing food and other items on the floor, but when the client sees that the RBT is collecting data regarding the frequency of this behavior, there is a marked decrease in its frequency. What is the most likely reason for this response?

    a. Compliance.
    b. Intimidation.
    c. Behavior modification.
    d. Reactivity.

42. The RBT has been working with a new and interesting client. With whom can the RBT share personal information about this client?

    a. An RBT who works with a different client.
    b. Friends on social media.
    c. The client's teacher.
    d. The supervising BCBA.

43. A chaining intervention planned for a client is one for which the RBT has been trained but is inexperienced with. What should the RBT do to prepare?

    a. Ask to observe the BCBA working with the client.

    b. Suggest a different intervention with which the RBT is more familiar.

    c. Practice the interventions.

    d. Write out a detailed description of the intervention.

44. When teaching a client to identify items, the RBT places the item (stimulus) to be identified closer to the client. What type of prompt is this?

    a. Modeling prompt.

    b. Extrastimulus prompt.

    c. Within-stimulus prompt.

    d. Physical prompt.

45. The RBT talks to the client throughout each visit, explaining the purpose of each intervention even though the client is nonverbal and does not make eye contact or respond in any way. What is the primary purpose of the RBT's behavior?

    a. As a nervous habit to fill the silence.

    b. To show respect for the client's dignity.

    c. To teach caregivers appropriate behavior.

    d. To teach the client the importance of communication.

46. Which one of the following verbal operants refers to the ability to label things appropriately, such as seeing a horse and saying "horse"?

    a. Echoic.

    b. Tact.

    c. Textual.

    d. Intraverbal.

47. The RBT is using shaping to teach a child to eat with a spoon. The child's first response is to pick up the spoon and lay it back down. Each time the child picks up the spoon, the RBT reinforces this. Then, the child picks up the spoon and puts it in the bowl. What should the RBT do at this point?

    a. Stop reinforcing the child's picking up the spoon and reinforce putting the spoon in the bowl.

    b. Reinforce both the child's picking up the spoon and putting the spoon in the bowl.

    c. Reinforce only the child's picking up the spoon.

    d. Stop all reinforcement until the child eats with the spoon.

48. A client is familiar with common fruits, and the RBT is teaching the client to identify fruits by showing the client an actual piece of fruit. The RBT begins with a banana and provides reinforcement when the client correctly identifies the fruit when shown by itself and with one and two other items. What level of mastery should the RBT expect before moving on to the next type of fruit?

    a. 80–90%.

    b. 70–80%.

    c. 60–70%.

    d. 50–60%.

49. A client often throws his books and school items on the floor during class; however, when the client picks up a book and drops it back on the desk, the RBT reinforces this behavior. What type of reinforcement is the RBT using?

   a. Differential reinforcement of alternative behavior.
   b. Differential reinforcement of other behavior.
   c. Differential reinforcement of incompatible behavior.
   d. Differential reinforcement of low rates.

50. Which one of the following variables is most likely to affect a client's ongoing behavior and should be reported to a supervisor?

   a. The client's father got a job promotion.
   b. The client's parents are separating and getting a divorce.
   c. The client slept poorly and is sleepy.
   d. The client got a new haircut.

51. Extinction procedures are primarily based on which one of the following?

   a. Providing reinforcement for alternative behaviors.
   b. Removing all reinforcement.
   c. Removing reinforcement for unwanted behavior.
   d. Providing reinforcement for wanted behavior.

52. The RBT is assisting with a preference assessment to determine appropriate reinforcers for a child. The RBT places several different toys on the floor in front of the child and observes her interacting with the toys. What type of preference assessment method is the RBT using?

   a. Ask.
   b. Indirect.
   c. Contrived free operant.
   d. Naturalistic free operant.

53. The RBT is working with an aggressive client who has acted violently in the past. Which one of the following is an appropriate personal preventive measure?

   a. Apply physical restraints on the client.
   b. Remind the client to behavior appropriately.
   c. Keep hair up and out of reach.
   d. Insist that a security guard be present.

54. An RBT has been working with a child who is reluctant to carry out tasks, often waiting 10–12 seconds before beginning. However, after 2 weeks, the client is now usually beginning tasks within 6–8 seconds. This represents an improvement in which type of measurement?

   a. Reactivity.
   b. Frequency.
   c. Latency.
   d. Duration.

55. **A young child who was developmentally challenged was unable to crawl until she was almost 2 years old. However, once she could crawl, she began exploring the environment and experiencing many different opportunities for behaviors. What does crawling represent for this child?**

   a. Behavioral cusp.
   b. Keystone behavior.
   c. Pivotal behavior.
   d. On-task behavior.

56. **When is it appropriate to use punishment-based procedures with a client?**

   a. In response to negative behavior.
   b. When they are included in the treatment plan.
   c. When positive-based procedures are ineffective.
   d. When the client engages in dangerous behavior.

57. **When using paired stimuli/forced-choice preference assessment with a client, the client always selects the item placed on the left. What does this suggest?**

   a. The RBT makes an effort to put items that the client likes on the same side.
   b. The client is not interested in participating.
   c. The child is left handed and favors the left side.
   d. This is not an effective assessment for this client.

58. **Under what circumstance is the RBT permitted to advertise services or be employed as an independent contractor?**

   a. Under no circumstances.
   b. When clients require only minimal assistance.
   c. When required for employment.
   d. Whenever desired to work independently.

59. **When graphing data on a line graph, for which one of the following is the *y* axis used?**

   a. Time.
   b. Behavior.
   c. Condition.
   d. Intervention.

60. **A client's teacher reports that the client has been acting out (yelling, throwing things) in class and has been placed in a time-out for 5 minutes each time. What type of reinforcement or punishment does this represent?**

   a. Positive punishment.
   b. Positive reinforcement.
   c. Negative punishment.
   d. Negative reinforcement.

61. A child frequently throws temper tantrums, resulting in the parent giving the child attention, and this attention has become a reinforcer for the behavior so that the frequency of tantrums has increased. Because of this, the parent has been asked to provide frequent attention at random periods to the child and to ignore the tantrums. What type of reinforcement does this represent?

   a. Conditioned fixed-ratio reinforcement
   b. Unconditioned variable-ratio reinforcement.
   c. Noncontingent variable reinforcement.
   d. Noncontingent fixed reinforcement.

62. A client was very frightened on a visit to a farm by a black pony. Since then, the client becomes panicked when he sees any black animal, such as a black cat or dog. What does this represent?

   a. Response generalization.
   b. Simultaneous prompting.
   c. Stimulus generalization.
   d. Stimulus control.

63. A client with Attention-deficit hyperactivity/disorder has difficulty completing school assignments/worksheets, so a token economy is being used to improve performance.

Tokens	Response Cost	Backup Reinforcer
2 per assignment	1 per missed assignment	5 tokens for 30 minutes of video game playing

In the first 2 days, the client hands in seven assignments and misses two. How many minutes of video game time has the client earned?

   a. 30 minutes.
   b. 45 minutes.
   c. 60 minutes.
   d. 75 minutes.

64. If a child has difficulty staying on task in the school setting and the RBT is measuring the client's progress, which measurement is most indicated?

   a. Frequency.
   b. Duration.
   c. Intensity.
   d. Latency.

65. According to the prompt hierarchy, which one of the following response prompts is the strongest?

   a. Modeling.
   b. Visual.
   c. Verbal
   d. Physical.

66. How many face-to-face contacts must the supervisor have with the RBT each month?

   a. One.
   b. Two.
   c. Three.
   d. Four.

67. The RBT is using no-no prompting with a client. With the first trial, the RBT asks the client to pick up a cup, but the client simply pushes the cup. What is the correct response for the RBT?

   a. "No, you pushed the cup."
   b. "I want you to pick up the cup."
   c. "You almost got it! Try again."
   d. "No, try again."

68. A client has been undergoing extinction for an unwanted behavior. Almost immediately after reinforcement has stopped, the client experiences an increase in the unwanted behavior. What does this represent?

   a. Extinction burst.
   b. Response variation.
   c. Spontaneous recovery.
   d. Extinction failure.

69. Before a BCBA can perform a functional analysis, what type of functional behavioral data collection must be carried out?

   a. Direct observation.
   b. Interviews with the client and family.
   c. Questionnaire for key observers, such as parents and teachers.
   d. Behavioral checklist.

70. When conducting a preference assessment with multiple stimuli with replacement, how many times should each item be included in the array of items in order to establish an order of preference?

   a. At least one time.
   b. At least two times.
   c. At least three times.
   d. At least four times.

71. Which one of the following is an example of short-circuiting the contingency?

   a. A parent allows a child to watch TV even though she has not completed her homework.
   b. A client consistently overeats and hoards food.
   c. A client turns in classwork only half of the time.
   d. A client takes candy from another client and is required to return it and give the other client an additional piece of candy.

72. A client frequently grabs at food items, so the RBT places a hand in front of the items so the client is unable to reach them. Which intervention is the RBT using?
   a. Personal restraint.
   b. Positive punishment.
   c. Response blocking.
   d. Negative punishment.

73. Which one of the following is an example of sensory stimulation, one of the functions of behavior?
   a. A client repeatedly grabs at a toy that the client wants.
   b. A client hides behind a desk when called on by a teacher.
   c. A client goofs off in class and makes other students laugh.
   d. A client rocks back and forth at his desk when anxious.

74. When a crisis or emergency situation occurs, what is the primary concern for the RBT?
   a. Client welfare and safety.
   b. RBT personal welfare and safety.
   c. Avoiding reinforcement for unwanted behavior.
   d. Establishing boundaries.

75. Which one of the following must be self-reported to the Behavior Analyst Certification Board (BACB)?
   a. A new episode of depression with a treatment plan in place.
   b. Court-ordered treatment for substance use disorder 2 years previously.
   c. A $650.00 traffic ticket.
   d. Personal bankruptcy procedures.

76. When faced with a series of associated behaviors, what is the behavior called whose change would most likely lead to changes in multiple behaviors?
   a. Behavioral cusp.
   b. Keystone behavior.
   c. Escape behavior.
   d. Avoidance behavior.

77. The RBT is using forward chaining to teach a client to do mouth care. The RBT has been prompting the first step, and the client is beginning to master that step. What should the RBT do next?
   a. Fade the prompt.
   b. Introduce the second step, and prompt both steps.
   c. Ask the client if she is ready for the next step.
   d. Continue prompting the first step until it is fully mastered.

78. Which one of the following is an example of an abolishing operation?
   a. A client has been running and playing and responds to reinforcement with a glass of juice.
   b. A client just ate a large lunch and does not respond to reinforcement with food items.
   c. A client skipped breakfast and responds to reinforcement with food items.
   d. A client sees a dog and runs in the opposite direction.

79. Because a client likes grapes, the RBT has been consistently using grapes as a reinforcer for wanted behavior. However, over time, the client's wanted behavior has decreased and the client seems less interested in the reinforcement. What does this suggest?

a. Extinction burst.
b. Response variation.
c. Behavior trap.
d. Satiation.

80. With habit reversal training, what does "response cost" refer to?

a. The time during which habitual behavior occurs.
b. Removing a reinforcer for habitual behavior.
c. Using distraction for a time period.
d. Substituting a competing behavior.

81. The RBT notes that during the day a client periodically exhibits unusual behaviors—running into a corner, sitting, and covering his eyes. What initial intervention is indicated?

a. Asking the client what the problem is.
b. Assessing reinforcement.
c. Assessing antecedents.
d. Withdrawing reinforcement.

82. How would the data in the following graph be categorized?

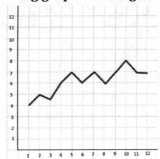

a. High level, high variability.
b. Medium level, high variability.
c. Low level, low variability.
d. Medium level, low variability.

83. In a written behavior reduction plan, which one of the following is an appropriate operational definition for the target behavior that needs to be changed?

a. The client reacts with anger and aggression when asked to do tasks.
b. The client runs to the nearest wall and bangs her head repeatedly (20–40 times) against the wall hard enough to cause bruising and swelling when stressed.
c. The client refuses to cooperate with any people in authority, such as her parents or teachers.
d. The client engages in repeated self-injurious behavior.

103

84. The RBT's certification expires on November 30. When should the RBT apply for renewal?

    a.   15 days prior to the expiration date.
    b.   30 days prior to the expiration date.
    c.   45 days prior to the expiration date.
    d.   60 days prior to the expiration date.

85. Which one of the following is an essential element of stimulus transfer control?

    a.   Prompting.
    b.   Prompt fading.
    c.   Shadowing.
    d.   Graduated guidance.

Answer Key and Explanations for Test #1

1. A: The BCBA has the responsibility to develop the written skill acquisition plan, but the role of the RBT is to assist the BCBA and to collect baseline and ongoing data. The RBT has a valuable role because the RBT has more contact and more observation time with clients, so the RBT can provide feedback regarding progress and the need to follow up and modify a treatment plan, although the RBT cannot independently implement modifications without the BCBA's approval.

2. B: The Americans with Disabilities Act (ADA) provides those with disabilities, including those with mental disabilities, access to employment and the community and also requires that communities provide transportation services for those with disabilities of all ages, including accommodations for people in wheelchairs. Additionally, public facilities, such as schools, must be wheelchair accessible. Telecommunications must be accessible through accommodations or devices for those who are blind and/or deaf. These include closed captioning, text for photographs, and web accessibility standards.

3. C: Total task presentation is appropriate for tasks that a client is familiar with and that involve few steps. Although both verbal and physical prompts may be used, graduated guidance is common, especially with young children. The RBT begins with hand-over-hand physical prompting, and as the client begins to show mastery of some steps, the RBT switches to shadowing, in which the hands are held over the client's hands but not touching, so that they can provide assistance if needed. As the client begins to show mastery of all steps, the shadowing is faded.

4. B: With fixed-ratio (FR) reinforcement, reinforcers are delivered after a specified number of responses, in this case, three, designated as FR:3. FR reinforcement may be used after a behavior has been learned in order to maintain the behavior. Typically, clients respond fairly rapidly until they get the reinforcement and then slow down for a brief period. The greater the ratio, the longer the pause. Additionally, if the ratio is high (e.g., FR:6), clients may begin to pause before the reinforcement, and clients may tire if responding too quickly or for too long in order to gain reinforcement.

5. D: Setting events are those that "set the stage" for unwanted behavior and may be internal (e.g., thirst, hunger, pain) or external (e.g., setting, activities, location, temperature) factors. Therefore, they are a type of antecedent event. For example, if a client has a headache, he may be more likely to exhibit unwanted behavior because of his discomfort. Setting events may occur hours, days, weeks, or even months before a behavior as opposed to trigger events, which occur immediately before a behavior.

6. D: The RBT should avoid transporting records that contain personal information about a client as much as possible. However, if the RBT does transport documents, they should be locked in the trunk of the car rather than left inside, even with the car locked. Taking them inside an assisted living facility may allow others to access the records unless the RBT holds them throughout the visit, but doing this may interfere with interventions. Records must be retained and stored for at least 7 years.

7. D: Functional behavioral assessment includes observation and recording of ABCs:

- Antecedent: What happens before the behavior occurs.
- Behavior: The target response.
- Consequence: What follows the behavior.

In this case, the math problem is the antecedent (A), the child's crying is the behavior (B), and comfort and cookie is the consequence (C) offered by the parent. Because the consequence is rewarding to the child, it may act as a reinforcer of the behavior, making it more likely that the child will cry the next time the child encounters difficult problems.

8. A: Descriptions of behavior and the environment should be provided in observable (i.e., what is seen) and measurable terms as much as possible. In this case, "Child threw himself on the floor, screaming and kicking for 5 minutes" is the correct response. Describing this only in terms of a "tantrum" or "temper tantrum" is unclear because children may carry out tantrums in different ways. The duration of time is also important for follow-up training to reduce tantrums. Descriptions of the training results should also be observable and measurable, for example, "Child correctly identified five out of eight pictures of animals." Description of the environment can include anything perceived by the senses: hearing, seeing, feeling, smelling, and tasting.

9. A: If the total count for each session is more important than the length of the time period, then frequency measurement is used. When tallying occurrences, it is important that the observation periods be the same so that meaningful comparisons can be made. If the behavior being observed is in response to a prompt, then the results may be reported as a percentage. Thus, if the client responded appropriately to a prompt 5 times out of 10 tries, the result would be 5 times out of 10, or 50%.

10. A: Before proceeding with any data collection, the RBT should be very clear about what is needed and expected. If not clear, the RBT should clarify any questions with the BCBA. Data collection is done not only to comply with insurance requirements but also to plot progress and determine the need for a change in strategies. Before beginning the collection, the RBT should understand its goals and purposes, review protocols, prepare all materials, and review time issues.

11. B: Unconditioned positive reinforcers are those necessary for survival and do not require learning or training in order to be perceived as reinforcers. Unconditioned positive reinforcers include such things as water, air, sex, and shelter. Unconditioned negative reinforcers include escaping such things as thirst and hunger. Conditioned reinforcers, on the other hand, are initially neutral but become reinforcers. Conditioned reinforcers may be edible (candy), sensory (music), an activity (watching TV), tangible (toy), or social (interaction, attention).

12. D: Reinforcers are more effective if they are given immediately after the desired response to ensure that a client begins to make the connection between a behavior (and this should be a specific behavior, not a range of behaviors) and the reinforcer. If there is a delay between the behavior and the reinforcer, the connection may be weak. Additionally, if an intervening behavior occurs before the reinforcer is provided, then the reinforcer may reinforce the intervening behavior rather than the intended behavior.

13. B: Informed consent must be obtained for all treatments that the client receives, including an explanation of treatments and procedures as well as their benefits and risks, duration, intensity, and frequency. Clients and/or parents or legal representatives should be informed of all options for care. Informed consent does not include the costs of treatment, but these should be covered in other documents. Outcome goals are not included in the informed consent but are included in the behavioral intervention plan.

14. A: Active listening involves careful observation of the speaker, including paying attention not only to the words but also to the body language, eye contact, and tone of voice. Feedback is especially important because it lets the speaker know that the listener is paying attention. Feedback

may include nodding the head, asking questions, or making comments about what the speaker is saying. The listener should avoid looking away or using a cell phone during communication because this indicates disinterest.

15. A: Feedback is an important element of supervision, and the RBT should avoid making any type of excuses but should ask for further information and should take advantage of the supervision to improve care, for example, by saying "Could you tell me what I should do to improve?" The purpose of feedback is to help the RBT improve his or her performance, develop new skills, and solve problems. The RBT's responsibility is to ask questions, clarify, and learn from the supervisor's feedback.

16. D: Differential reinforcement of low rates differs from other types of differential reinforcement in that it does not aim to eliminate a behavior (because the behavior in itself is desired) but to limit the behavior to appropriate situations. In this case, the undesired behavior is repeatedly asking for a cookie. With differential reinforcement of low rates, a time period is identified (such as every 15–30 minutes), and whenever the number of times the client uses the behavior decreases, he or she receives some type of reinforcement.

17. D: A conflict of interest occurs when an RBT (or even the spouse) can receive personal benefit from a professional relationship or when the RBT and another party (such as the client or supervisor) hold incompatible goals. Any time the possibility of a conflict of interest exists, the RBT should immediately report it to the supervisor. In a small town or community, avoiding all conflicts may be challenging, but the supervisor should review the situation and determine whether the RBT should be assigned to a different client (which is often the best solution) or if some other plan to manage the conflict should be developed.

18. D: A contingency is essentially an "if...then" situation: "If you turn in your homework, then you can watch TV." If the response (turn in homework) is appropriate, the consequence (reinforcing reward) is provided; therefore, a contingent relationship is present between the response and the consequence. One must be completed in order to obtain the other. In order to motivate the client and change behavior, the reinforcement (conditioned or unconditioned) must always follow the desired behavior.

19. A: The Individuals with Disabilities Education Act (IDEA) provides free and appropriate education to children with disabilities. Children must be placed in the least restrictive environment, which means that children are mainstreamed in regular classes whenever possible. The IDEA provides early intervention services for children birth through age 2 and special education and related services to children ages 3–21 (or older if state law permits). Children's educational services must include academic content as well as self-help and vocational skills.

20. B: Automatic negative reinforcement involves a behavior (in this case, scratching) reducing an aversive (negative) stimulus (anxiety) without any intervention from another individual. Automatic positive reinforcement, on the other hand, is an automatic response that results from a behavior, such as headbanging resulting in self-stimulation. Both automatic negative and automatic positive reinforcement may be difficult to manage, although substitutions that provide similar relief or stimulation may be effective.

21. D: For a child with limited speech, when carrying out manding trials, the child should be rewarded for any approximation of the target word. "Juuu" is the first sound in the word "juice," so it should be reinforced. Then, shaping should be used to help the child to say the whole word. As the child progresses and masters the word "juice" and uses it appropriately, the child may be prompted to say "Juice, please," so the progression with manding is typically from syllable to phrase to sentence, depending on the client's abilities.

22. C: A cumulative graph is used when the total over a designated time period is more important than the daily achievement. Cumulative graphs are typically done as a line graph with the cumulative totals on the *y* (vertical) axis and the duration of time on the *x* (horizontal) axis. Although it is possible to determine the daily totals, doing so requires calculation; therefore, if the daily totals are most important, then a different type of graph should be used.

23. D: Communication with a supervisor should be direct and timely. If the RBT is not familiar or comfortable with an intervention, then he or she should immediately tell the supervisor and ask for guidance, such as through modeling. A BCBA working with a newly certified RBT likely understands that the person lacks experience in some areas. Any time an RBT has a question, he or she should ask it promptly and should also report any important information to the supervisor.

24. C: Numerous individualized assessment procedures are used with clients. Criterion-referenced assessments compare clients with predetermined criteria or skill levels. The focus is not on the skills that the client lacks but rather on the skills that the client actually has in order to determine interventions needed to teach the client further skills. Common criterion-referenced tools include the VB-MAPP and the ABLLS-R. The skill levels tested must be appropriate for the child—not too easy and not too difficult.

25. D: With backward chaining, reinforcement is given only after the step that the client completes without prompting. To teach handwashing, typically the RBT would hold the child's hands and assist the child through each step, describing each step verbally, "Turn on the water," and so on until the last step, which is throwing the paper towel away. Because the child is able to do this step without assistance or prompting, reinforcement is given: "Great! You threw the paper towel away!" again describing the step. Once the child has fully mastered this last step, the second-to-last step is added, and so on.

26. C: A romantic relationship between an RBT and the supervising BCBA is an example of a dual, or multiple, relationship (RBT + client, RBT + BCBA). The RBT should not engage in a sexual relationship with a client or supervisor for at least 2 years after the end of the professional relationship. If an attraction develops, it should not be acted upon because it opens the possibility of other violations of professional boundaries, and it is often best to withdraw from the professional relationship. For example, if possible, a different supervisor should be assigned.

27. D: Momentary time sampling only measures the presence or absence of a behavior at the exact time of the sampling. It is not important that the behavior persists throughout the sampling period, only that it is present when the sampling period begins. Momentary time sampling is typically used for behaviors that persist for a longer duration of time, such as tantrums or staying on task. Momentary time sampling is not useful for short-duration behaviors, such as hitting or spitting; measures of frequency are used for those behaviors.

28. C: Receptive language is the ability to understand language or take in information. Although receptive language is sometimes described as listening, people without hearing engage in receptive language, which also includes such things as the ability to read and comprehend and the ability to understand graphs, symbols, gestures, and images. Expressive language, on the other hand, is the ability to speak or communicate in some other way. Expressive language includes turn-taking, pausing, body language, and eye contact as well as direct communications.

29. C: Discontinuous measurements are carried out in scheduled time periods during part of a day or session. With partial interval measurement, the RBT records the frequency of a behavior, but the results are calculated based on only whether or not a behavior was present during the interval, not the frequency. In this case, tics were present during four of the five intervals (4/5), or 80% of the time. Discontinuous measurements may not be as reliable as continuous measurements because behaviors may vary.

30. B: Incidental teaching (or naturalistic teaching) is carried out in the natural environment, such as at home, at school, or in a grocery store; it assumes that the skills the client needs are in those environments. Incidental teaching also includes taking advantage of natural opportunities for learning as they arise rather than planning all of the teaching. Skills taught in contrived situations, such as in a treatment center, do not always transfer well to the natural environment, so incidental teaching promotes the transfer and generalization of skills.

31. B: Because the purpose of discrete trial training is to teach, when a client makes an error, such as the child pointing at a cat instead of a fox, the correct response is to provide simple feedback that provides the correct answer. In this case, the RBT should simply point at the picture of the fox and say "This is a fox" and then move on to the next trial. The RBT should avoid any negative type of response, such as saying "No," or a negative tone of voice or facial expression.

32. A: Permanent product recording involves counting items (in this case, boxes) or outcomes and is used to assess production of tangible products. This is an indirect method of assessment because the RBT does not need to be present to observe the behavior. Examples of permanent products include the number of worksheets completed, the number of math problems completed, or the number of sandwiches made. One problem with permanent product recording is that it is not always possible to ensure that the client is the one who completes the product.

33. A: The purpose of prompt fading is to decrease and remove prompts so that the client responds appropriately to the stimulus independently in order to prevent prompt dependency. Time-delay prompting involves an increasing time delay between the stimulus and the prompt. The time may be slowly increased (progressive time delay or increased on a fixed delay time [constant time delay]). Other types of prompt fading include least to most, most to least, simultaneous prompting, and graduated guidance.

34. C: As a mandatory reporter of abuse, the RBT has a responsibility to report any signs of suspected child abuse or neglect to the local child protective services agency. The observations should be reported immediately to a supervisor, who can provide guidance. The RBT should not question the parent/guardian or the child about possible abuse. As well as physical signs of abuse (e.g., bruising, grab marks), children often display behavioral indications (e.g., fear, compliance, aggression toward others, depression, self-destructive behavior).

35. B: The RBT should avoid answering any question that ask for details about treatment, reasons for choosing particular interventions, or the behavioral intervention plan, but should refer these questions to the BCBA. The RBT may answer general questions, such as the purpose behind a treatment such as fading, but should avoid trying to justify the use with the client. The RBT may address issues such as respecting the individuality and dignity of the client.

36. C: Objective statements are based on verifiable observations and facts without added opinions: "When prompted to read a word, the child picked up the book and threw it at the RBT." Objective statements should be measurable whenever possible, for example, "The client responded to color prompts correctly six out of eight times." Subjective statements, on the other hand, involve an opinion and are always open to interpretation and may be influenced by biases. That is, if an individual has an expectation about someone, that individual may focus on behavior that supports that expectation and may ignore other behavior.

37. B: The RBT needs to evaluate situations and determine if information needs to be shared with the supervisor immediately, at the end of the session, or at a later date, such as when the supervisor makes a visit. In this case, because there is no imminent danger and the RBT can intervene to prevent the child from biting others, the RBT should communicate with the supervisor at the end of the session. Because this is new behavior, the RBT should try to assess any antecedent that may have triggered the behavioral change.

38. D: Intensity is the measurement that is most difficult to accurately carry out because it often depends on subjective assessment, so the results may vary depending on who is doing the observation. Thus, there is little interobserver reliability. For example, if assessing a client's temper tantrums, one observer may focus on the loudness of screaming and another on the duration of the tantrum although duration is a different measurement. Intensity measures often use a 1–10 scale to demonstrate results.

39. C: Professional boundaries are behaviors that separate the professional or paraprofessional and personal relationships. Violations of professional boundaries can interfere with the provision of safe and effective care. In this case, gossiping about a client is a violation: The RBT tells another RBT that a client is sexually active. Violations include any sexual contact with a client, injuring or harming a client, insulting or degrading a client, asking for unnecessary personal information, accepting gifts, and doing favors. Although bowing the head and standing quietly to respect another person's religious practice is appropriate, the RBT should not share, proselytize, or impose her own religious or political beliefs.

40. C: The RBT is responsible for implementation of the intervention plan for the client. This includes collecting data about progress and providing support. However, the BCBA is responsible for assessing the client's needs and progress and designing the intervention plan and any necessary modifications that may be needed. The RBT, who has the most contact with the client, can provide valuable information and may respectfully make suggestions, but the final decisions lie with the BCBA.

41. D: One of the problems that can occur when a client is aware of data collection is that the client may alter behavior so that the results do not accurately reflect the client's actual behavior. This is referred to as reactivity. For this reason, data should be collected as unobtrusively as possible. If the RBT notes that a client seems to exhibiting reactivity, then observations should be made at a different time or with a different method.

42. D: The Health Insurance Portability and Accountability Act (HIPAA) requires the privacy of personal and health information. Protected health information includes any identifying or personal information about an individual, including information in medical records and conversations between doctors and other healthcare providers. Applied behavioral analysis services must comply with HIPAA regulations. An RBT should share personal information about a client only with those directly involved in providing care, such as the BCBA.

43. C: The RBT may encounter interventions with which the RBT has been trained but has not used much with clients. To prepare, the RBT should practice the interventions, going through the steps and considering how to react to different client responses. If the RBT is completely unfamiliar with an intervention, then the RBT should ask the BCBA for guidance or modeling. The RBT may find it

helpful to write out a brief performance plan or checklist but should avoid writing out detailed descriptions because reading through them can be distracting for the RBT and the client.

44. C: Stimulus prompts serve as temporary discriminative stimuli to bring about a response. Stimulus prompts include some change that makes the stimulus more noticeable to the client. There are two types of stimulus prompts: within-stimulus prompts in which some characteristic of the stimulus, such as the size, color, shape, or the placement, changes and extrastimulus prompts, which involve the use of more than one prompt, such as a visual clue and a verbal clue.

45. B: Maintaining client dignity is essential, so the RBT should always communicate with clients in age-appropriate language as though they can understand, even if they do not respond or appear to understand. It is never appropriate to talk down to or belittle a client or talk over them as though they are not present, such as by discussing their progress with a parent or other caregiver without including the client in the conversation.

46. B: Tact is the term used to describe a client's ability to label something perceived in a nonverbal way, such as by sound, taste, smell, or sight, in the environment. For example, if a client smells popcorn, the client may say "popcorn." Typically, tact does not refer to something that the client actually wants (that would be a mand), so it is not a request. Echoic is the ability to repeat words. Textual is the ability to see a written word and say it, and intraverbal is the ability to think about something and respond appropriately.

47. A: Shaping involves differential reinforcement of successive approximations of a desired behavior, in this case, eating with a spoon. The first approximation (picking up the spoon) is reinforced, but as soon as a closer approximation (putting the spoon in the bowl) occurs, the first approximation is no longer reinforced and the new approximation is. It is important to avoid overreinforcing an approximation because this may delay progression. Two types of shaping are across-response topography (how behavior appears) and within-response topography (change in a characteristic, such as duration, intensity, or rate).

48. A: Discrimination training teaches clients to discriminate among different items, in this case, different types of fruit. The client should be familiar with the items in some way. For example, if asked to discriminate types of fruit, the client has likely eaten the different types before. With discrimination training, the RBT reinforces only correct responses. The client should be able to identify the item by itself and when placed with one and two other distracting items in random order. When the client achieves mastery 80–90% of the time, the RBT can move on to teaching the next item.

49. B: Differential reinforcement of other behavior is used to decrease undesired behavior by reinforcing other behaviors that are less undesirable. In this case, although dropping a book on the desk may be annoying, it is less distracting that the client throwing the book on the floor. Other behaviors may be reinforced any time they are observed or on an interval schedule. The aim is to slowly extinguish the undesired behavior and move toward desired behaviors.

50. B: Although almost any variable can affect a client's behavior in the short term, variables that cause a substantial disruption, such as the parents deciding to separate and get a divorce, are likely to cause ongoing changes in behavior because the client will have to deal with numerous issues, such as the absence of one parent, change in the economic status of family, visitation with the noncustodial parent or moving back and forth between homes with shared custody, and emotional distress. This type of variable should be reported to the supervisor.

51. C: Extinction procedures are primarily based on removing reinforcement for unwanted behavior in order to decrease this behavior. Before extinction can be carried out, the reinforcer for the behavior must be clearly identified through observation because it may not always be obvious, contrived, or conditioned. For example, for some clients, the attention gained for unwanted behavior serves as the reinforcer. For this reason, punishment sometimes backfires, such as when a parent gives a child a time-out that allows the child to escape a chore that the child does not want to do.

52. C: With contrived free-operant preference assessments, the client is observed interacting with items laid out in front of her. The items that the client chooses, the order of choice, and the duration of interaction with each item are recorded. Generally, the longer the client spends with an item, the greater the preference. With naturalistic free-operant preference assessment, the observations occur in the client's natural environment (such as in the home). Other methods of preference assessment include asking the client and indirect assessment (i.e., asking a parent/caregiver).

53. C: Personal preventive measures are those undertaken to prevent injury from a client, such as avoiding wearing jewelry that might be pulled, keeping hair up and out of reach (to avoid hair pulling), wearing long-sleeved clothes, wearing clothes and shoes that allow for easy running, and keeping any items that could be used as a weapon out of the environment. The RBT should avoid behavior that may provoke the client and should be alert to precursor behaviors.

54. C: Latency is the time between a cue (such as asking a child to carry out a task) and the behavior or response—that is, the time needed to start a behavior. Latency measures differ from duration measures, which begin with the behavior. In this case, the latency is decreasing, showing an improvement in behavior. Latency measures often focus on decreasing latency, but they may also be used when the goal is to increase latency. Latency measures are typically done with continuous measurement.

55. A: Behavioral cusps are behaviors or changes in behavior that open opportunities for new behaviors. For this client, the ability to crawl opens up a new world of possible contingencies: reaching for things and exploring her environment. Behavioral cusps, such as learning to read, crawl, or drive, may therefore be a training goal. Behavioral cusps are similar in some ways to and sometimes confused with pivotal behaviors, which occur when training a new behavior leads to other behaviors (untrained) that do not need to be directly taught.

56. B: According to section 2 of the Behavior Analyst Certification Board (BACB) RBT Ethics Code (2.0), punishment-based procedures should only be used when they are part of the treatment plan designed by the BCBA. Punishment-based procedures may include such things as time-outs and loss of privileges or tokens (in a token economy). Punishment-based procedures should be used sparingly because they may result in the behavior that they are intended to eliminate. Punishment-based procedures should not include physical punishments, such as spanking.

57. D: With paired stimuli/forced choice, the client is given a choice of two similar items to determine which one would be the most effective reinforcer. The RBT should vary the side that the item is placed on and watch to see if the client always picks the item on one side. In that case, this is not an effective assessment method. It is important when conducting this assessment to allow the client 1–2 minutes to interact with the chosen item before introducing another choice of items to avoid the client becoming frustrated.

58. A: In the United States, the RBT is not allowed to work as an independent contractor because RBT certification requires that the RBT work under supervision, which is contrary to the requirements of an independent contractor. Employers should not be hiring RBTs as independent contractors, and the RBT should avoid employment with any employer who does so because the RBT will not be receiving adequate supervision. Additionally, working as an independent contractor is a violation of the RBT Ethics Code (2.0).

59. B: The y (vertical) axis of the line graph is used for behavior (how much or how many), and the x (horizontal) axis is used for time. The line graph is used to provide a visual display of behavior changes over time. It may be used to plot increases and decreases in behaviors. If the line increases over time, this shows an upward trend, whereas if it decreases, it shows a downward trend. The first measurement is the baseline measurement.

60. A: Positive reinforcement and punishment involve adding something. Thus, positive punishment means to add something to discourage a behavior, such as adding a time-out to discourage acting out in class. Positive reinforcement, on the other hand, is adding reinforcement to encourage behavior. Negative reinforcement and punishment involve removing something. So, negative reinforcement involves taking something unpleasant away to encourage the desired behavior, and negative punishment involves taking something pleasant away to discourage unwanted behavior.

61. C: Noncontingent reinforcement is not dependent on a response and requires no preceding behavior. Thus, if the client throws tantrums to obtain reinforcing attention, providing the attention at other times can weaken the connection between the tantrum and getting attention. Noncontingent reinforcement can be given on a fixed schedule, such as every 5 minutes, regardless of behavior, or it can be given on a variable schedule, provided at random periods. Noncontingent reinforcement is often combined with extinction exercises.

62. C: Stimulus generalization occurs when a response to one thing (stimulus) extends to responses to other stimuli that are similar; in this case, from a black pony to other black animals. In training, it can mean that what the client learns in training sessions can transfer to other situations. For example, a client learns to say thank you to the RBT when receiving something to drink and then says thank you to a parent for a glass of milk.

63. C: A token economy uses conditioned reinforcers to improve client behavior. The tokens can be exchanged for a backup reinforcer, usually something especially desired by the client. In this case, the client earns 15 tokens for completing seven school assignments but loses 2 tokens (response cost) for failing to hand in two assignments, for a total of 12 tokens. Because 5 tokens are needed for 30 minutes of video game time, the client earns 60 minutes of playing time and still has 2 tokens remaining.

64. B: When a goal is to increase the time during which a client is engaged in a desired activity, such as staying on task in a school setting, then a measurement of duration is indicated. The RBT will note the onset (i.e., beginning) and offset (i.e., ending) of the behavior each time it occurs to determine if the client is making progress. Duration measurements may also be used to determine if a client is decreasing the duration of an unwanted behavior, such as withdrawing or refusing to cooperate.

65. D: Response prompts occur before a response in order to encourage the appropriate response. The prompt hierarchy ranks response prompts from the strongest to the weakest: Physical (the strongest and most intrusive prompts), modeling, gestural, verbal, and visual (the weakest prompts). Some clients may develop prompt dependence if prompts are used consistently without

113

fading. Note that although the visual clue is the weakest for most clients, this may not be true for all clients, such as those with impaired hearing.

66. B: The RBT's supervisor must carry out two face-to-face (i.e., not over the phone or mail) contacts each month. The RBT must ensure that the supervision is carried out and contact the supervisor if necessary. The supervisor should make an onsite visit and observe the RBT working directly with the client during at least one of the visits. However, supervision may be conducted via web camera or video conferencing if necessary. The RBT must also keep a record of the supervisor's visits, including the dates, duration, and format. If the RBT has more than one supervisor, each supervisor must make two monthly visits.

67. D: No-no prompting involves giving directions without a further prompt up to three times. The trial is stopped if the client responds correctly, but each time the client responds incorrectly, the RBT says "No, try again." Only after the client fails to respond correctly three times does the RBT repeat the directions and give a prompt of some kind (such as mimicking the action) to encourage the appropriate response. At this point, the client receives reinforcement with a correct response but no consequence or reinforcement for an incorrect response and the trials end.

68. A: An extinction burst (i.e., an increase in the frequency, duration, or intensity of a target behavior) is a common occurrence after reinforcement has stopped. In this case, the behavior is usually temporary, so reinforcement should not be reintroduced because it may interfere with the extinction. Spontaneous recovery is similar but delayed and may occur after an extended period of time. For spontaneous recovery, extinction is reintroduced. Other responses to extinction include aggression and emotional responses (e.g., crying, begging), especially if the client has developed a dependence on the reinforcer.

69. A: Although valuable data can be obtained for a functional analysis from indirect observations, which can include questionnaires, behavioral checklists, and interviews with client and family, a functional analysis requires that direct observations be made. A functional analysis uses information about the ABCs of behavior. With ABC continuous recording, problem behaviors (B) and their antecedents (A) and consequences (C) are monitored throughout the session. With ABC narrative recording, data are only collected when undesired behavior occurs. With scatterplot recording, data are only recorded in specific time periods.

70. B: With preference assessments with multiple stimuli, clients are presented with an array of three to eight items and asked to choose one. With multiple assessment without replacement, the first item selected is removed and so on until the client has the last item, noting the order of preference. With multiple assessment with replacement, the item chosen is kept in the array but the other items are replaced with each item being included in the array at least two times to establish an order of preference.

71. A: Short-circuiting the contingency means to provide reinforcement before the desired response, such as allowing the child to watch TV before she completes her homework. This results in reinforcing the unwanted behavior. If a client consistently overeats and hoards food, this represents a behavioral excess. If a client turns in classwork only half of the time, this represents a behavioral deficit. If a client takes candy from another client and has to return it, this is restitution; however, if the client has to give the other client additional candy, this is an example of overcorrection.

72. C: Response blocking involves preventing an unwanted behavior by using some type of barrier, such as placing a hand in front of items that a client is grabbing. Response blocking is one type of physical restraint, which should be used only in emergency situations. Other types include physical restraint, such as by holding a person's body part, and protective equipment, such as using a helmet to prevent head injury to a client who engages in headbanging or mittens to prevent scratching.

73. D: There are four main functions of behavior:

- Sensory stimulation: Rocking back and forth.
- Attention getting: Goofing off in class and making others laugh.
- Access to tangible items: Repeatedly grabbing at a toy.
- Avoidance/Escape: Hiding behind a desk.

Sensory stimulation is a form of automatic reinforcement and is common in children on the autism spectrum. The type of behavior that a client exhibits can help determine the function or the type of reinforcement that the client gains from the behavior.

74. A: Client welfare and safety is the primary concern during any emergency situation, even when the client is the instigator, although this does not mean that the RBT should not take steps to ensure his or her own personal safety as well. Crisis and emergency situations may result from behavioral problems, health problems, or environmental problems. The RBT should be familiar with all safety protocols, including how to respond to aggressive clients and where fire extinguishers, shelters, and escape routes are located.

75. B: The BACB has many different self-reporting requirements, which include a history of court-ordered treatment for substance abuse disorder within the previous 3 years. However, a new mental health or substance use disorder for which a treatment plan is in place and for which the disorder is unlikely to impact safe delivery of care does not need to be self-reported. Traffic tickets of $750.00 or less and bankruptcy procedures do not need to be reported.

76. B: Keystone behaviors are behaviors that affect other behaviors, so that if the keystone behavior changes, it will result in multiple other changes. For example, if a client is angry at the caregiver, the client may refuse to cooperate, may fall behind in assignments, and may lash out at others. If the anger issue with the caregiver can be resolved, the other behaviors may improve without further intervention. Keystone behaviors may be negative or positive and are often the key to changing other behaviors.

77. A: Forward chaining is teaching steps to a behavior in order from the first step to the last step. With this intervention, prompting is used initially for each step; when the client begins to show mastery of the step, the prompting is faded until the client can carry out that step independently; and then the next step is added. The RBT completes the rest of the steps. The goal of forward chaining is for the client to carry out the complete chain of behaviors without prompting.

78. B: Motivating operations include abolishing operations and establishing operations. It is important when working with clients to determine what may be motivating to them, keeping in mind that these may change according to circumstances. Abolishing operations decrease the likelihood that a discriminative stimulus will cause a behavior to occur; therefore, if a client just ate a large lunch, food will be less likely to reinforce positive behavior. Establishing operations are the opposite: They increase the likelihood that a discriminative stimulus will cause a behavior to occur.

79. D: Satiation occurs when the value of a reinforcer decreases, sometimes from overexposure, so the client has less motivation to carry out the desired behavior in order to receive the reinforcement. Thus, it is important to vary reinforcers rather than to use the same reinforcer for prolonged periods. Satiation is the opposite of deprivation, which is an increase in the value of a reinforcer after a period without it. For example, if candy is withheld from a child, the child is more motivated to carry out wanted behavior in order to get the candy.

80. B: Response cost is the removal of reinforcement for habitual behavior. This is a form of negative punishment because something is taken away. Response cost is often part of a token economy in which the client either gains or loses tokens according to behavior. Other elements of habit reversal training include differential reinforcement of other behavior, awareness training, self-monitoring, relaxation training, response prevention (barriers), and competing or alternative responses. Various types of habits (repetitive behaviors) include nervous habits (hair pulling, biting nails), tics (motor, vocal), and stuttering.

81. C: One of the first interventions to modify behavior is to stop the behavior from occurring in the first place through assessing antecedents rather than responding to the unwanted behavior. This requires carefully observing the client and making note of any triggering events that may occur before the behavior. Triggering events may vary widely and can include something in the environment, such as noise or lighting, or the presence or actions of another person or thing

82. B: On a scale of 1–12, this client has a baseline of 4 and a top reading of 8, which represents medium level, high variability. Middle-level points lie near the middle of the graph (these totals average ~6.5). Variability represents a significant difference between the low (4) and high (8) points. When graphing, trend (whether going up- or downward), level, and variability are the three elements to consider during evaluation.

83. B: The operational definition of a target behavior should clearly describe the undesired behavior in such a way that anyone working with the client can immediately recognize the behavior and can measure it: When stressed, the client runs to the nearest wall and bangs her head repeatedly (20–40 times) against the wall hard enough to cause bruising and swelling. The behavior reduction plan should contain the objective description of the behavior and the reinforcement that the client receives from that behavior. In this case, the headbanging reduces the client's stress. The most effective method of identifying the reinforcement is through functional analysis.

84. C: RBT certification must be renewed annually. Applications should be completed 45 days prior to the expiration date of the current certification, and 2 weeks should be allowed for processing of the application. The renewal application must include a renewal competency assessment, which is completed by a supervisor and assesses the RBT's skills in measurement, assessment, skill acquisition, behavior reduction, professionalism, and requirements. The assessment may include observations of the RBT with a client or role-playing as well as interview questions.

85. B: Stimulus transfer control involves prompt fading. For example, if the RBT is teaching a client to identify a bird, the RBT might give the prompt "Say 'bird.'" When the client is able to respond to the verbal prompt "bird," the RBT then shows the client a picture of a bird and says "What is this?" so the prompt has now changed from verbal (i.e., the word) to visual (i.e., the picture). Reinforcement is given when the client responds appropriately. The client is now responding to a different stimulus with the same action.

RBT Practice Test #2

1. A student allows herself one piece of chocolate each time she completes her homework assignments for the day. What type of reinforcement does this represent?

    a. Self-reinforcement.
    b. Automatic positive reinforcement.
    c. Automatic negative reinforcement.
    d. Unconditioned reinforcement.

2. A client's schedule of reinforcement indicates that the client should receive variable interval reinforcement, specifically, VI5. When should the RBT provide reinforcement?

    a. Every 5 minutes.
    b. After an average of 5 minutes.
    c. Every fifth response.
    d. Five times every hour.

3. The RBT is working with a child diagnosed with autism spectrum disorder, and the parent of a different child with the disorder asks the RBT which child is progressing faster. What is the best reply?

    a. "I'm not sure."
    b. "Why do you want to know?"
    c. "Every child progresses differently."
    d. "I can't discuss another child with you."

4. A young child tries to poke a pencil into an electrical outlet, and the caregiver grabs the child's hand away and yells "NO!," frightening the child, who begins to cry. What is the best way to describe the caregiver's action?

    a. Positive punishment.
    b. Negative punishment.
    c. Positive reinforcement.
    d. Aversive stimulus.

5. An adolescent is throwing a tantrum and yelling at others to "Get away!" What is the most appropriate response?

    a. Give the adolescent a safe space and speak calmly.
    b. Place the adolescent in restraints.
    c. Remind the adolescent of the consequences for negative behavior.
    d. Ignore the adolescent's behavior.

6. What role does the RBT have in the individualized assessment and the skill acquisition plan for a client?

    a. The RBT has no role in the assessment.
    b. The RBT implements interventions outlined in the plan of care.
    c. The RBT carries out the assessment under BCBA supervision.
    d. The RBT carries out the assessment independently.

7. The RBT is working with a client with obsessive-compulsive disorder. What is the primary goal of exposure and response prevention interventions?

    a.   To delay or eliminate compulsive responses.

    b.   To eliminate all symptoms of obsessive-compulsive disorder.

    c.   To promote relaxation and mindfulness.

    d.   To reduce the need for medication treatment.

8. Which one of the following is an example of unconditioned reinforcement?

    a.   Toy.

    b.   Candy.

    c.   Water.

    d.   Attention.

9. A client is using self-monitoring to help decrease hair-pulling and is showing much more progress than when monitored by others. What does this exemplify?

    a.   Reactivity.

    b.   Cognitive restructuring.

    c.   Positive reinforcement.

    d.   Negative reinforcement.

10. The RBT has been directed to carry out a contrived free operant preference assessment for a 4-year-old child. Which one of the following procedures should the RBT follow?

    a.   Ask the child what his or her favorite toy is.

    b.   Observe the child in the home environment, noting the items chosen, the order, and the duration of interaction.

    c.   Ask the parent or caregiver what the child's favorite toy is.

    d.   Place a number of toys in front of the child, noting the items chosen, the order, and the duration of each interaction.

11. The RBT plans to use competing response training to help a client substitute a different behavior for hair-pulling. Which one of the following is the first step?

    a.   Ask the client to describe the behavior in detail.

    b.   Carry out a number of observations of the behavior.

    c.   Ask the client to report each time the urge or behavior occurs.

    d.   Determine establishing operations.

12. As a personal protective measure, which one of the following should the RBT avoid?

    a.   Wearing long-sleeved clothing.

    b.   Wearing loose-fitting clothing.

    c.   Wearing the hair tied back.

    d.   Wearing a necklace.

13. The RBT is teaching a child to put toys away after playtime and providing reinforcement each time. Over time, the child has begun to put the toys away on prompting. In the home environment, the mother, father, and an older sister have tried to get the child to put toys away, but the child is uncooperative. Which one of the following interventions is most indicated?

    a. Stimulus control transfer.
    b. Generalization training.
    c. Parent training.
    d. Peer modeling.

14. A child frequently acts out or calls out in class to get the teacher's attention, so the teacher must deal with constant interruptions. What type of antecedent intervention may help reduce this behavior?

    a. Prime.
    b. Time delay.
    c. Noncontingent reinforcement.
    d. High-probability sequence.

15. A client writes swear words on a wall and is required to clean the wall and the adjacent wall as well. What does this exemplify?

    a. Negative punishment.
    b. Positive reinforcement.
    c. Aversive response.
    d. Overcorrection.

16. At what age do peers begin to take on more influence with a child, sometimes leading the child to challenge parents and other adults?

    a. Ages 7–8.
    b. Ages 9–10.
    c. Ages 11–13.
    d. Ages 14–16.

17. The parent of a client of the RBT has many questions about the client's behavior reduction plan, including the purpose of each intervention and the goals. How should the RBT respond?

    a. Explain as much as possible.
    b. Tell the parent to ask the BCBA.
    c. Ask the BCBA to discuss the plan with the parent.
    d. Tell the parent it is not the RBT's responsibility.

18. A child has developed a habit of chewing on crayons. In order to change this behavior, the RBT has provided the child with gum to chew. What type of strategy is the RBT using?

    a. Competing response training.
    b. Abolishing operation.
    c. Differential reinforcement of alternative behavior (DRA).
    d. Differential reinforcement of incompatible behavior (DRI).

19. What is the role of the RBT with regard to informed consent?

    a. The RBT obtains the informed consent.
    b. The RBT answers questions and ensures compliance.
    c. The RBT ensures that clients/families understand informed consent.
    d. The RBT has no role with regard to informed consent.

20. During the yearly renewal competency assessment, an RBT does not demonstrate competency in one task. What action will this result in?

    a. Failure of the assessment.
    b. Further training for the RBT.
    c. Suspension from work and reassessment.
    d. Corrective feedback and reassessment.

21. An 18-year-old client with an intellectual disability has the language skills of a typical 4- to 5-year-old. When speaking with the client, how should the RBT communicate?

    a. As the RBT would to any 18-year-old.
    b. As the RBT would to a 5-year-old.
    c. As the RBT would to a toddler.
    d. Primarily by using gestures and pictures or illustrations.

22. The RBT is working with a child recently adopted after 3 years in foster care. The child has been diagnosed with reactive attachment disorder and has been withdrawn and listless and exhibits distrust and avoidance of interactions with the adoptive parents. What approach to behavioral modification is most commonly used with children with reactive attachment disorder?

    a. Parent focused.
    b. Anger management focused.
    c. Anxiety focused.
    d. Attachment focused.

23. Which type of tic is characterized by brief movements, such as eye blinking and head jerking?

    a. Complex motor tics.
    b. Simple motor tics.
    c. Complex vocal tics.
    d. Simple vocal tics.

24. Which one of the following is an example of a positive social reinforcer?

    a. An indication of praise, such as smiling.
    b. The pleasure of listening to music.
    c. A favorite food.
    d. Coins.

25. A student has often missed turning in homework, so the RBT is working with the student to better manage time and to turn in completed work. Which one of the following measurements may provide the best information about the student's progress?

 a. Momentary time sampling.
 b. Frequency.
 c. Permanent product recording.
 d. Discrete categorization.

26. A child diagnosed with autism spectrum disorder is having a meltdown. The RBT knows that the child is fascinated with building blocks, so the RBT sits near the child and begins to lay out the blocks and build a tower. What strategy is the RBT using?

 a. Positive reinforcement.
 b. Noncontingent reinforcement.
 c. Distraction.
 d. Competing response training.

27. The RBT is working with a client on communication skills. Which one of the following is an example of a receptive communication skill?

 a. Body language.
 b. Command of turn-taking.
 c. Ability to understand pictures.
 d. Eye contact.

28. The RBT has a scheduled meeting with a new BCBA to report the progress of four different clients. What should the RBT do in preparation for the meeting?

 a. Organize and outline the report.
 b. Practice the report.
 c. Memorize the report.
 d. Relax and stay calm.

29. Part C of the Individuals with Disabilities Education Act includes services for children from birth to age 2. Which one of the following is a service included for this age group?

 a. Family training.
 b. Supplementary aids.
 c. Individualized education plan.
 d. Special education services.

30. A playroom has a snake in an enclosed glass container, but a child screams each time he sees the snake and refuses to enter the room. Which one of the following may serve as the most effective modification of antecedents?

 a. Show the child pictures of the snake in preparation.
 b. Explain that snakes are not harmful.
 c. Cover the snake container with a cloth.
 d. Allow the child to avoid the room.

RBT Practice Test #2

31. Restraints can generally be used in which one of the following circumstances?

    a. Imminent danger.
    b. At the RBT's discretion.
    c. As punishment for various behaviors.
    d. For lack of cooperation.

32. A 16-year-old male client has a history of bullying of peers, abuse of animals, destruction of property, aggression, defiance, and truancy. These behaviors are most consistent with which one of the following conditions?

    a. Conduct disorder.
    b. Oppositional defiant disorder.
    c. Obsessive-compulsive disorder.
    d. Fetal alcohol syndrome.

33. Which one of the following is the correct term to use to describe a client learning and gaining a new skill?

    a. Absorption.
    b. Acquisition.
    c. Interaction.
    d. Transition.

34. The RBT is making observations and gathering data about the antecedents and consequences associated with a problem behavior. What type of assessment does this represent?

    a. Preference.
    b. Functional.
    c. Skill.
    d. Norm based.

35. A child is trained to reduce headbanging when upset but also reduces hand-flapping with no further training. What term is used to describe the tendency of behaviors to change together?

    a. Cross training.
    b. Response covariation.
    c. Learning transfer.
    d. Stimulus generalization.

36. A client must take medications at specified times but has had difficulty remembering to do so, so he keeps a written record of medications for 3 days and notes that four doses were missing. The client is provided an automatic timer that rings each time medications should be taken to help him manage them independently. What do these actions represent?

    a. Self-reinforcement.
    b. Self-monitoring.
    c. Positive reinforcement.
    d. Negative reinforcement.

37. A parent gives a child a sticker on a chore chart each time the child completes a chore without being reminded. Once five stickers are earned, the child can exchange them for privileges such as television time. What strategy is the parent using?

    a. Shaping.
    b. Guided compliance.
    c. Modeling.
    d. Token economy.

38. An RBT notices injuries on a child. Which one of the following injuries is most suggestive of child abuse?

    a. Scraped knee.
    b. Facial bruising and swelling.
    c. Fractured ankle.
    d. Cut on a finger.

39. Which one of the following conditions increases the effectiveness of a reinforcer?

    a. Satiation.
    b. Deprivation.
    c. Delayed reinforcement.
    d. Overuse.

40. How many days does an RBT have to inform the BCBA of a change in personal contact information?

    a. 15.
    b. 30.
    c. 45.
    d. 60.

41. If the RBT only uses prompts with a client when necessary and gradually stops using the prompts, what type of prompt fading is the RBT using?

    a. Simultaneous prompting.
    b. Graduated guidance.
    c. Time delay.
    d. Most to least.

42. For which one of the following situations is intensity measurement the best choice?

    a. A child frequently hits other children.
    b. A child screams very loudly when upset.
    c. A child has difficulty staying on task.
    d. A child withdraws in the presence of other children.

43. To what does "observer drift" refer?

    a. Forgetting to record data.
    b. Interacting less frequently with clients.
    c. Boredom from prolonged measurement affecting results.
    d. Burnout from overwork.

44. A child has been practicing responding to the fire alarm by leaving the classroom and walking toward the exit. When a car alarm goes off outside, the child immediately begins to leave the classroom. What does this exemplify?

    a.   Learning transfer.
    b.   Response generalization.
    c.   Stimulus generalization.
    d.   Guided compliance.

45. A child responded well to extinction of temper tantrums, but 2 weeks later the child begins to throw temper tantrums again. What is the most appropriate intervention?

    a.   Ignore the behavior.
    b.   Reintroduce extinction.
    c.   Use positive punishment.
    d.   Use shaping.

46. A 3-year-old child with developmental delay has been diagnosed as being on the autism spectrum. Whom would the parents contact to begin early and intensive behavioral interventions for the child?

    a.   The local public elementary school.
    b.   The local early intervention program.
    c.   The local public health department.
    d.   The nearest hospital with a pediatrics department.

47. In addition to impairment of social interactions and impairment of communication, which one of the following characteristics is most common to people on the autism spectrum?

    a.   Predictable behavior patterns.
    b.   Lack of empathy and compassion.
    c.   Restrictive repetitive or stereotypical behavior.
    d.   Marked intellectual disability.

48. The RBT is observing an adolescent with Down's syndrome and is collecting data. Which one of the following is an indication of possible reactivity on the part of the adolescent?

    a.   The adolescent's behavior is consistent with previous observations.
    b.   The adolescent appears to be ignoring the RBT.
    c.   The adolescent's behavior is atypical and inconsistent.
    d.   The adolescent's behavior appears confident.

49. A stopwatch is frequently used for which type of measurement?

    a.   Frequency.
    b.   Intensity.
    c.   Discrete categorization.
    d.   Duration.

50. The RBT is using noncontingent reinforcement with a child who has been throwing temper tantrums in order to get attention. What is the primary purpose of using noncontingent reinforcement in this situation?

    a. Eliminate the need for reinforcement.
    b. Increase the effectiveness of reinforcement.
    c. Change the relationship between the behavior and reinforcement.
    d. Strengthen the relationship between the behavior and reinforcement.

51. A student persists in playing with toys during class time, so the teacher places the student in a time-out for 5 minutes. What strategy does this represent?

    a. Negative reinforcement.
    b. Negative punishment.
    c. Positive reinforcement.
    d. Positive punishment.

52. The BCBA tells the RBT that the RBT is carrying out an intervention incorrectly, even though the RBT is performing the intervention as taught during training. How should the RBT respond?

    a. "This is the way I was taught."
    b. "Would you please model this intervention for me?"
    c. "I guess there is more than one way to do this."
    d. "I'm sure that I'm doing it correctly."

53. The RBT begins to teach a behavior chain by guiding the hands of the client physically through all but the last step in a behavior chain and then prompting the client to carry out the last step independently. What type of chaining does this represent?

    a. Forward.
    b. Backward.
    c. Backward with a leap ahead.
    d. Reverse.

54. The RBT notes that after asking a client a question, there is a significant pause before the client responds. What type of measurement is best used to assess this slowed response?

    a. Latency.
    b. Duration.
    c. Frequency.
    d. Intensity.

55. What type of relationship does a contingency represent?

    a. Stimulus-response relationship.
    b. Cause-and-effect relationship.
    c. Risk-reward relationship.
    d. Response-consequence relationship.

56. The RBT is showing a child flash cards, asking the child to identify colors and shapes during a 15-minute session, and recording the number of correct responses. What type of continuous measurement procedure is the RBT using?

    a. Duration.
    b. Latency.
    c. Event/Frequency.
    d. Interval.

57. The RBT notes that a client continually taps a foot, rubs hands together, and fidgets in the chair. Which one of the following should the RBT suspect?

    a. The client is nervous.
    b. The client is bored.
    c. The client is angry.
    d. The client is tired.

58. An RBT who has worked with two clients on the autism spectrum states, "All autistic clients avoid eye contact and have delayed speech." Which type of logical fallacy does this represent?

    a. Hasty generalization.
    b. Overgeneralization.
    c. Post hoc.
    d. Slippery slope.

59. Which type of graph is most suitably used to compare successful completion of assignments by different age groups of students?

    a. Bar graph.
    b. Line graph.
    c. Pie chart.
    d. Cumulative graph.

60. When carrying out a trial-based preference assessment with multiple stimuli with replacement and a child chooses one item in an array and interacts with it for a short period of time, what should the RBT do next?

    a. Remove the chosen item, and present the remaining items in a different arrangement.
    b. Remove the chosen item, but keep the other items in the array.
    c. Keep the chosen item in the array, but replace the other items.
    d. Replace all items in the array.

61. Which one of the following is an example of a cognitive process?

    a. Problem solving.
    b. Playing with toys.
    c. Watching a movie.
    d. Reading a book.

62. The BCBA has developed a schedule of reinforcement for a new client. During the initial treatment periods, which type of reinforcement is usually most effective?

  a. Continuous.
  b. Intermittent.
  c. Both are equally effective.
  d. Alternate between continuous and intermittent.

63. When using error correction, on the first trial, the RBT provides a direction: "Touch the yellow card." The child's response is to touch the green card, so the RBT removes and then replaces the cards. What should the RBT do next?

  a. End the trial.
  b. Repeat the direction.
  c. Repeat the direction and point at the picture.
  d. Show the child the yellow card, and then repeat the direction.

64. A student is very anxious about a presentation and claims to be sick the morning that it is due in order to avoid having to give the presentation, thereby reducing anxiety. Which one of the following does this represent?

  a. Self-reinforcement.
  b. Automatic positive reinforcement.
  c. Automatic negative reinforcement.
  d. Negative punishment.

65. The RBT accompanies a client to a grocery store and answers questions and provides different information about the items in the store and checkout procedures. What type of teaching does this represent?

  a. Chaining.
  b. Modeling.
  c. Incidental.
  d. Task analysis.

66. The RBT has home visits scheduled for four clients: two in the morning and two in the afternoon. When is the best time to complete session documentation?

  a. Immediately after the first two visits.
  b. Immediately after each visit.
  c. Immediately after the fourth visit.
  d. After returning to the office after the visits.

67. An RBT failed to complete the needed hours of supervision, so the BCBA found the RBT substantially noncompliant. What action should the RBT expect the BCBA to take?

  a. Suspension of certification for 6 months.
  b. A reprimand and a specific period of time to complete supervised visits.
  c. Termination of certification.
  d. No action is required with the first failure to have adequate supervision.

68. A 16-year-old with Down syndrome tries to kiss the RBT and touches the RBT intimately during a session. Which one of the following responses is most appropriate?

    a. Reprimand the client.
    b. Request that the client be reassigned.
    c. Immediately leave the session.
    d. Reinforce boundaries.

69. The RBT is working with a client using a strategy outlined by the BCBA but believes that the client is responding negatively to the intervention. How should the RBT discuss this issue with the BCBA?

    a. "I think this is the wrong strategy."
    b. "This intervention is not working at all."
    c. "Do you think there may be a better strategy for this client?"
    d. "The client's response rate has fallen 50%."

70. An RBT documents that a client is "angry and belligerent." What is a better way to describe the client?

    a. "Client is very unhappy and uncooperative."
    b. "Client is yelling 'I hate you' and refusing to comply with requests such as 'Please sit down.'"
    c. "Unable to calm client or obtain cooperation."
    d. "Client expressing dislike of staff and refusing cooperation."

71. A child on the autism spectrum dislikes wearing clothes and the feeling of different textures and refuses to wear any clothes other than sweatpants and sweatshirts. What type of behavior is the child exhibiting?

    a. Covert.
    b. Sensory stimulation.
    c. Escape.
    d. Avoidance.

72. Which one of the following is appropriate for an RBT to post about work on a social media platform, such as Instagram or Facebook?

    a. The problems with employment.
    b. The nature of a client's condition.
    c. A specific case without naming the client.
    d. The RBT should post nothing about work on social media.

73. A child often refuses to eat any foods except junk foods or fast foods (e.g., chips, cookies, and hot dogs), so the parent has told the child that in order to watch television, the child must eat other foods. However, when the child throws a tantrum, the parent repeatedly gives in and allows the child to watch television even though the child refuses the other foods. What does this represent?

    a. Behavioral deficit.
    b. Behavioral trap.
    c. Short-circuiting the contingency.
    d. Noncontingent reinforcement.

74. A 5-year-old child throws crayons on the floor four times in a row and then draws a picture the fifth time. The RBT immediately gives the child an animal cracker as a reinforcer. The child then continues to repeatedly throw the crayons on the floor. How should the RBT respond?

    a. Reinforce only after a series of correct responses.
    b. Continue providing reinforcement after correct responses.
    c. Reprimand the child each time the child responds incorrectly.
    d. Ask the BCBA for guidance.

75. A client who was bitten by a dog has an extreme fear of dogs, so the RBT is accompanying the client to a shelter where dogs are safely enclosed. The RBT provides encouragement as the client walks by the enclosures. What strategy does this represent?

    a. Extinction.
    b. Flooding.
    c. Systematic desensitization.
    d. Guided compliance.

76. The registered behavior technician (RBT) is assisting the board certified behavior analyst (BCBA) with data collection. How does the RBT ensure that the integrity of the data is maintained?

    a. By recording all objective and subjective data.
    b. By avoiding personal interpretations and subjective observations.
    c. Through careful observation.
    d. By verifying all data with the BCBA.

77. The Assessment of Basic Language and Learning Skills, Revised, is what type of assessment tool?

    a. Criterion referenced.
    b. Norm referenced.
    c. Curriculum based.
    d. Social.

78. An RBT is using momentary time sampling at six 15-second intervals to assess the duration of a child's temper tantrum.

- First interval: Present.
- Second interval: Present.
- Third interval: Present.
- Fourth interval: Present.
- Fifth interval: Absent.
- Sixth interval: Absent.

How are these responses recorded?

    a. 4/6.
    b. 3/6.
    c. 2/6.
    d. 6/6.

79. A student has been throwing temper tantrums in class and when working with the RBT, so the RBT is applying the ABCs of functional assessment. What is the purpose of applying the ABCs in this situation?

    a. To determine an appropriate intervention.
    b. To apply consequences for the negative behavior.
    c. To understand what is triggering the negative behavior.
    d. To assess the frequency and duration of the behavior.

80. The RBT has been using simultaneous prompting to teach a child to drink water from a cup. The RBT tells the child, "Take a drink of water," and mimics doing so. During the assessment trials, the RBT only tells the child, "Take a drink of water," but the child does not take a drink. What is the appropriate RBT response?

    a. Mimic taking a drink.
    b. Repeat the instruction.
    c. Repeat the instruction and mimic taking a drink.
    d. End the trials with no consequence or reinforcement.

81. The RBT has been assigned a new client, but during the home visit, the RBT recognizes the client as a young cousin of the RBT's partner. What should the RBT do next?

    a. Provide services as assigned.
    b. Ask the parent if the RBT can proceed.
    c. Apologize and leave.
    d. Contact the BCBA for guidance.

82. A client's mother tells the RBT in confidence that she is not feeling well and has not been able to carry out interventions with her child because she recently suffered a miscarriage. When reporting on the child's lack of progress for the week, how should the RBT report this to the BCBA?

    a. Say that the child's mother is not feeling well.
    b. Say nothing about how the mother is feeling.
    c. Say that the child's mother had a recent miscarriage.
    d. Say that the child's mother has a health problem that the RBT cannot discuss.

83. The RBT is using whole-interval measurement to assess a child's ability to stay on task during five 20-second intervals:

- First interval: 15 seconds on task.
- Second interval: 12 seconds on task.
- Third interval: 20 seconds on task.
- Fourth interval: 9 seconds on task.
- Fifth interval: 13 seconds on task.

How would these results be scored?

    a. 5/5.
    b. 4/5.
    c. 2/5.
    d. 1/5.

84. **If an adolescent on the autism spectrum appears agitated and upset, which one of the following is the best description?**

    a. Adolescent appears agitated and upset.
    b. Adolescent's attitude appears markedly deteriorated.
    c. Adolescent is having a meltdown.
    d. Adolescent is pacing around the room for 20 minutes and refuses to respond verbally or to follow directions.

85. **A client with Down syndrome usually responds well to crackers as reinforcement, but during one session, the client does not seem motivated to carry out a target behavior to get rewarded with crackers. Upon questioning, the RBT discovers that the client had eaten a large bag of cookies before the RBT arrived. What does this behavior represent?**

    a. Establishing operation.
    b. Abolishing operation.
    c. Covert behavior.
    d. Avoidance behavior.

RBT Practice Test #2

Answer Key and Explanations for Test #2

1. A: With self-reinforcement, the client provides the reinforcement for target behaviors, such as completing homework assignments, without an observer present. Advantages to self-reinforcement include increased motivation and autonomy (the client chooses the reinforcer and controls its application) and immediate feedback (because no outside observer is needed). However, there are some disadvantages including a lack of objectivity (i.e., the client judges her own behavior), an increased need for extrinsic rewards, self-sabotage (i.e., a reward can be given without completion of the task), and inconsistency (i.e., the client follows the program intermittently).

2. B: With variable interval reinforcement (VI5), reinforcement is provided with the first response following an average of 5 minutes. Performance tends to be more consistent than with fixed interval reinforcement, and variable reinforcement is more resistant to extinction. However, because clients are unable to predict reinforcement, they may be less motivated to carry out the behavior, so the response rate may be low. Additionally, VI5 reinforcement may increase the difficulty of shaping behavior.

3. C: The RBT should not compare the progress of one child with that of another with one of the parents or anyone except for a supervisor. The best reply, if asked by a parent to do so, is "Every child progresses differently." The RBT can take this opportunity to discuss the progress that the parent's own child is making and can compare that with the child's baseline, stressing that every child on the autism spectrum is an individual with different strengths and challenges than other children.

4. D: While the child cries when the caregiver grabs the child's hand away from the electrical output and yells "NO!," the caregiver is using an aversive stimulus (i.e., one that causes some type of discomfort) to prevent injury. Although this is a form of punishment because it can result in emotional upset, pain, or discomfort, the intention in this case is immediately stopping an unsafe behavior, so safety concerns may take precedence over other concerns. However, aversive stimuli should be used sparingly because they can result in negative effects, such as promoting fear or a lack of trust.

5. A: If an adolescent is throwing a tantrum and yelling at others to "Get away!" the most appropriate response is to give the adolescent a safe space (which means ensuring that there is nothing there that the adolescent can use to injure the self or others) and to speak calmly. It is important to remain nonthreatening and to validate the client's feelings, by saying, for example, "I understand why you are upset." The adolescent may need time to recover, so the RBT should remain close by but should avoid infringing on the adolescent's need for space and time.

6. B: The individualized assessment and development of a skill acquisition plan is the responsibility of the BCBA, but the RBT may assist the BCBA with the assessment if requested to do so. The primary responsibility of the RBT, however, is to implement the interventions outlined in the plan, communicate with the BCBA, and report progress. The individualized assessment is used to identify the client's skill level, needs, and barriers and to establish or update goals. The BCBA may gather information through direct observation, from interviews with caregivers or others who interact with the client, and by assessment of existing data, such as from various types of assessment.

7. A: The gold standard for treatment of obsessive-compulsive disorder is exposure and response prevention, whose goal is to gradually expose the individual to triggers for obsessions while delaying or preventing the compulsive responses. Exposure and response prevention usually

132

begins with development of an exposure hierarchy (from least to most) and is followed by exposure therapy, beginning with exposure to the least distressing triggers and support to resist compulsive behaviors. For example, if a client has an obsession with contamination, the least distressing action may be entering a public bathroom whereas the most distressing may be touching a surface in the bathroom. A beginning strategy would be for the client to enter the bathroom and resist the urge to immediately wash his or her hands.

8. C: Unconditioned reinforcement involves reinforcers that are necessary for survival. For example, if a person suffers from thirst (a negative unconditioned reinforcer), then the person will seek water (a positive unconditioned reinforcer). These are unconditioned reinforcers in the sense that they are not learned and are generally biologically important. Conditioned reinforcement, on the other hand, involves secondary reinforcers that are initially neutral (such as a toy) and have no inherent value as a reinforcer but become reinforcers when paired with a primary reinforcer.

9. A: Reactivity is a desired result of self-monitoring because, when individuals are self-monitoring, the behavior (in this case, hair-pulling) often changes toward that which is desired. During self-monitoring, the individual has increased self-awareness, is engaged in setting goals and tracking progress, and receives immediate and ongoing performance feedback. Additionally, self-monitoring can help the individual identify personal strengths and weaknesses and help the individual feel more responsible and accountable for his or her behavior.

10. D: There are different methods to use for preference assessments:

- Contrived free operant: Place a number of toys in front of the child, noting the items chosen, the order, and the duration of interaction.
- Naturalistic free operant: Observe the child in the home environment, noting the items chosen, the order, and the duration of interaction.
- Direct: Ask the child directly: "What is your favorite toy?"
- Indirect: Ask the parent or caregiver what the child's favorite toy is.
- Trial-based: Place a set of similar toys in front of the child, ask the child to choose one to play with for a short period of time, and then create a new array of toys that includes the chosen toy from the previous selection to see if the same toy is chosen when it is within a different set of toys.

11. A: Competing response training (a form of habit reversal training) involves teaching and reinforcing an incompatible behavior in order to reduce the target behavior. Steps include the following:

- Identify the target behavior and help the client to describe the behavior in detail, include antecedent movements, to increase awareness.
- Ask the client to acknowledge each time the urge or behavior occurs. Provide positive reinforcement if the client acknowledges the urge or behavior, and give a reminder if the client does not.
- Use competing behaviors that prevent the target behavior.

12. D: Personal protective measures are those that help prevent injury to the RBT. The RBT should avoid wearing jewelry that may be grabbed, pulled, or used to choke, such as dangly earrings and necklaces or neck scarves. Hair-pulling is common, so long hair should be pulled back, in a bun, or under a cap. Wearing clothing with long sleeves can help prevent scratching or other injuries to the arms. Wearing tight-fitting clothes, high heels, and flip-flops may make it difficult to retreat or run.

Answer Key and Explanations for Test #2

13. A: Because the child has learned to put toys away in response to prompting by the RBT (the stimulus), the RBT has stimulus control over the behavior. In order to switch stimulus control to others, the intervention that is needed is stimulus control transfer so the client will respond to different stimuli (e.g., prompting by family members) with the same behavior. Before stimulus control transfer can take place, the initial stimulus control must be established. Stimulus control transfer involves prompt fading and prompt delay and changing the stimulus that brings about a response.

14. C: Noncontingent reinforcement is a type of antecedent intervention that involves providing reinforcement before a behavior begins in order to break the connection between the behavior (acting/calling out) and the reinforcement (attention). In this case, for example, the teacher might set a timer for every 5 minutes and then call on the child or acknowledge the child in some way regardless of the child's behavior at the time. Noncontingent reinforcement not only often results in reducing difficult behavior, but it also establishes a positive environment and increases cooperation.

15. D: Overcorrection is a type of punishment in which the client must (1) make restitution or correct the consequences of a behavior, such as by cleaning the wall, or (2) carry out positive practice (by repeatedly practicing the target behavior). The purpose of overcorrection is to help the client associate negative consequences with unwanted behavior. Overcorrection should be appropriate for the situation and should be combined with positive reinforcement (by saying, e.g., "You cleaned that wall really well!") and teaching alternative behaviors.

16. D: Ages 14–16 is a transitional time period for children. Peers begin to take on more influence, and children sometimes begin to challenge parents and other adults as they form a sense of personal identity. Children of this age especially want to fit in with peers and do not want to appear "different." During this period, children may be less cooperative with the RBT, so it is important to recognize this stage, to maintain open communication, show empathy, offer choices, and compromise but also to set clear boundaries and outline consequences.

17. C: If a parent asks about the behavior reduction plan, the RBT should explain that the BCBA develops the plan based on the BCBA's assessment of the client and should tell the parent that the RBT will ask the BCBA to discuss the plan with the parent. Even though the parent may have gone over the plan with the BCBA initially, it is common for a parent to have many questions as the plan is implemented because people often are unsure what to ask before interventions begin.

18. D: Differential reinforcement of incompatible behavior (DRI) involves substituting a behavior that makes it difficult to carry out the problem behavior. In this case, chewing gum would be incompatible with chewing on crayons, so chewing gum is likely to decrease the client's desire to chew on crayons. DRI is a variation of differential reinforcement of alternative behavior (DRA), which involves substituting a different behavior, such as drawing with the crayon rather than chewing on it. DRI and DRA may be used for such things as nail-biting, hair-pulling, and thumb-sucking.

19. B: The BCBA is responsible for explaining the importance of informed consent and obtaining informed consent from clients or their legal representatives. However, the RBT has an important supporting role. The RBT should be aware of the importance of informed consent and should be prepared to answer questions and ensure compliance. Informed consent includes a thorough explanation of all procedures and treatments that are part of the plan of care, options, and any associated benefits or risks.

20. D: The renewal competency assessment is part of the annual recertification process. The assessment may be carried out with a client by role-playing or through interview or some combination by a qualified BCBA with or without the help of an assistant assessor. If an RBT does not demonstrate competency in one task, the BCBA should provide feedback and reassess on a different day or days as needed until the RBT demonstrates competence without the need for feedback.

21. A: Maintaining client dignity is essential in all interactions with clients. If a client has an intellectual disability that limits language skills to that of a typical 4- or 5-year-old, the RBT should still communicate with client with age-appropriate language for an 18-year-old but may adjust some vocabulary to ensure comprehension and should break down tasks into simple steps and may supplement instructions with pictures and illustrations. The RBT should avoid using terms of endearment, such as "Honey," that are commonly used with small children.

22. D: Reactive attachment disorder is common among children who are neglected or abused during the first 2–3 years of life, are unable to form an attachment to caregivers, or are separated from caregivers for a prolonged period, such as those with a parent who is ill or deceased or those in foster care. Behavior modification is typically attachment focused to help the child develop a healthy trusting relationship with the caregivers. Caregivers should have an active central role in the implementation of interventions.

23. B: Simple motor tics are characterized by brief movements, eye blinking, head jerking, grimacing, shrugging the shoulders, nose twitching, and pursing the lips. Motor tics are often transient (usually lasting <1 year) but may persist for prolonged periods. Tic onset is usually during childhood (it peaks at approximately age 7) or early adolescence, although late-onset tics may occur after age 18. Simple motor tics may be a sign of Tourette syndrome, but they may also occur in people without the disorder.

24. A: Positive reinforcers, which can take various forms, follow a behavior and reinforce that behavior. Positive reinforcers may be intrinsic (such as feeling personal pride or satisfaction) or extrinsic (i.e., coming from outside the individual):

- Social: Indications of praise, such as smiling.
- Consumables: Favorite foods, such as cookies, crackers, grapes, or candies.
- Tangible items: Coins and toys.
- Activity privileges: Phone, television, computer, or tablet use; movies; concerts; and sports.
- Sensory: Music, fragrance, and photos/pictures.

25. C: With permanent product recording, which is an indirect method of measurement, behavior is assessed based on a tangible product, such as the number of homework pages that a student turns in. Permanent product recording does not require direct observation because the RBT can obtain the report from the teacher's accumulated record. Permanent product recording provides objective data. However, because direct observation is not required, it is possible, for example, that someone else is completing the homework for the student.

26. C: Distraction is a technique used to shift a client's attention from the thing or situation that is causing a crisis to something that the client enjoys in order to diminish the power of the triggering event. Distraction can help a client to break a pattern of unwanted behavior and provide alternatives. Additionally, distraction may make it more difficult for the client to focus on the cause of the crisis. When using distraction, it is important to change the client's focus to something that is meaningful or enjoyable for the client—in this case, the building block toys.

27. C: Receptive communication skills involve the ability to take in, process, and comprehend information to include spoken and written words, pictures, graphs, symbols, and body language. Receptive skills include following directions and active listening—that is, focusing on the message sender, providing feedback, and asking questions. A person's receptive vocabulary is often much larger than their expressive vocabulary. For example, a child who is nonverbal or has limited verbal ability may be able to comprehend the spoken word very well, so receptive and expressive skills should be assessed independently.

28. A: Although it is always good for the RBT to be relaxed and calm when meeting with a BCBA, it is more important to be organized and to prepare a brief outline of the report so the RBT is sure to cover all important points because the BCBA is ultimately responsible for the clients. The RBT should respect the time constraints of the BCBA and report the functional progress of the clients by summarizing highlights in measurable terms.

29. A: The Individuals with Disabilities Education Act, Part C, applies to children from birth to age 2. Children with disabilities are entitled to early intervention services, which can include a comprehensive assessment, family training, occupational therapy, physical therapy, speech therapy, hearing services, nutritional services, assignment to a social worker, assistive technology and devices, counseling, and home visits. Additionally, the child and family receive a written individualized family service plan that outlines the child's stage of development and future goals.

30. C: An antecedent is the trigger for a behavior. In this case, it is the sight of the snake that triggers the response (i.e., screaming and refusing to enter the room). A modification of antecedents may include covering the snake container with a cloth. Modification of antecedents (i.e., changing something in the environment) is done to prevent a behavior from occurring, so this occurs before (the antecedent) the discriminative stimulus (the snake). Determining an antecedent (A) requires careful observation of undesirable behavior (B) and any triggering events as well as any consequence (C) resulting from the behavior.

31. A: Restraints should be avoided as much as possible, with the RBT using behavioral support measures instead. Generally, RBTs must be trained in the use of different types of restraints, such as through the Crisis Prevention and Intervention Training course, before they are permitted to use them. Restraints should be restricted for use only if the client or others are in imminent danger and then for the shortest time necessary. A client in any type of restraints should not be left unattended.

32. A: Conduct disorder is characterized by bullying, animal abuse, destruction of property, aggression, defiance, and truancy. Conduct disorder is more common in males than females, and onset may be during childhood (if onset is before age 10, the signs are usually more severe) or adolescence. Although there may be neurological factors associated with conduct disorder, a dysfunctional family and environment as well as the influence of peers may affect behavior and treatment outcomes. Comorbidities, such as attention deficit hyperactivity disorder, mood disorders, and substance use disorders, are common.

33. B: The process by which a client learns and gains a new skill is referred to as acquisition. The acquisition phase may vary widely. In some cases, a new skill may be acquired rapidly. For example, a child may quickly learn to jump rope after watching peers and engaging in minimal practice. On the other hand, learning to read often requires many steps, beginning with recognition of the letters and their sounds. With all types of learning, some clients may progress more quickly than others, so expectations should always be individualized.

34. B: Functional assessments are used to determine the antecedents and consequences that are associated with a problem behavior in order to find out what function the problem behavior serves. Four possible functions include:

- Social positive reinforcement: Reinforcement provided by another person, such as through increased attention.
- Social negative reinforcement: Removal of an aversive stimulus by another person, such as being allowed to skip chores.
- Automatic positive reinforcement: Personal reinforcement, such as through reduced anxiety after stimming.
- Automatic negative reinforcement: Personal escape from aversive stimulus, such as reducing unpleasant emotions that were present behavior before behavior.

35. B: The term used to describe a tendency toward behaviors changing together is response covariation. This is a specific type of response generalization, which occurs when a learned response generalizes to other situations. For example, treating hair-pulling tends to reduce thumb-sucking as well. Both of these are self-soothing behaviors, and one may substitute for the other when the child is stressed. As another example, treating nail-biting tends to decrease skin-picking. Both of these are repetitive compulsive behaviors. With response covariation, the behaviors are different but tend to serve the same underlying purpose.

36. B: Self-monitoring is a method that encourages clients to observe and record their own behavior—in this case, remembering to take medications. Self-monitoring helps clients become more aware of their behaviors and to be accountable. Steps to self-monitoring include identifying the target behavior (i.e., taking medications), establishing goals (i.e., 100% compliance), selecting the monitoring method (i.e., a written record), collecting data (e.g., by keeping a written record), analyzing the data (i.e., reviewing the record), receiving feedback (e.g., intrinsic or extrinsic), and modifying behaviors (e.g., by using a timer).

37. D: A token economy uses some type of reward token (e.g., check marks, stickers, points, or poker chips) to reinforce desired behaviors. The tokens can be exchanged for something that the client values. Usually the number of tokens needed for exchange is low at the beginning and greater over time. Some may also use a response cost (a type of negative punishment), that is, removing a token for unwanted behavior. Steps to using a token economy include (1) specify the target behavior, (2) identify a reinforcement schedule, (3) identify the tokens and the number of tokens needed for privilege exchange, and (4) identify the backup reinforcers.

38. B: Although state laws vary regarding who is a mandatory reporter, employees in any organization that provides services to children and who have direct contact with children are generally included in all states. Physical abuse indicators can vary, and some abusers are careful to hit children under areas of clothing so that any bruises are not clearly evident. Head and facial injuries (e.g., bruising and swelling) are common, as are bite or burn marks. Hand or finger marks may indicate forceful grabbing. Unusual bruising, such as across the buttocks, or any bruising, swelling, or tearing of the genital area can also indicate abuse.

39. B: Deprivation typically involves keeping a reinforcer from an individual for a prolonged period of time so that, when it is provided, the deprivation increases the effectiveness of the reinforcer. Immediate provision of reinforcement also increases effectiveness, and the greater or more valued the reinforce, the stronger the effectiveness. Things that decrease the effectiveness of an enforcer include satiation and overuse, which both decrease the value of the reinforcer to the individual, and delayed reinforcement because this weakens the connection between the behavior and its consequence (reinforcement).

40. B: The RBT must ensure that the BCBA has accurate information by which to contact the RBT, so the RBT must update the BCBA within 30 days of a change, such as a change in name, address, or other contact information. The RBT does not, however, need to use the self-reporting forms to do so: These are used to report professional or personal conduct that may pose a risk to others, such as violations of ethical standards.

41. B: The different methods of prompt fading include the following:

- Graduated guidance: Using prompts as needed and gradually stopping them.
- Simultaneous prompting: Giving the prompt immediately after describing the task with no delay.
- Most to least: Providing prompts and decreasing or increasing them as necessary.
- Time delay (a modification of most-to-least prompt fading): Increasing the time delay between the stimulus and the prompt. With constant time delay, a fixed delayed time is used; however, with progressive time delay, the delay time is slowly increased with each prompt.
- Least to most: Allowing the client to respond independently without prompts unless prompts are needed and then beginning with a weak prompt, adding stronger prompts if needed.

42. B: Intensity measurement assesses the strength, force, or severity of a response rather than its frequency or duration. Intensity is more difficult to assess; the use of monitoring devices, such as a sound meter, may be helpful and may avoid a primarily subjective evaluation. Intensity measurement may be used, for example, when teaching an individual to reduce the loudness of his or her voice. In some cases, a point system is used for intensity measurement to assess the intensity of behaviors, such as acts of aggression.

43. C: Observer drift may occur if measurement is carried out for a prolonged period of time, resulting in boredom or fatigue, which can affect the results and interfere with the reliability and validity of the data. With observer drift, the observer may lose motivation or become inattentive without being consciously aware. Solutions to observer drift include carrying out measurements for shorter periods of time when possible, carrying out interrater reliability assessments, and using regular training sessions and standardized protocols.

44. C: Stimulus generalization occurs when different stimuli elicit the same response. In this case, the child has learned to respond to a fire alarm by leaving the building, so when a similar alarm sounds, the child carries out the same behavior. Part of training must include planning for generalization. In this case, the child needs to learn to differentiate other sounds and alarms from the fire alarm sound. If a control stimulus, such as the fire alarm, is often accompanied by other sights or sounds, such as the teacher clapping hands to get attention, the child may respond the same way to the clapping as to the control stimulus.

45. B: Spontaneous recovery of previously extinguished behaviors is not uncommon because extinction results in a gradual reduction in behavior. When this occurs, the most appropriate intervention is to reintroduce extinction. Typically, the unwanted behavior will extinguish faster than when extinction was initially carried out. Other clients may respond in different ways to extinction. Some exhibit aggression and may hit, kick, or hurt others or engage in self-injury; others may have an emotional response (e.g., crying, arguing).

46. A: Early and intensive behavioral interventions are available in all states and US territories for children with development delays, autism, and other disabilities to help them develop basic skills that are typically acquired during the first 2 years of life. Programs are described as follows:

- Children younger than 3 years: Contact the local early intervention program. Each state runs its own program, which go by various names.
- Children 3 years and older: Contact a local public elementary school and the district's special education director to determine what services are available.

47. C: The characteristics that are common to those on the autism spectrum include impairment of social interactions, impairment of communication, and restrictive repetitive or stereotypical behavior. Behavior patterns may vary widely and are not predictable. Although people on the autism spectrum may have difficulty expressing emotions or recognizing the feelings of others, this does not mean that they are unable to feel empathy or compassion. Many people on the autism spectrum have normal or superior intelligence, although approximately 40% demonstrate some degree of intellectual disability.

48. C: Reactivity occurs when behavior is influenced by observation; that is, the individual changes behavior when he or she becomes aware of the observation. Indications of reactivity include displaying atypical, unusual, or inconsistent behavior or exhibiting self-consciousness (i.e., by showing anxiety or discomfort) during activities. Mitigating actions include habituating the individual to data collection so that he or she no longer reacts to it, conducting naturalistic observations, and conducting blind observations (such as by videotaping) so that the individual is not aware of any observation taking place.

49. D: Duration measurement is the time period during which a specific behavior persists. The target behavior monitored may be positive (desired) or negative (undesired). When collecting data, a stopwatch is typically used to measure the duration of time between when the behavior begins and when it ends. Duration measurement is used for behaviors that can occur over different periods of time, such as while exercising, or for behavioral states, such as periods of agitation or withdrawal from activities.

50. C: With noncontingent reinforcement, enforcement is given either at fixed (most commonly) or variable intervals rather than immediately after the behavior. For example, if the child gains attention by throwing a tantrum, the child learns to throw a tantrum to get the attention he or she craves. If, however, the child receives no reinforcement after a tantrum but receives reinforcement at other times, this changes the relationship between the behavior (tantrum) and the reinforcement (attention). Noncontingent reinforcement is often combined with extinction exercises to decrease incidences of the unwanted behavior.

51. D: Positive punishment involves adding something (e.g., an aversive stimulus, such as a time-out) to discourage an unwanted behavior (in this case, playing with toys). To be effective, positive punishment should occur immediately following an unwanted behavior and should be appropriate for the age and the behavior. One downfall is that positive punishment may cause resentment and may only temporarily suppress a behavior without teaching an alternative behavior. Positive punishment is often used with positive reinforcement and other strategies.

52. B: There are variations in how interventions are carried out, so the RBT should avoid any defensive remarks if the BCBA's feedback indicates that there is an issue with how the BCBA wants interventions done. The best response is to be open to learning, by saying, for example, "Would you please model this intervention for me?" If a BCBA is continually or unfairly critical of the RBT, then

139

this is a different issue that may need to be addressed directly with the BCBA or the BCBA's supervisor.

53. B: Backward chaining involves teaching a behavior chain by assisting the client with all but the last step in a chain in order and then teaching the last step first by prompting. One variation of backward chaining is reverse chaining, in which the client is physically guided, such as by holding the client's hands through the behavior chain, until the last step, which is then taught. Once the last step is mastered, then the next-to-last step is taught until all steps have been mastered.

54. A: Latency measurement is used to assess the time between a cue (stimulus), in this case a question, and the target behavior (the response). Latency measurement may be used when the goal is to lengthen or shorten the latency period. For example, if a client often responds to the stress of interacting with others by throwing a tantrum, one goal may be to lengthen the latency time. Latency measurements are used when there is a specific stimulus and response.

55. D: A contingency represents a response-consequence relationship based on an "if, then" statement: "If you eat your lunch, then you can watch a cartoon." If the response (eating lunch) results in the consequence (watching a cartoon), then a contingent relationship has been established between the response and the consequence. Consequences can be positive (such as a reward being provided), which increases the likelihood that a behavior will be repeated. Consequences can also be negative (such as a privilege being removed), which increases the likelihood that a behavior will not be repeated.

56. C: Event recording (aka frequency recording) typically involves the RBT observing the individual and recording each correct response or incidence of a target behavior. The RBT keeps a running tally during the observation, such as by pencil and paper or a tally counter, in order to determine trends or patterns of behavior or changes in behavior. The duration of event recording may vary, depending on the type of behavior that is measured and the age and developmental stage of the individual.

57. A: Although individuals' behavior can vary widely, some types of behavior are typical signs of nervousness, including being restless, pacing, tapping feet, trembling, avoiding eye contact, speaking rapidly, and nail-biting. Being nervous can make it difficult for clients to focus on the interaction between the RBT and the client, and the client may resort to self-comforting measures, such as rubbing the hands together, touching the body in some other way, or taking deep breaths. The RBT should respond by remaining calm and speaking clearly. Offering the client a choice of some kind may help him or her feel more in control.

58. A: A hasty generalization is assuming that one example (or even more) applies to a whole group and drawing conclusion with insufficient evidence. In this case, the RBT worked with two clients on the autism spectrum who both happened to avoid eye contact and had delayed speech, and the RBT, without evidence, assumed that this applied to all people on the autism spectrum. Although these are common signs, they are not universal. Signs of autism may vary widely.

59. A: Bar graphs are often used to demonstrate performance or data, such as for one individual, or to compare different categories or groups, such as students by ages. Bar graphs may be vertical or horizontal and have an *x* (horizontal) and a *y* (vertical) axis. The values represented by the *x* and *y* axes may vary, although for a vertical bar graph, the *y* axis typically represents value and the *x* axis represents time or categories. Bar graphs provide a simple visual display of differences and are easy to interpret.

60. C: With a trial-based preference assessment with multiple stimuli with replacement, the client is presented three to eight similar items (such as toys), is asked to choose one, and is allowed a short period of time to interact with the item. Then, the chosen item is kept in the array but the other items are replaced. Each item should be presented at least twice. If a client consistently chooses the same item a number of times, demonstrating a strong preference, that item should be removed from the array.

61. A: Cognitive processes are those associated with the mind, such as problem-solving, thinking, believing, and expecting. Cognitive processes are not visible externally. Most activities, such as playing with toys or watching a movie, involve observable behavior as well as cognitive processes. For example, if a client watches a movie, an observable behavior, the client may think about the story, wonder what will happen next, and have expectations about the ending. However, there is no way to predict what the person is thinking about.

62. A: A schedule of reinforcement is the plan for how reinforcement is to be carried out. Continuous reinforcement is often used in the initial treatment period because it helps the client understand the desired response and helps to quickly establish a new behavior. However, continuous reinforcement can result in dependency, a situation in which the client expects a reward each time for the target behavior, or satiation, a situation in which the value of the reward lessens over time and the behavior diminishes. Therefore, continuous reinforcement is usually switched to intermittent reinforcement once the target behavior is consistently achieved.

63. C: Error correction is used when a client makes a mistake, such as incorrectly identifying the yellow card. If the first trial, which involves only giving a direction, fails, then up to three transfer trials with directions plus a prompt are carried out:

Trial 1:

- Direction (discriminative stimuli [S^D]): "Touch the yellow card."
- Response: Touches the green card.

Transfer trial (up to three times): Remove the cards and then replace.

- Direction (S^D): "Touch the yellow card."
- Prompt: Point toward the yellow card.
- Response: Touches the green card.

Prompts should be more directive at first and then fade.

64. C: With automatic negative reinforcement, a behavior (such as claiming to be sick) stops an aversive stimulus (the presentation). If claiming sickness results in being able to avoid giving the presentation, the student is more likely to use sickness as a means of avoiding other unpleasant or anxiety-producing situations in the future. Once the pattern is recognized, then the student needs to learn more adaptive behaviors to reduce anxiety rather than strategies leading to avoidance. Steps include identifying the behavior, determining its function, teaching other coping skills, gradual exposure/desensitization, and reinforcing other behaviors.

65. C: Incidental teaching takes place in a natural environment, such as a home, school, park, or store, rather than under contrived or artificial conditions. With incidental teaching, the teaching is client initiated, but the RBT makes observations and uses them as learning opportunities and provides prompts and reinforcement, such as by giving praise if the client correctly identifies an item or a process. Incidental teaching may be used to improve generalization and communication

141

skills. The RBT may guide the client to use skills in the natural environment that were learned in contrived situations.

66. B: Although documentation should be done within at least 24 hours, the best time to complete session documentation is immediately after each visit when the information is still fresh in the RBT's mind. It can be difficult to remember details about each client if documentation is delayed, especially if clients have similar issues and interventions. Records are legal documents, and this means that the RBT cannot delete information that was previously documented or alter any existing information.

67. C: It is the responsibility of the RBT to ensure that the necessary hours of supervision are completed. If the BCBA finds an RBT substantially noncompliant with the required supervision hours, the RBT is subject to termination of certification and/or termination of the ability to be recertified. Under either condition, the RBT cannot apply for recertification for a period of 6 months and if recertified may be subject to increased auditing to ensure that adequate supervision is occurring. The BCBA may take action against the RBT as well.

68. D: Middle adolescence, ages 15–17, is a time of sexual exploration. If an adolescent with Down syndrome makes sexual advances, the RBT should stay calm and respectful but reinforce boundaries, explaining why the behavior is inappropriate and beginning a discussion of consent. The adolescent may need some basic education regarding relationships and boundaries and practice with social skills. The RBT should report this behavior to the BCBA because, if it persists, the adolescent may need further intervention, but the RBT should protect the adolescent's privacy and maintain confidentiality as much as possible while ensuring the safety of others.

69. D: Although the BCBA is responsible for devising the intervention plan, input from the RBT can be invaluable. The RBT should express opinions directly but respectfully using assertive communication and by considering the value of the information. Saying "I think this is the wrong strategy" or "This intervention is not working at all" provides criticism but no helpful information. Saying "The client's response rate has fallen 50%" provides measurable information that the BCBA can use to assess the intervention.

70. B: When documenting, subjective descriptions such as "angry and belligerent" should be avoided in favor of objective descriptions such as "Client is yelling 'I hate you' and refusing to comply with requests such as 'Please sit down.'" Subjective observations are based on opinions and are open to interpretation. For example, some may view the client as angry and belligerent, whereas others may view the client as being terrified and trying to run away. Objective descriptions include data and verifiable facts.

71. D: Avoidance behavior involves evading an aversive stimulus (in this case, different textures) that the client can predict. If avoidance behavior is successful, it is more likely to be used again. Escape behavior is similar; however, it results in not only escape but also the end of the event. For example, if a student does not want to take a test and skips school, the student escapes the test (at least for that day). Avoidance behavior sometimes follows escape behavior: A client may escape from a noisy room the first time and then avoid returning to that room later.

72. D: The RBT should post nothing about work on social media because, even if a social media site is private and the information is quite general, someone can share that information. It is a violation of confidentiality to post anything at all about a client even if the name is withheld because someone familiar with the client may be able to determine to whom the RBT is referring.

Additionally, the RBT should avoid all contact with clients or their families/caregivers on social media and should avoid searching for them online to gain information.

73. C: Short-circuiting the contingency involves providing reinforcement (in this case, television time) without carrying out the appropriate response (i.e., eating other foods). Because the child receives reinforcement when throwing a tantrum and when not eating appropriately, the reinforcement begins to strengthen these behaviors rather than the desired behavior. Short-circuiting the contingency is common in natural environments, such as the home, and it often results in persistent undesirable behavior

74. A: One difficulty that can arise with reinforcement is that it may reinforce not only a correct response (drawing) but also the incorrect responses (throwing the crayons on the floor) that precede the correct response, especially if the correct response is an isolated one. The solution is to avoid reinforcing a single correct response that is preceded by incorrect responses and only providing reinforcement after a series of correct responses so the child stops associating the reinforcement with both behaviors.

75. B: Flooding is a form of exposure therapy in which the client is exposed to the thing that causes anxiety (in this case, dogs) in order to decrease the anxiety response. Although the RBT may provide some encouragement or reassurance (e.g., by saying "I'll be right here with you"), the RBT should make no attempt to relieve the client's anxiety or fear during the experience. Systematic desensitization, on the other hand, takes place in small, incremental steps; for example, the client may first be asked to look at a picture of a dog. Flooding is most successful with clients who are highly motivated.

76. B: The RBT has an important role in collecting data as directed by the BCBA. Maintaining the integrity of the data is essential and requires that the RBT avoid reporting or interpreting data according to subjective observations or while being influenced by personal biases. All data should be objective and consistent so that they are valid and reliable. The RBT should remain in close contact with the BCBA and should discuss any concerns regarding the observations or methods of collecting data.

77. A: The Assessment of Basic Language and Learning Skills, Revised, is a criterion-referenced assessment intended for clients ages 0–12 years on the autism spectrum or with other developmental disabilities. Criterion-referenced tools compare the client with a predetermined criteria or skill level. This tool assesses 25 different skill areas including the skills that most children will need to enter kindergarten. Skills are broken down into specific steps so the child's skill level can be more easily identified.

78. A: With momentary time sampling (a form of discontinuous measurement), during each interval, a behavior is scored simply as being present or absent—the duration is not counted. Momentary time sampling is best used for behavior of a longer duration. In this example, the behavior stopped after 4/6 intervals, or 60 seconds. Momentary time sampling does not require constant monitoring, although intervals are often spaced closely together, and the accuracy and value of the results will vary depending on the intervals selected.

143

79. C: When trying to understand a behavior, it is important to understand the circumstances associated with the behavior, or the ABCs:

- Antecedent: What happens before the behavior occurs.
- Behavior: The target response.
- Consequence: What follows the behavior.

In this case, the primary purpose of applying the ABCs is to understand what is triggering the behavior, that is, the antecedent (A). Triggers may include specific cues, situations, people, environmental changes, or interactions. Once the ABCs have been determined, then interventions can be designed to decrease or extinguish the problem behavior.

80. D: Simultaneous prompting, in which a prompt is given immediately after a direction (in this case, the verbal direction and the mimicking prompt), is used only for instructional trials. This is typically used only when the client is able to consistently carry out the behavior. During assessment trials, the direction is given but without the additional prompt:

- Directions: "Take a drink of water."
- Response:
  - Takes a drink of water: Provide praise/reinforcement.
  - Does not take a drink of water: End the trial with no consequences or reinforcement.

81. D: If an RBT recognizes a possible conflict of interest, the supervising BCBA should be contacted immediately for guidance, with an explanation of the conflicting relationship. The BCBA may reassign the RBT or may determine that the RBT can provide services to the client. The RBT must adhere closely to any guidelines provided by the BCBA and must establish appropriate boundaries and respect the privacy and confidentiality of the client and the client's family.

82. A: The RBT should be careful to always respect the privacy and confidentiality of the client and family members and should not divulge confidential information without permission. In this case, the RBT is told about the miscarriage in confidence, but not feeling well is nonspecific, so the RBT should report that the child's mother is not feeling well and has not been able to carry out interventions with her child. This explains the child's lack of weekly progress without violating confidentiality.

83. D: Whole-interval measurement (a form of discontinuous measurement) is used to assess such things as the ability to stay on task, stereotypic/self-stimulatory behavior, and sleep and sedentary behavior. With whole-interval measurement, the duration of the target behavior is measured during each interval, but when scoring, a score is given only if the behavior occurred during the entire interval—in this case, 20 seconds. Only interval three resulted in the child staying on task for the full 20 seconds, so this is scored as 1/5, or 20%.

84. D: Descriptions of a client's behavior or the environment should be based on what is observable and should be described in objective and measurable terms as much as possible. If, for example, the RBT observes that an adolescent on the autism spectrum appears "agitated and upset," these terms are judgmental and subjective and can be interpreted by others in different ways. Rather, the RBT should record the observable behavior: "Adolescent is pacing around the room for 20 minutes and refuses to respond verbally or to follow directions."

85. B: Abolishing operations and establishing operations are different types of motivating operations. Abolishing operations are those that will likely diminish the effects of a reinforcer. In

144

this case, because the client is likely full from eating a bag of cookies, more food is not effective as a reinforcer. Establishing operations, on the other hand, will likely increase the value of a reinforcer. In this case, if the client had not eaten before the session and was hungry, the value of the reinforcer (the crackers) would likely increase.

RBT Practice Test #3

1. A client becomes angry during a session and throws materials off the desk and onto the floor. As a consequence, the RBT requires that the client pick up the materials and replace them on the desk. What type of strategy is the RBT using?

    a. Positive practice.
    b. Restitution—overcorrection.
    c. Restitution—simple correction.
    d. Response cost.

2. A child tries to grab a pair of scissors by the blades, and the RBT immediately places a hand in front of the child's hand to prevent the child from grabbing the scissors. What type of restraint does this represent?

    a. Personal.
    b. Seclusion.
    c. Mechanical.
    d. Response blocking.

3. Which one of the following is required before an RBT submits a self-report to the Behavior Analyst Certification Board?

    a. Disclosure to the supervising BCBA.
    b. Consultation with an attorney.
    c. Consultation with an applied behavioral analyst.
    d. The submission occurs within 60 days of a situation/incident.

4. When the RBT first meets a new client, the client avoids eye contact with the RBT. What should the RBT assume about the client?

    a. The client is not being truthful.
    b. The client is fearful.
    c. The RBT needs more information about the client.
    d. The RBT is making the client uncomfortable.

5. An employer has offered an RBT a position as an independent contractor with an increase in per diem pay from the RBT's current position but no benefits. The RBT wants to take the job because of the increased income. What is the most appropriate response?

    a. Decide based on the actual financial benefit.
    b. Decline the position immediately.
    c. Take the position because it pays more.
    d. Seek advice from other professionals.

6. If using discrimination training to teach a client to discriminate different items used in eating (e.g., plates, spoons, cups), what is the appropriate response if the client identifies a glass incorrectly?

    a. Say "Try again. You drink water from this."
    b. Say nothing but move to the next item.
    c. Say "Good try, but this is a glass."
    d. Say "Wrong" and then move on to the next item.

7. What is the primary purpose of the Americans with Disabilities Act?

    a. Provide services to those with disabilities.
    b. Prevent discrimination and provide equal opportunities for those with disabilities.
    c. Provide employment for those with disabilities.
    d. Fund research into treatments for disabilities.

8. A loud noise sounds outside the facility, and a child hears it and runs and hides. What does the loud noise represent?

    a. Backup reinforcer.
    b. Conditioned stimulus.
    c. Reinforcer.
    d. Unconditioned stimulus.

9. A client appears to have good receptive communication skills but limited expressive communication skills. Which one of the following is an expressive communication skill?

    a. Active listening.
    b. Understanding illustrations.
    c. Reading.
    d. Body language.

10. Which one of the following is one of the strengths that clients with trisomy 21 (Down syndrome) often exhibit?

    a. Long attention span.
    b. Good memory of spoken words.
    c. Good visual learning ability.
    d. General good health.

11. The RBT had been using animal crackers as reinforcers, but the child is responding less frequently, so the RBT withdraws the reinforcer for a period of time and will reintroduce it later. What is the term for this type of withdrawal of a reinforcer?

    a. Escape behavior.
    b. Fading.
    c. Extinction.
    d. Deprivation.

12. The schedule of reinforcement calls for fixed-ratio (FR) reinforcement and specifies FR3. When should the RBT provide reinforcement to the client?

    a. Every 3 minutes.
    b. Every correct response except for the third.
    c. Every third correct response.
    d. After an average number of three responses (2, 4, 3).

13. For which one of the following behaviors is frequency measurement most indicated during a specified period of time?

    a. Engaging in an activity.
    b. Effect of the environment.
    c. Time to complete a task.
    d. Hitting.

14. The RBT shows a child a green card and asks the child, "What color is this?" The child responds "Green," and the RBT says "Yes, it's green. Good job!" Which one of the following is the discriminative stimulus?

    a. "What color is this?"
    b. The green card.
    c. "Green."
    d. "Yes, it's green. Good job!"

15. If a student scores 38% on a norm-referenced test, what does this mean?

    a. Compared to set criteria, the student correctly responded to 38% of questions.
    b. The student is at 38% of normal developmental skills.
    c. Compared to the scores of his or her peers, the student scored lower than 37%.
    d. Compared to the scores of his or her peers, the student scored lower than 62%.

16. The RBT has been assigned a new client. What is the first step in preparation for a session with a new client?

    a. Gather all of the necessary supplies and equipment.
    b. Read through the skill acquisition plan.
    c. Ask the supervisor for guidance.
    d. Review the skill acquisition plan to determine if any parts need clarification.

17. A client repeatedly picks at her skin, so the RBT has set a timer for 3 minutes. When the timer goes off, the client receives no reinforcement if she is picking at her skin but she receives reinforcement if she is not picking at her skin. What strategy is the RBT using?

    a. DRO.
    b. DRL.
    c. DRA.
    d. DRI.

18. Which one of the following terms is used to describe the relationship between behavior and its consequence when the consequence occurs only if the behavior occurs?

    a. Reinforcement.
    b. Stimulus.
    c. Contingency.
    d. Antecedent.

19. An RBT has developed a friendly relationship with the parent of a client the RBT sees often and has accepted an invitation to dinner with the parent and the client. According to the RBT Ethics Code (2.0), Section 1, General responsibilities, what does this represent?

    a. Acceptable friendship.
    b. Bad judgment.
    c. Coercion.
    d. Multiple relationship.

20. The RBT is to meet the BCBA to discuss a client's progress and suggests meeting at a busy coffee shop; however, the BCBA prefers to meet in the car in the parking lot. Why does the BCBA likely want to avoid meeting inside the coffee shop?

    a. The coffee shop is probably too noisy.
    b. To avoid the possibility of being overheard.
    c. There will be no interruptions.
    d. Meeting for coffee is too social.

21. The RBT is working with a student who has been diagnosed with mild intellectual disability (i.e., having an IQ in the range of 55–69). To which grade should the RBT expect the student to be educable?

    a. 2nd.
    b. 4th.
    c. 6th.
    d. 8th.

22. Which one of the following descriptions is objective?

    a. Client angry and upset about the change in schedule.
    b. Student confused about assignments.
    c. Client very distracted this morning.
    d. Child tore six pages out of a book and threw them on the floor.

23. Which one of the following is true about reinforcers?

    a. They should be provided for every response.
    b. They should remain consistent over time.
    c. They should be provided only for a desired response.
    d. They should be changed frequently.

24. What should the communication between an RBT and a supervising BCBA focus on?

    a. The concerns of the RBT.
    b. The needs and progress of the client.
    c. The recommendations of the BCBA.
    d. The areas of concern.

25. A student often refuses to do assignments in math class, so the teacher sends the student to study hall as a punishment. However, the student enjoys reading in study hall and does not want to do the math assignments, so being sent to study hall solves the student's problem and serves as reinforcement for the problem behavior. What does this exemplify?

    a. Behavior trap.
    b. Abolishing operation.
    c. Establishing operation.
    d. Short-circuiting the contingency.

26. Following a duration measurement, the RBT reports to the board certified behavior analyst (BCBA) that the child was able to stay on task for 6 minutes in a 30-minute observation period. This would be reported as what percentage of the observation time?

    a. 6%.
    b. 12%.
    c. 20%.
    d. 30%.

27. When the RBT arrives to work with an adolescent client diagnosed with autism spectrum disorder, a parent tells the RBT that the adolescent has exhibited a sudden change in behavior and has been increasingly agitated and resistive. How should the RBT initially respond?

    a. Immediately report this to the supervising BCBA.
    b. Reassure the parent that this is normal for adolescents.
    c. Ask about any variables or changes that have occurred recently.
    d. Observe the client carefully during the session.

28. What three characteristics are common to those with attention deficit hyperactivity disorder (ADHD)?

    a. Heightened intelligence, hyperactivity, and good recall.
    b. Inattention, heightened intelligence, and hyperactivity.
    c. Impulsivity, hyperactivity, and creativity.
    d. Inattention, impulsivity, and hyperactivity.

29. Which one of the following is an accurate reflection of using aversive statements to modify behavior?

    a. It can result in escalation of unwanted behaviors.
    b. It promotes generalization of behavior.
    c. It promotes learning of a new behavior.
    d. It can increase the rate of extinction.

30. Which one of the following therapies is often used as part of behavior modification strategies for clients with Tourette's syndrome?

    a. Hypnosis therapy.
    b. Medication therapy.
    c. Dialectical behavior therapy.
    d. Habit reversal therapy.

31. According to the prompt hierarchy, which type of prompt is the weakest?

    a. Visual.
    b. Gestural.
    c. Verbal.
    d. Modeling.

32. What is the primary role of the RBT in development of the skill acquisition plan?

    a. To develop appropriate interventions.
    b. To outline goals for skill deficits.
    c. To collect baseline and ongoing data.
    d. To collaborate with the client and family.

33. For which one of the following is a line graph most commonly used?

a. To display discrete data.

b. To show trends and changes over time.

c. To compare two variables.

d. To show the relationships among multiple variables.

34. Which one of the following behaviors is considered covert?

a. Frowning.

b. Speaking.

c. Gesturing.

d. Daydreaming.

35. By what age are children with normal fine motor skills expected to be able to tie their shoes?

a. 5–7.

b. 4–5.

c. 3–5.

d. 4.

36. The registered behavior technician (RBT) is collecting data regarding the frequency of repetitive or self-injurious behavior in a 7-year-old child diagnosed with autism spectrum disorder after a period of activity when the child is becoming tired. During the scheduled observation period, construction begins on the property next to the facility with jackhammering and other loud noises, causing the child to markedly increase these repetitive or self-injurious behaviors. Which one of the following actions is most appropriate?

a. Delay the observation and data collection.

b. Continue with the data collection as planned.

c. Explain the construction noises to the child and continue data collection.

d. Move the child to a different area further from the construction.

37. A parent reports using time-outs by sending an adolescent to his room for 1 hour when he refuses to do his homework, but the parent reports that the problem is becoming worse instead of better. What is the most likely problem?

a. The time-out is too long for the behavior.

b. The time-out is reinforcing the behavior.

c. The adolescent is resistive to authority.

d. The adolescent is inherently unmotivated.

38. If using no-no prompting and the client gives an incorrect response with trial 1, how should the RBT respond?

a. Repeat the direction.

b. Say "No, try again."

c. End the trial.

d. Repeat the directions and add a prompt.

39. The RBT has received a friend request from a client on a social media platform. How should the RBT respond?

    a. Explain and deny the request.
    b. Ask the BCBA about what to do.
    c. Accept the request.
    d. Ignore the request.

40. Latency measurement is always used with which type of relationship?

    a. Sender-receiver.
    b. Stimulus-response.
    c. Cause-effect.
    d. Input-output.

41. When applying the ABCs of functional behavioral assessment, the A stands for which one of the following?

    a. Activity.
    b. Antecedent.
    c. Abnormality.
    d. Analysis.

42. A parent had taken an adolescent's cell phone away because of falling grades but allows the adolescent to have the phone back when the grades begin to improve. What strategy is the parent using when taking the phone away in order to encourage continued academic improvement?

    a. Positive reinforcement.
    b. Positive punishment.
    c. Negative reinforcement.
    d. Negative punishment.

43. With behavioral modification, which one of the following occurs first?

    a. Discriminative stimulus.
    b. Prompt.
    c. Reinforcement.
    d. Motivating operation.

44. Which one of the following is considered a common function of behavior?

    a. Sexual satisfaction.
    b. Avoidance or escape.
    c. Enlightenment.
    d. Spiritual comfort.

45. The RBT carries client data regarding the diagnoses, conditions, and interventions planned for the individuals whom the RBT sees in their homes each day. Where is the best place to safeguard these documents?

    a. Carry them at all times.
    b. Place them in the glove compartment of the car.
    c. Place them in the locked trunk of the car.
    d. Place them in a locked container inside the home.

46. The RBT is using total task presentation to teach a child to wash hands after playing outside. Which one of the following techniques is usually used initially with total task presentation?

    a. Shaping.

    b. Modeling.

    c. Graduated guidance.

    d. Shadowing.

47. A client has a habit of pulling her hair, resulting in bald spots. The client has discussed the nature and impact of her habit with the BCBA and the RBT, and the RBT is to use habit reversal training with the client. What should the RBT do to help the client increase her awareness of hair-pulling?

    a. Make careful, detailed observations.

    b. Ask the client to do self-monitoring with a habit log.

    c. Ask the client to wear a device that signals when hair-pulling occurs.

    d. Interview family members.

48. While working with a client with developmental delay, the fire alarm goes off. Which one of the following should be the RBT's primary concern?

    a. The location of the fire.

    b. The safety of the child.

    c. The location of the nearest exit.

    d. Calling for help.

49. A client was in a car accident 1 month earlier and has recently been having nightmares about the accident and is exhibiting periods of anger and aggression. How would the car accident be categorized?

    a. Behavior cusp.

    b. Behavior trap.

    c. Setting event.

    d. Stimulus generalization.

50. Which one of the following is a positive strategy to help a client prevent unwanted behavior?

    a. Use silent signals.

    b. Say "NO!"

    c. Apply a respond cost.

    d. Immediately interrupt unwanted behavior.

51. An RBT is using stickers as reinforcers when a child completes worksheets. However, the child refuses to cooperate and demands a sticker in advance. To encourage cooperation, the RBT gives in and provides the child with a sticker, and then the child happily completes a worksheet. What type of strategy does this represent?

    a. Bribery.

    b. Indirect reinforcement.

    c. Intrinsic motivation.

    d. Negative reinforcement.

52. The RBT is using discontinuous measurement to assess a client's behavior. Which one of the following is a disadvantage associated with discontinuous measurement?

    a. It may require several days of measurement.
    b. It is difficult to organize.
    c. It requires hours of constant assessment.
    d. It may provide an inaccurate representation.

53. Which one of the following reinforcement schedules is typically the most resistant to extinction?

    a. FR.
    b. FI.
    c. VI.
    d. VR.

54. The BCBA has encouraged the RBT to ask for clinical direction or report changes whenever the RBT thinks that it is needed rather than to wait until the next scheduled meeting. Which one of the following should the RBT report to the BCBA immediately?

    a. A client is responding to positive reinforcement.
    b. A client would like a change in the schedule.
    c. A client has a black eye and unexplained bruises.
    d. A client has a doctor's appointment for a physical exam.

55. What is the term used to describe behaviors that, when changed, also affect clients' other behaviors or overall functioning?

    a. Keystone.
    b. Core.
    c. Foundational.
    d. Oppositional.

56. The RBT has been teaching a student to raise a hand in class and wait to be called on before calling out an answer. If the teacher asks a question and the student responds appropriately, what should be the RBT's next action?

    a. Continue to observe.
    b. Provide reinforcement.
    c. Record data.
    d. Provide feedback to the BCBA.

57. An individual diagnosed with autism spectrum disorder frequently engages in various types of aggressive behavior such as shouting, hitting, and throwing things. Which type of measurement is likely to provide the most useful information?

    a. Discrete categorization.
    b. Duration.
    c. Frequency.
    d. Intensity.

58. For an adolescent, which one of the following likely represents a behavioral cusp?

a. Playing video games.
b. Learning to drive.
c. Washing dishes.
d. Watching videos.

59. Which one of the following is a criterion-referenced functional assessment tool intended for school-aged children to adults?

a. Essential for Living test.
b. ABLLS-R.
c. PEAK.
d. AFLS.

60. Which one of the following addresses the rights of individuals related to the privacy of their health information?

a. Health Insurance Portability and Accountability Act (HIPAA).
b. Americans with Disabilities Act (ADA).
c. Individuals with Disabilities Education Act (IDEA).
d. Occupational Safety and Health Administration (OSHA).

61. At what age should the RBT expect that a child will be able to name at least five body parts?

a. 1–2.
b. 2–3.
c. 3–4.
d. 4–5.

62. The RBT takes a child into a playroom and gives the child a number of colored blocks; the child begins to stack the blocks, one on top of the other, while the RBT engages in continuous measurement procedures to determine how successful the child is at this activity. The RBT introduces sounds, such as music, to determine if the child becomes distracted. What type of observation is this?

a. Natural
b. Contrived.
c. Interval.
d. Latency.

63. If an RBT receives sanctions as part of a disciplinary review and wishes to file an appeal, how many days does the RBT have to do so?

a. 15.
b. 30.
c. 45.
d. 60.

64. A student with ADHD has difficulty paying attention in class, so the RBT is using praise and tokens to reward the child for staying on task, with an ultimate goal of 10 minutes. The RBT starts with an initial goal of 1 minute and gradually increases the duration of time needed to receive reinforcement. What strategy is the RBT using?

    a. Shaping.
    b. Modeling.
    c. Chaining.
    d. Prompt fading.

65. The RBT has become frustrated with a child who is not cooperative, so the RBT tells the child that there will be no dessert with lunch unless the child cooperates. What does this exemplify?

    a. Battery.
    b. Coercion.
    c. Harassment.
    d. Assault.

66. What is the purpose of a manding trial?

    a. To identify reinforcers.
    b. To teach a client to ask for something.
    c. To evaluate readiness.
    d. To teach a client to delay gratification.

67. When the RBT arrives at a home, the adolescent client with cerebral palsy is found tied to a bed, soiled with urine and feces, and hungry and thirsty. The only other person in the home is a 5-year-old sibling. What should the RBT do?

    a. Call 9-1-1 to report the findings.
    b. Contact the BCBA and the local child protective services agency.
    c. Try to contact the parents to ask when they are returning.
    d. Call the police on a nonemergency number.

68. An RBT is observing eye-blinking in a child using partial interval measurement, during five 60-second intervals:

- First interval: 0 blinks.
- Second interval: 1 blink.
- Third interval: 2 blinks.
- Fourth interval: 3 blinks.
- Fifth interval: 0 blinks.

How are these observations scored?

    a. 6/5.
    b. 3/5.
    c. 2/5.
    d. 5/5.

69. How frequently must the RBT certification be renewed?

   a. Annually.
   b. Biannually.
   c. Biennially.
   d. Every 3 years.

70. The BCBA tells the RBT that a client would benefit from speech therapy. The RBT recommends a speech therapist who is a close friend of the RBT and whom she believes would work well with the client. What does this represent?

   a. Collaboration.
   b. Client-centered care.
   c. Communication.
   d. Conflict of interest.

71. The RBT has been working with a student to decrease speaking out in class without first raising a hand and waiting to be acknowledged by the teacher. During a period of observation and data collection, the RBT notes that the student has markedly decreased interruptions. Which type of reactivity does this likely represent?

   a. Hawthorne.
   b. Novelty.
   c. Demand.
   d. Response to measurement instrument.

72. The RBT has seen a marked improvement in a child's behavior over the past 6 months, and, when making observations, the RBT scores the child higher than three other observers. Which one of the following is likely the reason for this discrepancy?

   a. The other observers use a different method of scoring.
   b. The RBT falsifies the child's score.
   c. The RBT is influenced by expectations.
   d. The other observers are more critical of the child.

73. Which one of the following is best assessed through permanent product recording?

   a. Assessing an individual's ability to pack a product into boxes.
   b. Monitoring a child's ability to identify colors.
   c. Assessing a student's problem-solving ability.
   d. Assessing a child's behavioral development.

74. When carrying out a trial-based preference assessment using paired stimuli, or forced choice, what should the RBT do?

   a. Place two similar items in front of the client and observe the interaction.
   b. Place a number of pairs of similar items (e.g., toys, candy, books) in front of the client and observe the interaction.
   c. Place items one at a time in front of the client and observe the interaction.
   d. Ask the client to choose between two similar items.

75. A child frequently engages in masturbation in the presence of adults, resulting in social reinforcement in the form of a reprimand. The BCBA has recommended that the RBT and others stand nearby to shield the child from others but withhold the reprimand when the child masturbates. What strategy is the BCBA recommending?

    a. Positive punishment.
    b. Short-circuiting the contingency.
    c. Overcorrection.
    d. Extinction.

76. The RBT asks for guidance from the supervising BCBA but does not understand the explanation. What should the RBT do?

    a. Research independently.
    b. Ask another RBT.
    c. Ask the BCBA's supervisor.
    d. Ask the BCBA for further clarification.

77. During a class observation, the RBT notes that a teacher is using guided compliance (by pointing at a chair) to ensure that a child sits in a chair during class. What type of reinforcement or punishment does this represent?

    a. Positive punishment.
    b. Negative punishment.
    c. Positive reinforcement.
    d. Negative reinforcement.

78. The VB-MAPP test is most frequently used to assess which one of the following groups?

    a. Adults with Down syndrome.
    b. Adults with autism spectrum disorder.
    c. Children with autism spectrum disorder.
    d. Any child or adult with a language delay.

79. A child with autism spectrum disorder self-soothes by stimming (i.e., self-stimulation) by repeatedly flapping his hands. What type of reinforcement does this represent?

    a. Automatic negative.
    b. Self-reinforcement.
    c. Automatic positive.
    d. Negative punishment.

80. If a client is able to see a cat and say "Cat," what verbal operant is the client using?

    a. Textual.
    b. Transcriptive.
    c. Tact.
    d. Intraverbal.

81. A child learns to button a shirt and is then able to button a jacket and other items of clothing. What does this exemplify?

    a. Cross-training.
    b. Learning transfer.
    c. Stimulus generalization.
    d. Response generalization.

82. Which one of the following terms is used to describe a series of discriminative stimuli and responses?

    a. Behavior chain.
    b. Behavior model.
    c. Discrete trial.
    d. Block trial.

83. The RBT is conducting discrete trial training with a client. The RBT holds several different pictures of items and shows them to the client in different orders, moving to the next picture when a client has successfully identified a picture. What type of discrete trial training does this represent?

    a. Errorless learning.
    b. Massed trial.
    c. Block trial.
    d. Random rotation trial.

84. An adolescent exhibits many different behavior problems, so the BCBA has developed a behavior contract with the adolescent. The RBT, the adolescent, and the parents are responsible for enforcing the contract. A behavior contract should generally be limited to how many target behaviors?

    a. Four or five.
    b. Two or three.
    c. One or two.
    d. Only one.

85. What percentage of the RBT's hours worked should be supervised by a BCBA each month?

    a. 2%.
    b. 5%.
    c. 10%.
    d. 15%.

Answer Key and Explanations for Test #3

1. C: Restitution with simple correction involves correcting the effects of the behavior with no additional actions. Restitution with overcorrection involves not only correcting the effect of the behavior but carrying out additional actions to compensate (an overcorrection). Positive practice involves repeatedly practicing a desired behavior. Restitution and positive practice are often used together. For example, if a client throws trash on the floor, the client may be required to pick up the trash and dispose of it properly (i.e., restitution) and then go around the room and pick up all trash and dispose of it (i.e., positive practice).

2. D: Response blocking, preventing unwanted behavior, should only be used when an individual (such as the child grabbing at the blades of a pair of scissors) is in immediate danger. Minimal force should be used to ensure that the blocking does not result in injury. When using response blocking, the RBT should clearly communicate the reason so that it is not misconstrued as punishment, by saying, for example, "It's dangerous to grab scissors by the blades because they can cut you." The RBT should treat the individual in a respectful manner.

3. A: An RBT must disclose to their supervising BCBA any situation or incident about which the RBT plans to submit a self-report to the Behavior Analyst Certification Board, and the discussion should be documented. Although it is recommended that the RBT consult an attorney or applied behavioral analyst, it is not a requirement. Submissions must occur within 30 days of the situation/incident. All relevant documents should be attached as PDF files so they cannot be altered. Ongoing situations require quarterly submissions (i.e., every 3 months).

4. C: Eye contact is typically valued in Western culture as a sign of caring and honesty; however, people may avoid eye contact for many reasons: fear, discomfort, shame, respect, untruthfulness. Some ethnic groups avoid direct eye contact as a sign of respect. Some individuals on the autism spectrum feel uncomfortable with direct eye contact. The RBT should not make an assumption based on an initial contact but should spend more time with the client and gather more information before the RBT can begin to understand the reason for the client's avoidance of eye contact.

5. B: If the RBT is offered a position as an independent contractor or sees a job advertised as such, the RBT should immediately decline the position because it is a violation of the RBT Ethics Code to work as an independent contractor and is also a violation of the US Internal Revenue Service definition for employees. An independent contractor must be in control of duties performed without the need for supervision, but certified RBTs must work under supervision.

6. D: Discrimination training, which teaches a client to discriminate among different items with which the client has some familiarity, involves providing reinforcement for only an appropriate response. If a client incorrectly identifies an item, the RBT simply says, "Wrong," and then moves on to the next item. Discrimination training is used to teach basic academic skills, such as recognizing letters. Discrimination training may also be used to teach clients to differentiate facial expressions or sounds and to learn safety skills (such as the meaning of warning signs).

7. B: The Americans with Disabilities Act of 1992 is a civil rights act that aims to prevent discrimination and provide equal opportunities for those with disabilities. Employers, for example, must make reasonable accommodations. Communities must provide transportation services for those with disabilities, and all public facilities must be accessible with ramps and/or elevators as needed. Telecommunications must also be accessible to those who are hearing or visually impaired. Individuals with disabilities should have equal access to goods, programs, activities, and services.

8. D: An unconditioned stimulus is one (such as the loud noise) that elicits a response (e.g., running and hiding). The response is natural and instinctive rather than thought out or planned. An unconditioned stimulus may be perceived in different ways, positive or negative, but may effect a physiological response, such as an increased heart rate. Unconditioned stimuli, such as thirst, may motivate the client to take action (e.g., to get a drink of water).

9. D: Expressive communication skills involve the ability to share information in some way, such as through spoken words as well as turn-taking, body language, gestures, eyes contact, and other nonverbal methods of communication. Expressive communication is used to discuss needs and desire and convey thoughts and ideas. Much communication among individuals is now through electronic means, such as instant messaging, that incorporate the use of symbols to express meaning.

10. C: Although clients with trisomy 21 (Down syndrome) often face many challenges (e.g., intellectual disability, developmental delays, multiple health problems, communication difficulties, increased risk of infections), they often exhibit strengths in other areas. For example, although clients may have a short attention span, they often have very good visual learning ability and respond well to illustrations, photos, and videos. Additionally, they are often friendly and outgoing and have good social skills. If the intellectual disability is mild, clients may be able to learn, live, and work independently.

11. D: Deprivation, a form of establishing operation, involves removing a specific reinforcer for a period of time in order to make the reinforcer more powerful when it is reinstated so the client will be more motivated to carry out the wanted behavior in order to receive the reinforcer. Deprivation is often associated with satiation, in which the value of a reinforcer decreases. In this case, the animal cracker became less valuable because of satiation and had increased value after deprivation.

12. C: With fixed-ratio (FR) reinforcement, reinforcement is given after a specific number of correct responses. FR1 represents continuous reinforcement because reinforcement is given after every response. With FR3, reinforcement is given after every third correct response. Some advantages of FR reinforcement include a high response rate, especially if clients recognize the pattern of reinforcement, leading to consistent performance and a short, uniform interresponse time. However, some disadvantages are that clients may develop satiation and pause after reinforcement and may lose motivation. Also, the behavior may have limited generalization because clients may respond only in the situations/environment in which the behavior has been reinforced.

13. D: Frequency measurement is best used for discrete, countable behaviors, such as hitting or throwing things. Frequency measurement is often used to assess target behaviors, both positive and negative, and it may be used to assess social interactions, such as turn-taking, and verbal behavior, such as correct responses to questioning. Frequency measurement is typically not used for actions of a longer duration, such as playing a game or completing a task, or to assess the effects of environmental conditions.

14. B: The event that occurs before a response and reinforcement is the discriminative stimulus. In this case, the green card is the cue that triggers a behavioral response. "What color is this?" is the prompt, and the child's answer, "Green," is the response. The consequence (the reinforcement) is the praise, "Yes, it's green. Good job!" Discriminative stimuli may include a wide variety of things, such as visual cues (such as the yellow card), words, smells, and sounds.

15. D: Norm-referenced tests, such as the SAT, compare a client's performance to those of his or her peers. Thus, if a student scores 38% on a norm-referenced test, this means that, compared to his or her peers, the student scored higher than 37% and lower than 62% of other test takers. With norm-referenced tests, a representative sample of individuals from a specific group (such as school grade level), referred to as a normative sample, takes the test under standardized conditions, and the scores are used to establish normal scores.

16. B: The RBT should be fully prepared to work with the client before beginning a session. The first step should be to carefully read through the skill acquisition plan to make sure that the RBT fully understands the plan and can ask a supervisor for clarification if necessary. Additionally, the RBT should practice interventions if necessary and gather all of the required supplies and equipment. Writing out a brief checklist or performance plan can help ensure that no elements are overlooked.

17. A: Differential reinforcement of other behavior (DRO) is used to decrease undesirable behavior by reinforcing any other, more desirable behavior. Momentary reinforcement is given whenever another behavior is observed; however, interval reinforcement, given at specified intervals, is more commonly used. In this case, every 3 minutes, the RBT observes the client and provides reinforcement if she is not picking at her skin. If, however, the client substitutes another undesirable behavior for the first, this undesirable behavior is not reinforced.

18. C: Contingency is the term used to describe the relationship between a behavior and its consequence when the consequence occurs only if the behavior occurs. For example, if a child raises a hand when asking the teacher a question and receives a sticker, the sticker is contingent on the child raising a hand. Effectively applying contingencies is essential in behavioral modification, including techniques such as shaping. Operant conditioning proposes that behaviors are influenced by the consequences, which weaken or strengthen the behavior.

19. D: Multiple, or dual, relationships occur when the RBT has more than one relationship with a client, supervisor, or family member. In this case, the RBT has an established professional relationship with the client and with the parent and is also engaging in a relationship as a friend. Although the RBT should be friendly with clients and family members, this should not cross over into a friendship because this can compromise the professional relationship.

20. B: The RBT should never discuss clients in any sort of public area, such as a coffee shop or cafeteria, where others may overhear because this would constitute a HIPAA violation of privacy and confidentiality. Also, the RBT should use care if discussing a client with the BCBA over the telephone and should do so where no one else can hear. The RBT should always avoid making any comments or discussing clients with anyone who is not involved in the care of those clients.

21. C: A student with a mild intellectual disability is typically educable to approximately the 6th-grade level.

Classifications (IQ)	Description
55–69: mild (85%)	Educable to approximately the 6th-grade level. Usually able to learn skills and be self-supporting but may need assistance and supervision.
40–54: moderate (10%)	Trainable and may be able to work and live in sheltered environments or with supervision.
25–39: severe (3–4%)	Can learn only basic academic skills and perform simple tasks.
<25: profound (1–2%)	Require constant care and supervision.

22. D: Objective descriptions describe what is actually observed without the addition of judgmental/subjective opinions, such as that described in answer option (D). While it may seem obvious that the child is angry and upset, the child may, in fact, be afraid, anxious, worried, or feeling ill and may be unable to adequately express his or her feelings. Objective descriptions should be factual and impartial and should contain concrete details and avoid ambiguous descriptions.

23. C: Reinforcers are provided to reward a client and should only be given when a response is appropriate. Preference assessments are carried out to determine the reinforcers that are most motivating under different circumstances. Reinforcers that are commonly used include food, toys, videos, television viewing, and cell phone use. Reinforcers may change, so what is reinforcing on one day may not be reinforcing on another day or in a different situation.

24. B: Communication between the RBT and a supervising BCBA should focus on the needs and progress of the client. The BCBA and RBT should share information and ensure that their goals are in alignment. Data should be reviewed and analyzed to determine if interventions are effective or need to be modified. The RBT may seek advice and receive feedback on how to better implement interventions and discuss any challenges or concerns that have arisen with the client.

25. A: A behavior trap occurs when unwanted behavior (e.g., refusal to do math assignments) is inadvertently reinforced (e.g., by sending the student to study hall where the student enjoys reading). Behavior traps are common in the natural environment (such as at work, in the home, or at school) when punishment results in reinforcement, especially if the pattern repeats frequently. Behavior traps become habits over time, and habits are difficult to break. The only way this pattern of behavior can be extinguished is to stop providing the reinforcement and insist on compliance.

26. C: Duration measurements are most often reported as a percentage of the observation period. Thus, if a child stayed on task for 6 minutes out of 30, this represents 20% of the time:

$$6/30 = 0.2 \times 100 = 20\%.$$

The time the behavior begins is the onset, and the time the behavior ends is the offset. Duration measurement is not suitable for actions of a short time duration, such as hitting or throwing things, but it is suitable for activities that are carried out for variable time periods, such as watching television or engaging in play with other children.

27. C: A sudden change in a client's behavior should always be reported to a supervisor, but before doing so, the RBT should gather as much information as possible, including when the behavior was first noted and if there are any variables or changes that may have affected the adolescent. Variables can include a wide variety of things, such as new medications, medical conditions (e.g., infection, pain), changes in family dynamics, environmental changes, poor sleep, loss/acquisition of a pet, and/or a change of caregiver. Clients with autism spectrum disorder often respond poorly to any type of change.

28. D: The three characteristics that are common to those with attention deficit hyperactivity disorder (ADHD) include inattention (e.g., daydreaming, mind wandering), impulsivity (e.g., making careless mistakes, forgetting things, getting along poorly with others), and hyperactivity (e.g., talking too much, squirming, fidgeting). Up to approximately 5% of children and 2.5% of adults have been diagnosed with ADHD. The three subtypes of ADHD include (1) predominantly inattentive, (2) predominantly hyperactive/impulsive, and (3) combined.

29. A: Aversive statements may initially reduce an unwanted behavior, but, over time, the behavior may escalate because these statements may result in the suppression of a behavior rather than the learning of a new one. Aversive statements may include the following:

- Criticism: "You are so messy and disorganized."
- Insults and name-calling: "You are so dumb!"
- Threats/Warnings: "If you don't sit down, you will lose television time."
- Reprimands: "You are not supposed to talk during quiet time!"
- Sarcasm: "That was a genius action."
- Guilt-tripping: "I worked really hard on this, and you don't even appreciate it."

30. D: Habit reversal therapy is often used to help clients with Tourette's syndrome manage their symptoms. This therapy typically begins with awareness training to help clients recognize the urges that trigger tics and then involves competing response training, which replaces tics with an incompatible behavior. For example, if a person has the urge to move the fingers, the person may be taught to make a fist or to flex or stretch the fingers. Habit reversal therapy also includes strategies to recognize and treat underlying factors that contribute to tics.

31. A: The prompt hierarchy categorizes different types of prompts from strongest to weakest:

- Physical (strongest): Ranges from full (i.e., physically guiding) to partial (i.e., shadowing).
- Modeling: RBT demonstrates.
- Gestural: Nodding of the head, pointing, mimicking a behavior, looking at something.
- Verbal: "Show me the cat."
- Visual (weakest): Media, such as pictures, videos, posters, illustrations.

When choosing the appropriate prompt, things to consider include the ability of the learner, the complexity of the task, the effectiveness of the prompt with the learner, the potential for prompt fading, the learner's motivation, and the task analysis.

32. C: The BCBA is responsible for the development of the skill acquisition plan, including identifying skill deficits, goals for dealing with the deficits, identifying prompting, and reinforcing strategies and consequences. The role of the RBT is to help by obtaining baseline and ongoing data and providing feedback to the BCBA, such as regarding the possible need for modification of the plan. However, the RBT does not independently change the plan or implement modifications.

33. B: Line graphs are used most often to show trends and changes over time. Line graphs contain two axes: horizontal (x) and vertical (y). Measurements occur on the vertical (y) axis, whereas the vertical axis represents time. Thus, if measuring the frequency of a behavior, this would be noted on the vertical access, starting with a beginning or baseline value. Each measure provides a data point that is connected in a line to the next data point, and so on.

34. D: Covert behaviors are not observable because they take place within the mind. Covert behaviors include thinking, daydreaming, calculating, remembering, and processing information. Covert behaviors may occur when the individual is active or inactive and cannot be assessed. Overt behaviors, on the other hand, are observable and include facial expressions (e.g., frowning, smiling), speaking, and gesturing. Overt behaviors are those that are assessed as part of behavior modification. Covert behaviors may trigger overt behaviors, which, in turn, trigger more covert behaviors.

35. A: Between ages 3 and 6, the child moves from toddlerhood to childhood and gains many new skills. Most children with normal fine motor skills are able to tie their shoes by age 6, but this may vary from age 5 to age 7 because some children are more motivated to learn early and others are not or are not taught how to tie their shoes. By age 6, children typically have a large, complex vocabulary; are beginning to read; can draw shapes and color in the lines; and can climb, run, and jump.

36. A: Because children diagnosed with autism spectrum disorder are very sensitive to sensory stimuli such as noise, if construction and loud noises are occurring and these are not part of the usual environmental sounds, the most appropriate action for the RBT is to delay the observation and data collection. The intention is to assess whether repetitive or self-injurious behavior increases when the child is becoming tired, but the data obtained when construction is occurring will instead be assessing the child's response to noise.

37. B: Time-outs remove an individual from a situation (e.g., refusing to do homework) and place the individual in another situation (e.g., stay in his room for 1 hour). One problem with time-outs is that they may be preferable to the individual, thus reinforcing the unwanted behavior. Additionally, if an adolescent is sent to his room, the room may be full of distractions (e.g., computer, tablet, cell phone, television) that the adolescent enjoys, so the punishment essentially becomes a reward.

38. B: With no-no prompting, directions are repeated up to three times after an initial incorrect response. The RBT provides reinforcement with correct responses (e.g., by saying "Good") or feedback (e.g., by saying "No, try again") with errors. On the third trial, the RBT gives directions and adds a prompt, such as mimicking the action desired. If the client responds correctly with the third trial, the RBT provides feedback; however, if the client responds incorrectly, the trial ends with no consequences or reinforcement.

39. A: If the RBT receives a request for a client to become a friend on a social media platform, such as Facebook, the RBT should first explain that it is against policy for the RBT to have a social media relationship with clients and then deny the request. A client may feel offended or hurt if the request is simply ignored or if the RBT denies the request without first discussing it with the client. The RBT should use privacy controls on social media to avoid clients accessing the RBT's site and learning personal information about the RBT.

40. B: Latency measurement is always used with a stimulus-response relationship. For example, the RBT requests that a child identify a shape (the stimulus), and the child waits 15 seconds (the latency period) to identify the shape (the response). Latency measurement may be used when trying to decrease the latency periods, such as when trying to get a child to respond more quickly, or to lengthen a latency period, such as when trying to get a child to decrease aggressive responses.

41. B: Functional behavioral assessments are carried out to determine why a behavior is occurring and what purpose it serves for the client in order to develop effective interventions. The ABCs of functional behavioral assessment include the following:

- Antecedent (A): Possible triggers for behavior, which may include sensory stimulation, confusion, biological distress, shame/embarrassment, lack of attention, and delayed gratification.
- Behavior (B): Outline the observed behavior in objective detail.
- Consequence (C): Observe how others respond to the client's behavior and what the client appears to gain or lose from the behavior.

165

42. C: When something unpleasant (i.e., an aversive stimulus, such as removing the adolescent's cell phone) is removed in order to increase the probability that a behavior (in this case, better academic performance) will occur, this is an example of negative reinforcement. The adolescent improves academic performance in order to avoid losing phone privileges again. Negative punishment, on the other hand, occurs when something is taken away until behavior changes. This was the initial strategy of the parent when taking away the phone.

43. D: When considering behavioral modification, the sequence (first to last) is as follows:

1. Motivating operation: Decreases (abolishing operation) or increases (establishing operation) the value of reinforcement.
2. Discriminative stimulus: The signal to carry out a behavior.
3. Prompt: The cue or instructions for an action.
4. Reinforcement: A reward for correct behavior.
5. Consequence: The result of a behavior.

44. B: There are four basic functions of behavior that are targeted with behavioral modification. The function of a behavior must be assessed before interventions are developed. The four common functions of behavior are as follows:

- Attention-getting: Behaviors include throwing tantrums, interrupting others, and gesturing.
- Access to tangible items: Behaviors include crying, grabbing, begging, grabbing, hitting, and biting in order to gain a desired item.
- Avoidance or escape: Behaviors include hiding, running away, and refusing to cooperate.
- Sensory stimulation: Behaviors include rocking back and forth, flapping the hands, and picking at a scab.

45. C: Client data in any form are covered under HIPAA regulations regarding confidentiality and privacy. Although the RBT may carry a client's data into that client's home, the RBT should not carry other clients' data into the client's home because someone in the home may look at the data. Client data, whether in paper or electronic form, should be securely locked in the trunk of a car. Data left inside the car, even if the car is locked, are more vulnerable to theft.

46. C: Total task presentation involves teaching a task by carrying out all of the steps each time. Graduated guidance, or hand-over-hand physical prompting in which the RBT guides the client's hands, is often used initially with total task presentation. As the client begins to master the steps, the RBT begins shadowing (e.g., by holding the hands over the client's but not touching so they can intervene if necessary) and then fading the shadowing. Total task presentation is best used for simple tasks rather than complex ones with many steps.

47. B: A habit log is a valuable tool for habit reversal training because it helps increase the client's awareness of the behavior. A habit log typically includes the date and time, the description of behavior and the urge to carry out the behavior, the triggers or antecedents, the intensity or duration of the habit, the consequences (e.g., pain, hair removed, reprimands, reminders), as well as any contextual information (e.g., people present, activities being carried out, the environment).

48. B: In any type of emergency, the primary concern of the RBT should always be the safety of the client. This does not mean that other concerns, such as the location of the nearest exit or calling for help, cannot also be attended to. Each organization should have a written emergency plan in place with specific protocols to follow in various situations: health problems (e.g., seizures, injury, illness)

behavioral problems (e.g., hitting, kicking, hair-pulling), or environmental problems (e.g., fire, hurricane, tornado, flood).

49. C: Internal or external factors that set the stage for unwanted behavior are setting events (in this case, the accident); setting events may occur hours, days, weeks, or months before a behavior manifests (setting events are different from triggering events, which occur immediately before the behavior). Setting events are often traumatic in some way and may include things that happen only once (such as the client's accident) or repeatedly (such as domestic violence). Establishing operations and abolishing operations are two specific types of setting events.

50. A: Positive strategies use encouragement and constructive interventions to help a client prevent unwanted behavior rather than any type of response cost or punishment. Strategies may include helping a client establish a routine so that the client knows what to expect; outlining expectations and helping the client set behavioral goals; and using unobtrusive signals, such as pointing or other gestures, to remind the client or to provide positive reinforcement.

51. A: If a child receives a reward before the target behavior rather than after, the reward is no longer serving as a reinforcer but rather as a bribe because the reward is provided to influence the subsequent behavior. It can be challenging to switch from bribery to reinforcement because the child may become resistive, especially if bribing the child has become a pattern. The RBT must be consistent in outlining expectations and providing reinforcement only after the target behavior occurs.

52. D: One of the disadvantages of discontinuous measurement is that it may provide an inaccurate representation because missed behavior that occurs before or after the designated assessment period may provide additional information that would change the behavioral assessment. Additionally, some behavior is highly variable; therefore, assessment at intervals may not capture the degree of variability. Additionally, the intervals chosen for assessment may not coincide with the target behavior or the behavior may occur more or less frequently in a different time period.

53. D: Variable-ratio (VR) reinforcement tends to be the most resistant to extinction because the unpredictability of VR reinforcement results in less dependency on the reinforcement. Therefore, the behavior is more likely to persist even without reinforcement. Additionally, VR may result in better generalization so that the behavior persists in different situations and environments. The response rate is often high because clients are motivated to receive reinforcement but are unsure about when it will occur.

54. C: Urgent situations about which the RBT should immediately notify the BCBA include any safety concerns for the client or the RBT—in this case, the client's black eye and other bruises. These types of injuries may indicate abuse, and the BCBA and RBT are mandatory reporters. Other urgent situations include an unexpected change or an environmental change that may affect the client or the behavior intervention plan. If the RBT is unable to implement interventions and this is impacting the behavior intervention plan, this should also be reported.

55. A: Keystone behaviors are those that, when changed, also affect clients' other behaviors or overall functioning. Keystone behaviors may result in negative or positive changes, but they have a significant pivotal impact. When looking at a series of associated behaviors, it is important to assess which change in behavior (i.e., the keystone) would be most impactful in changing multiple behaviors. For example, if a nonverbal child learns to use an electronic tablet to communicate, this one change can increase the child's independence, decrease tantrums and frustration, expand educational opportunities, and improve social interactions.

Answer Key and Explanations for Test #3

56. B: Reinforcement should immediately follow a target behavior so that the reinforcement strengthens the behavior. Reinforcers vary widely and are dependent on the client's age, developmental level, and personal preferences. The required elements of reinforcement include the following:

- A behavior or response must have a consequence.
- The behavior or response is more likely to occur with the consequence than without it.
- An increase in a behavior or response is directly related to the consequence.

57. A: Discrete categorization is a form of continuous measurement with an onset (beginning) and an offset (ending) that can be used to categorize behavior. For example, if an individual has episodes of various types of aggression (e.g., shouting, hitting, or throwing things), then discrete categorization can help determine the frequency and duration of each type of aggression. This information can help the BCBA develop goals for behavior modification and can also help with setting priorities for interventions.

58. B: Behavioral cusps are pivotal behaviors that lead to important new behaviors and have a significant impact on the person's life and development. Once an adolescent learns to drive, he or she can use this skill to get a job, go on dates, engage in risk-taking behavior, and become more independent. Some significant behavioral cusps include acquiring language, learning to read, learning to walk, and toileting. Each new skill that a client learns has the potential to become a behavioral cusp.

59. D: The Assessment of Functional Living Skills (AFLS) is a criterion-referenced assessment tool intended for school-aged children to adults. The tool contains six different assessment protocols, so one can choose which protocols are most appropriate. The AFLS is used primarily to assess functional skills in those with developmental disabilities in order to identify the client's areas of strength as well as areas that may require support, to assist with developing the plan of care and necessary interventions, to monitor progress, and to assist with transition planning.

60. A: The Health Insurance Portability and Accountability Act (HIPAA) addresses the rights of individuals related to the privacy of health information. Healthcare providers cannot release protected health information (PHI) about a client without consent. HIPAA also protects the privacy and security of all information in medical and health records and in conversations among healthcare providers. Although RBTs are not typically considered healthcare workers, they may be subject to HIPAA if dealing with PHI or are considered a business associate of a healthcare provider.

61. B: At ages 2–3, a child typically is able to talk in short sentences of three words and can name at least five body parts, identify colors, and recognize the difference between big and little. A child of this age can usually run steadily, jump on two feet, and climb. Most children are potty trained between ages 2 and 3, although some (often girls) may be potty trained earlier, and some parents may choose to do so later. During play, the child should be able to throw overhand and should be able to play side by side with other children and engage in some social interactions.

62. B: Contrived observations (aka structured) are those done under conditions in which something is deliberately planned to evoke certain behavior—in this case, blocks and sounds. The primary purpose of contrived observations is to study specific behaviors. Typically, the setting should reflect real-life situations. Contrived observations usually follow a specific protocol to elicit a certain behavior. Often, environmental factors, such as sounds, are manipulated to determine how they affect the target behavior.

63. B: An RBT has 30 days after receiving sanctions as part of a disciplinary review to file an appeal. Sanctions include certification or eligibility invalidation, certification or eligibility revocation, certification or eligibility suspension, practice restriction, and mandatory disciplinary supervision. The RBT has the right to be present at the appeal process through videoconferencing, although the RBT may not question any witness or the notifier but can file documents questioning the veracity of the information that was presented. If, on the other hand, corrective actions were required rather than sanctions, the RBT may not be present at the appeal process.

64. A: Shaping involves the differential reinforcement of successive approximations of a target behavior. In this case, the RBT has set a goal of 10 minutes on task for a child with ADHD but begins with 1 minute. When the child reaches this goal, then the time is extended before the child receives reinforcement until eventually the child reaches 10 minutes. Shaping can be used to teach a child to say words or to change other types of behaviors, such as tying shoelaces or making eye contact.

65. B: Coercion is a form of negative punishment in which something is taken away to control behavior. Coercion can include carrying out punishments, threatening punishments, or removing punishments for compliance. Coercion, or forcing a client of any age to do something the client does not want to do, should be avoided. It is almost always more productive to use positive reinforcement, even though clients may not always respond. Because the RBT has a position of authority over the client, coercion can be viewed as a form of abuse.

66. B: Manding is derived from the word "demand"; therefore, the purpose of a manding trial is to teach a client to ask for something. "Asking" can refer to different means other than just verbal. For example, a nonverbal child may learn to point at something the child wants or to choose a symbol on a tablet application rather than to cry or grab for the desired object. The first step is to model the desired behavior, for example, by saying, "This is a cracker," while giving the child the cracker. Then, the RBT shows the child the cracker and waits for the child to show interest but then withholds the cracker until the child provides a mand.

67. B: If an RBT encounters a situation in which neglect is evident, such as the adolescent client tied to a bed, soiled, hungry, and thirsty in the company of only a young sibling, the RBT should stay with the children to ensure their safety and notify the BCBA and the local child protective services agency (in some organizations, the BCBA will do the notification). The RBT should carefully document all observations regarding the environment, the children's conditions, and signs of neglect or abuse and should provide comfort and try to meet the children's immediate needs.

68. B: With partial interval measurement (a form of discontinuous measurement), the frequency of the eye-blinking is counted during each interval, but when scoring, the frequency is not counted. The score is simply based on whether the behavior occurred or did not occur during the interval. In this case, eye-blinking was observed during intervals 2, 3, and 4, so the score is 3/5, or 60%. Partial interval measurement may be appropriate for such things as assessing nail-biting, motor tics, and verbal interruptions.

69. A: RBT certification must be renewed annually. As part of the renewal process, the RBT must pass the Renewal Competency Assessment, which consists of 20 items in four broad areas: measurement (3 items), assessment (2 items), skill acquisition and behavior reduction (10 items total, 3 of which must be demonstrated directly with a client), and professionalism and requirements (5 items). The assessment cannot be taken more than 45 days prior to the RBT's certification expiration date.

70. D: Regardless of how well-meaning the RBT may be in this situation, recommending a friend to work with a client is a conflict of interest. Even if the friend may be an ideal fit for the job, the first thing the RBT should do is to report the relationship before any recommendation. Any existing or potential conflicts of interest should be disclosed immediately to a supervisor and should be appropriately documented. In some cases, the RBT may be removed from a situation in which a conflict of interest may occur.

71. C: Reactivity occurs when individuals change behavior when they are aware that they are being observed. Different types of reactivity include the following:

- Demand: The individual reacts by increasing behaviors that the individual believes are desired, such as occurs with this student.
- Novelty: The individual exhibits temporary changes in behavior and may appear curious or more alert.
- Hawthorne: The individual modifies his or her behavior in some way when aware of being observed.
- Response to measurement instrument: The individual alters behavior when observing instruments, such as when being videotaped.

72. C: Expectations can influence observations and scoring. For example, this RBT has noted a marked improvement in a child's behavior over the past 6 months, so the RBT may inadvertently overlook behavior that is different from what the RBT expects based on the child's progress and may focus on behavior that supports the expectations. This is a form of confirmation bias (i.e., seeking data to confirm expectations) as well as observer bias (i.e., expectations govern what is recorded).

73. A: Permanent product recording provides objective data about performance because it depends on production of a tangible product. For example, if a client with a disability is in a sheltered employment situation and is to pack a product into boxes, the number of boxes completed is the permanent product. Keeping a daily tally during workdays can indicate whether the client is showing improvement. Permanent product recording is an indirect measurement that does not require direct observation; therefore, it is possible that someone else is doing the work.

74. A: Trial-based preference assessments are especially useful when assessing reinforcers with clients who have difficulty communicating or expressing their preferences. Trial-based preference assessments typically present the client with choices while the RBT notes the order of preference, the type of engagement, and the duration of time spent with the chosen item. With single stimulus assessment, one item is presented at a time and the client's reaction are noted. With paired stimuli assessment, two similar items (such as two different action figures) are presented to the client and the order of choice, the type of interaction, and the duration are noted.

75. D: Extinction is used to eliminate unwanted behavior, in this case, masturbation. The child has been receiving reprimands, but this brings social attention, which serves as a reinforcer. With extinction, the reinforcer (i.e., the reprimand) is withheld consistently because reintroducing the reprimand, even occasionally, will likely set back extinction. During extinction, appropriate behavior, such as playing with a toy, should be reinforced. During extinction, some may respond differently, sometimes with worsening behavior and sometimes bettering, for a time. Additionally, following extinction, some will exhibit an extinction burst, an increase in the unwanted behavior, for a time.

76. D: If the RBT asks a BCBA for guidance and is still not clear about what to do, the RBT should address the problem at that time, by saying, for example, "I'm still not really sure about this; could you explain it to me again or model it for me?" This provides feedback to the BCBA as well about how clear the BCBA's information was initially presented. Open and clear communication is essential for the working relationship between the RBT and the BCBA, and the RBT is responsible for clarifying any information about which the RBT has a question.

77. A: Guided compliance is a type of positive punishment (e.g., by adding something to prevent unwanted behavior) for noncompliance. In this case, the teacher wants the child to sit in a chair during class. With guided compliance, the teacher provides prompts, such as pointing at the chair, so that the child must comply. If the child fails to follow the prompt, then the prompts become more intrusive. Physically guiding the child to the chair is the most intrusive prompting, but coercion or physical force should never be used because it is a form of assault.

78. C: Although the Verbal Behavior Milestones Assessment and Placement Program (VB-MAPP) test can be used with other groups, it is most frequently used with children ages approximately 2–6 with either autism spectrum disorder or other types of language delay. The three components of the test are (1) milestone assessment (e.g., mand, tact, echoic, intraverbal, independent play, and social play), (2) barrier assessment (e.g., skill deficit, challenging behavior), and (3) transition assessment (e.g., moving from one environment to another).

79. C: Automatic positive reinforcement occurs naturally as a result of carrying out a behavior rather than an extrinsic reward of some type. For example, when a child with autism spectrum disorder carries out a behavior as a means to self-stimulate (stimming), the reinforcement occurs as a natural response to the stimming action. Because the child finds pleasure in the stimming, this behavior is more likely to occur. Other examples of common automatic positive reinforcement include tapping the fingers or other repetitive actions, such as rocking back and forth or repeating the same words or phrases.

80. C: Verbal operants (identified by BF Skinner) include tact. Tacting is the ability to name or label things or events that the individual observes through sensory input: smell, sound, taste, sights, and touch. Tacting is an essential element of communication, allowing individuals to share information and provide descriptions. Textual refers to the ability to read, whereas transcriptive refers to the ability to hear a word and write (i.e., spell) it. Intraverbal is the ability to think about something and respond correctly.

81. D: Response generalization occurs when a client learns a new response (e.g., buttoning a shirt) and extends that response to similar situations (such as to other items with buttons). Response generalization is very common. Some clients more readily generalize knowledge than others. Encouraging clients to practice the same behaviors in different contexts and providing consistent reinforcement and feedback can help develop response generalization.

82. A: A behavior chain is a series of discriminative stimuli and responses. Most activities require a series of steps rather that a single step. A task analysis is required before developing a behavior chain. Each step in the chain becomes a stimulus (or a discriminative stimulus [SD]) for a response, which is reinforced. For example, if teaching a client to dress, the first step may be to open a drawer:

- SD1—Pants in the drawer. Response 1—Opens the drawer. ("Great job!")
- SD2—Drawer is open. Response 2—Takes out a pair of pants. ("That's right!)
- SD3—Holding pants. Response 3—Unfolds the pants. ("Good!")

83. D: With random rotation trials, the client is given multiple different targets (such as pictures of different items) in random order. A goal of random rotation trials is to promote generalization and discrimination. The client must focus on each individual discriminative stimulus rather than relying on a pattern (such as all color cards). Random rotation trials may be used to assess different tasks or skills. During the trial, clients receive reinforcement for correct responses and feedback for incorrect ones.

84. C: A behavior contract is individualized and developed by the client and the BCBA to make the client more accountable and should be limited to one or two behavior targets. Components of the behavior contract include the following:

- Identify target (i.e., undesired) behaviors that need to be changed—usually limited to one or two per contract.
- Outline who will be in charge of enforcing the contract, such as parents, teachers, caregivers, or the client (if he or she is self-managing).
- Identify desirable behaviors and reinforcers (e.g., type, quantity, frequency).
- Identify consequences for undesired behaviors.
- Establish expectations, including limits.
- Determine how progress will be assessed and measured.

85. B: An RBT must be supervised by a qualified BCBA for 5% (or 20 hours) of working time each calendar month. During supervision, the RBT must be engaged in providing applied behavioral analysis therapy with clients. The RBT must ensure adequate supervision, keep track of the hours of work and supervision, and maintain supervision records for 7 years. Failure to comply with appropriate supervision may result in loss of certification. Additionally, the RBT will be ineligible to reapply for recertification for at least 6 months.

Tell Us Your Story

We at Mometrix would like to extend our heartfelt thanks to you for letting us be a part of your journey. It is an honor to serve people from all walks of life, people like you, who are committed to building the best future they can for themselves.

We know that each person's situation is unique. But we also know that, whether you are a young student or a mother of four, you care about working to make your own life and the lives of those around you better.

That's why we want to hear your story.

We want to know why you're taking this test. We want to know about the trials you've gone through to get here. And we want to know about the successes you've experienced after taking and passing your test.

In addition to your story, which can be an inspiration both to us and to others, we value your feedback. We want to know both what you loved about our book and what you think we can improve on.

The team at Mometrix would be absolutely thrilled to hear from you! So please, send us an email at tellusyourstory@mometrix.com or visit us at mometrix.com/tellusyourstory.php and let's stay in touch.

173

Additional Bonus Material

Due to our efforts to try to keep this book to a manageable length, we've created a link that will give you access to all of your additional bonus material:

mometrix.com/bonus948/rbt